Studies in African American History and Culture

Edited by
Graham Hodges
Colgate University

A Routledge Series

STUDIES IN AFRICAN AMERICAN HISTORY AND CULTURE

GRAHAM HODGES, *General Editor*

SWINGING THE VERNACULAR
Jazz and African American
Modernist Literature

Michael Borshuk

Routledge
New York & London

Published in 2006 by
Routledge
Taylor & Francis Group
270 Madison Avenue
New York, NY 10016

Published in Great Britain by
Routledge
Taylor & Francis Group
2 Park Square
Milton Park, Abingdon
Oxon OX14 4RN

Printed in the United States of America on acid-free paper
10 9 8 7 6 5 4 3 2

International Standard Book Number-10: 0-415-97447-X (Hardcover)
International Standard Book Number-13: 978-0-415-97447-9 (Hardcover)
Library of Congress Card Number 2005016644

Library of Congress Cataloging-in-Publication Data

Borshuk, Michael.
   Swinging the vernacular : jazz and African American modernist literature / Michael Borshuk.
      p. cm. -- (Studies in African American history & culture)
   Includes bibliographical references (p.) and index.
   ISBN 0-415-97447-X
   1. American literature--African American authors--History and criticism. 2. African Americans--Intellectual life--20th century. 3. Music and literature--History--20th century. 4. Modernism (Literature)--United States. 5. African Americans in literature. 6. Jazz in literature. I. Title. II. Studies in African American history and culture.

PS153.N5B636 2005
810.9'112'08996073--dc22
                                                   2005016644

Taylor & Francis Group
is the Academic Division of Informa plc.

Visit the Taylor & Francis Web site at
http://www.taylorandfrancis.com

and the Routledge Web site at
http://www.routledge-ny.com

for a house filled with music, 623 Tournier:
for Mom, Jenny, and in memory of Dad.

Contents

Acknowledgments

This book straddles two different cities (Edmonton, Alberta and Lubbock, Texas); two different English departments (the University of Alberta and Texas Tech University); and two different stages in my academic career (graduate student and assistant professor). Accordingly, I wish to thank a number of people for helping me with this project on either side (or in some cases, both sides) of those various divides.

First off, I am overwhelmingly grateful to Teresa Zackodnik, who helped this book immeasurably at the dissertation stage with a virtuoso performance of generosity, patience, and intellectual insight. She remains an academic model for me. Secondly, I would like to thank the following faculty members from the University of Alberta for their hands–on assistance with this work throughout its early period: Garry Watson, Adam Krims, Susan Smith, Brad Bucknell, and Heather Zwicker. I appreciate too the patience and assistance of the English department support staff at Alberta, and want to make special note of Mary Marshall Durrell and Kim Brown. I am grateful for the Canada Research Chair Post–Doctoral Fellowship in Culture and the Modern State I was awarded at the University of Alberta, for post–doctoral research over the 2002–03 academic year. As well, I appreciate less "obvious" assistance I received in Edmonton from the following friends and colleagues: Russell Chace, Ernst and Alice Gerhardt, Paul Hjartarson, Melissa Jacques, Shauna Mosbeck, Linda Tucker, and especially Rob Brazeau, who has extended so much generosity over the duration of our friendship as to attain an avuncular position in my life.

From the English department at Texas Tech University I would like to thank the following colleagues for warm welcomes, administrative assistance, and intellectual support: Scott Baugh, Sam Dragga, Angela Eaton, Art Fricke, Sean Grass, Ann Hawkins, Stephen Jones, Miles Kimball, Jacqueline Kolosov-Wenthe, Feisal Mohamed, Jill Patterson, and William Wenthe. I would also like to acknowledge the assistance of the English departments at both the University of Alberta and Texas Tech University for travel money, which allowed me to present excerpts of this book at various academic meetings. I am immensely grateful, as well, to Jim Brink and the Provost's Office at Texas Tech, and Caryl Heintz and Jane Winer and the College of Arts and Sciences at Tech, for generously providing subvention money that allowed me to secure copyright permissions for material I quote at length.

I am thankful to the students of English 461: "Improvising America": Jazz and African American Literature, which I taught at the University of Alberta in the winter of 2003, and English 5324: Jazz and African American Literature, which I taught at Texas Tech University in the fall of 2004. The discussion you provided was essential to sharpening many of the ideas I present here.

Beyond my two "home" departments, I have received invaluable commentary and assistance from colleagues at other universities. I would especially like to single out Herman Beavers, from the University of Pennsylvania, an exceedingly generous scholar who influenced this project long before there even was a project—through an encouraging conversation at the 1995 Modern Languages Association Convention and a rich correspondence that has carried on since. I would also like to thank Michael Coyle, Christopher C. DeSantis, John Ditsky, John Gennari, Mark Osteen, and the editorial board from *Langston Hughes Review.*

I am grateful for the opportunity to have presented portions of this material at the following academic meetings: the Annual Meeting of the George Moses Horton Society for the Study of African American Poetry; the Guelph Jazz Festival Colloquium; the Langston Hughes Centennial Conference; and the Annual Meeting of the Midwest Modern Languages Association. I am also thankful to the University of Georgia for allowing me to reprint portions of Chapter One which were originally published in *Langston Hughes Review;* and to Oklahoma University for allowing me to reprint portions of chapters 2 and 3 which originally appeared in *Genre: Forms of Discourse and Culture.* And I appreciate the assistance I have received from Benjamin Holtzman and Kimberly Guinta at Routledge.

On a personal level, I would like to acknowledge the longtime friendship of John Deck, Sebastian Magierowski, Max Nelson, and Roland Ouellette. I would also like to thank extended families in Ontario and Saskatchewan for providing unshakeable foundations. And a note of appreciation to all those Windsor–Detroit musicians who kept my family's summer parties lively and our backyard joyful with the sounds of jazz, blues, and soul back in the late eighties and early nineties.

Finally, while this book is dedicated to the musical household in which I grew up, I also want to pay loving tribute to the song–filled home in which I live now. To my incredible partner and best friend, Karen, who provides me with so much sweet melody, and, at the risk of seeming silly, to our pets, Mingus and Wallace, who follow with plenty of rhythm.

Really, who could ask for anything more?

Introduction

The Language of Jazz as American Culture Becomes Modern

Episode Three of director Ken Burns's titanic documentary on the history of jazz begins in striking montage, with stock footage of Prohibition–Era nightlife, cast in sepia tones and black-and-white. Devoted to the years 1924–28, the period of the music's initial advance on the national scene, the program opens with an aerial view of the streets of New York, showing the city alive with prosperity after the Great War. Skyscrapers, perilously grand, burst from the urban landscape while traffic presses the thorough-fare at center screen, a host of cars in crowded motion toward the far hori-zon. A second shot brings us to street level, to a horde of black and white pedestrians in topcoats and straw hats on the sidewalks of Manhattan. Next, Burns takes us indoors, into a cabaret and a tight close–up of a bar-tender pouring spirits, the forbidden elixir at the heart of this vitality. A series of indoor scenes follows. We see African American patrons in a cabaret, smoking and drinking while a small jazz combo performs onstage. The drummer juggles his sticks while he keeps time, all maverick style and undaunted poise. Then a jump cut to the Cotton Club dancers, a scantily clad group of light–skinned black women. They mimic musical perform-ance with plastic clarinets and toy saxophones, as white spectators in tuxe-dos and evening gowns look on. This image gives way to that of a young white woman, a brazen flapper with short hair and a loose chemise, danc-ing the Charleston. She hikes up the hem of her skirt to allow for freer movement while her fellow nightclub patrons—mostly young white men—look on in bewilderment. Burns then offers shot after shot of young Jazz Age whites, men and women, making their own attempts at the Charleston, the signature step of that lively period. Arms akimbo, legs splayed, heads bobbing, and smiles all around. Finally, we are back to our flashy drummer

1

from the jazz combo of before. His sticks continue to fly in energetic display. There is a smile on his face that says, "This is just small–time. Kid stuff. You ain't seen nothing yet."

Overtop these arresting images, actor Samuel L. Jackson reads from Rudolph Fisher's essay, "The Caucasian Storms Harlem," originally published in *The American Mercury* in 1927. "What occasions the focusing of attention," he begins, "on the Negro" (81)?[1]

> Granted [. . .] white people have long enjoyed the Negro entertainment as a diversion, is it not something different, something more, when they bodily throw themselves into Negro entertainment in cabarets? "Now Negroes go to their own cabarets to see how white people act."
>
> And what do we see? Why, we see them actually playing Negro games. I watch them in that epidemic Negroism, the Charleston. I look on and envy them. They camel and fish–tail and turkey, they geche and black–bottom and scronch, they skate and buzzard and mess–around— and they do them all better than I! This interest in the Negro is an active and participating interest. It is almost as if a traveler from the North stood watching an African tribe–dance, then suddenly found himself swept wildly into it, caught in its tidal rhythm [. . .] Maybe these Nordics at last have tuned in to our wavelength. Maybe they are at last learning to speak our language. (81–82)

Behind Jackson's poignant reading of Fisher's shrewd commentary and ironic reflection we, of course, hear music. It is the trumpet of Louis Armstrong, in his early recording of "St. Louis Blues," performed for Columbia Records in December 1929. The record offers a striking sonic moment: the greatest of early jazz improvisers—a path–setter for generations of virtuosi ranging from Coleman Hawkins to Wynton Marsalis—performing one of the music's ur–texts, penned by W.C. Handy, self–proclaimed "Father of the Blues," in 1914. It is a fitting soundtrack for the images onscreen and the words that Jackson reads, a sound that seems to relate so perfectly to the montage, to the text, and to the history narrated therein. It is the "velocity of celebration," to borrow Albert Murray's astute term for swing music; it is exquisite art wrought from the vernacular, a socially complex form that observes the vicissitudes of racial inequity as it works to redress them. And it is the sound of American culture becoming modern, emerging from its antecedents, sassily and confidently willing itself into secure existence.

Though this segment of Burns's film is brief—a mere ninety seconds out of the full nineteen–hour extravaganza—so much of what it addresses and observes corresponds to the concerns of this book: the emergence of a self–assured twentieth–century American culture informed by the vernacular; the importance of creative interaction between white and black Americans, however imbalanced, in the development of that unique culture; the aesthetic and political significance of jazz in the birth of an American modernist ethos; the insidious effects of racialized phenomena like the "cult of primitivism" and an enduring voyeuristic economy between whites and African Americans in the material history of the music and a modernist literature; and the notion that jazz constitutes a "language," a singular expressive mode that simultaneously allows for the articulation of African American experience, the creation of a representatively American modernist aesthetic style, and the sundry forms of "cross–racial" appropriation and sympathetic exchange on which that national modernism has depended so often.

My argument might appear far–fetched to those scholars who subscribe to the notion that modernism is only the tangled, erudite geography of "high–art" explorers like James Joyce, Pablo Picasso, or Igor Stravinsky, but the savvy drummer whom Burns showcases in the above montage seems to be, in a number of ways, the embodiment of modernist expression.[2] Though ostensibly removed from the dense allusiveness of *Ulysses* or the jagged anti–representationalism of *Les Demoiselles d'Avignon*, the flashy drummer of Burns's film is not unlike the artists who gave birth to those accepted modernist landmarks in his break from expectation and his assertion of an individualistic expressive style. As Malcolm Bradbury and James McFarlane suggest in their essay, "The Name and Nature of Modernism," which has come to define literary modernism, "[I]n any working definition of [modernism] we shall have to see in it a quality of abstraction and highly conscious artifice, taking us behind familiar reality, breaking away from familiar functions of language and conventions of form" (24). In his self–conscious disruption of the staid reserve of classical musicians in the concert hall, the jazz drummer highlights the performativity of musical presentation in an aggressively modernist way. There is no assumption of transparency here; the musician is not the humble conduit of the music performed. His brash display at the drum kit evokes "the shock, the violation of expected continuities," which Bradbury and McFarlane maintain "is a crucial element *of* the [modernist] style" (24, original emphasis). And the drummer's uncompromised individualism unites him with received innovators of the so–called high arts in modernism, as well. As Bradbury and McFarlane insist, one of the key "qualities which we associate with painters like Matisse, Picasso and Braque, with musicians like Stravinsky and Schoenberg, novelists like Henry James, Mann, Conrad, Proust, Svevo, Joyce, Gide, Kafka, Musil, Hesse and Faulkner, poets like Mallarmé, Valéry, Eliot, Pound, Rilke, Lorca, Apollinaire, Breton and Stevens, with dramatists like Strindberg, Pirandello and Wedekind, [is] indeed their remarkably high degree of self–signature" (29).

Observing Bradbury and McFarlane's definition of modernist style, one is hard–pressed to deny jazz performance a place among modernism's traditionally accepted signal works. Indeed, the various formal qualities that Bradbury and McFarlane highlight—a disruptive engagement with tradition, the shock of the new, the push for self–signature—are uncannily close to the characteristics Ralph Ellison argues define jazz in his 1958 essay, "The Charlie Christian Story," written for the legendary guitarist:

> Jazz [. . .] is fecund in its inventiveness, swift and traumatic in its developments [. . .] There is [. . .] a cruel contradiction implicit in the art form itself, for true jazz is an art of individual assertion within and against the group. Each true jazz moment [. . .] springs from a contest in which each artist challenges all the rest; each solo flight, or improvisation, represents (like the successive canvases of a painter) a definition of his identity as individual, as member of the collectivity and as a link in the chain of tradition. Thus, because jazz finds its very life in an endless improvisation upon traditional materials, the jazzman must lose his identity even as he finds it. (266–67)[3]

While Ellison's description of a jazz aesthetic here seems to correspond so uniformly to Bradbury and McFarlane's description of a modernist style, his insistence elsewhere on jazz as language, as the product of each improviser's individual voice, brings to mind Fisher's suggestion that through jazz and black entertainment whites were learning to speak an African American language.[4] And language, as even the most conservative critics of the style will attest, is crucial to the development of modernist expression.

As Randy Malamud argues in *The Language of Modernism,* one of the central unifying qualities in the formation of a collective modernist literary style is a search for new language and a restlessness with old modes of linguistic expression. "Regardless of the specific novelty," Malamud writes, "the mere affirmation of novelty—in literature as well as within language—unites writers who have made the quest for a new language a fundamental facet of their literature" (4). Thus, while the individual literary and linguistic styles of "accepted" modernist luminaries like James Joyce, T.S. Eliot, and Gertrude Stein are unique, these writers are similar in their shared desire to expand and explode standard English:

> They have in common a fixation on language and on the challenge of language. They announce the inadequacy of the old language, and the

myriad possible alternatives for a replacement. Their linguistic experiments reflect a conviction that language, in the modern age, had to stretch—had to say more than it had been able to say before; had to reveal more, embody more. (4)

While Malamud's astute attention to modernist language is decidedly "traditional" in its focus—examining the language of Joyce, Eliot, Pound and their contemporaries as a somewhat unified transatlantic phenomenon, marked by its avant–garde "literariness" and its semantic complexity—other studies consider both the importance of national divisions in modernism's development and the importance of vernacular influence in the form's linguistic expansion.

In *The Dialect of Modernism,* for example, Michael North argues that a willingness to create linguistic distance from the orthodoxy of the King's English was paramount in the development of a distinctly American modernist literature. As North suggests, the notion of a "proper" English language was a key cultural vehicle for social control among Britain's power elite during the Victorian era. For instance, though work on the *Oxford English Dictionary,* begun in the 1880s, was intended to grant an ostensibly objective unity to Britain's understanding of its national tongue, thereby "deny[ing] the possibility of tense and tangled relationships within the language," it also facilitated an economy of exclusion based on academic elitism and ideologically suspect notions of cultural purity (12). The guardians of so–called standard English made claims to altruism in their attention to the language's preservation, but their intolerance of variation, dialect, and slang constituted an insidious push for homogenization that restricted the cultural expression of the disenfranchised. These efforts seemed designed to alleviate upper–class anxiety about the corruption of the nation in the face of class hierarchy and cultural difference. For these custodians, North suggests, "language [became] the cornerstone of national identity and an index of cultural health. Over and over, the linguistic conscience [told] its captive audience that linguistic unity [was] not just crucial to national identity but actually synonymous with it" (14). Moreover, "defense of the language became a way of defending England against the cultural consequences of the implosion of the empire" (16).

It was precisely these conservative associations that made standard English a target for attack by American modernist writers. While some of that rigid protectionism of standard English traversed the Atlantic and found its way into channels like the American Academy of Arts and Letters—which devoted institutional energy to preserving the integrity of the language—American literature seemed dominated by a recognizably rebellious tendency.

This stateside insurgent spirit was born, as North writes, from the "claim that Americans speak a more vital, natural speech than their decadent co–linguists" (20). As such, American–born modernists like T.S. Eliot, Gertrude Stein, William Carlos Williams, and Wallace Stevens, all of whom "grew up at a time when the English language was being pulled apart by competing political and social forces," fomented a collective linguistic rebellion against the inflexibility of standard English (North 24). In their experiments with dialect and slang, these writers answered Ezra Pound's 1915 imperative "[t]o use the language of common speech," rather than the elevated diction of the Royal tongue (135). But this literary insurrection was not limited to "serious" literature; the insolent turn from standard English fashioned by the moderns was more ubiquitous, wide scale, a trend among the entire generation of Americans who came of age in the 1920s. As Ann Douglas notes in *Terrible Honesty,* "the American moderns repudiated the long ascendant English and European traditions and their genteel American custodians as emblems of cultural cowardice; they were proud to learn that they spoke, not English, but 'The American Language,' as H.L. Mencken officially named it in a monumental and witty study of 1919" (4). This American Language was decidedly impudent and deliberately outrageous, a calculated gesture in the face of Victorian conservatism. The American generation of the 1920s, Douglas explains,

> introduced into what was left of polite society the full spectrum of long–tabooed profanity and a slang idiom that specialized in terms for reality or the facts (the "lowdown," the "scoop," the "dope," the "dirt") and the fake or meretricious ("bunk," "bogus," "baloney," "applesauce," "balls," "bull[shit]"); they tried to eliminate from their lexicon all the words like "sacred," "sacrifice," and "soul" that their Victorian predecessors had disfigured by overuse and misuse. Slang in the 1920s was the speech of bootlegging criminals and fast–talking vaudevillians, people who knew how to "fix" everything from the World Series to bathtub gin, the language of the instincts wised up to their own vicissitudes and insistently critiquing human claims to anything but strictly mortal turf. The rudely insistent "Who sez?" was a 1920s retort. (54)

However, as both North and Douglas show, this linguistic rebellion, widespread among white Americans during the 1920s, was an insurrection dominated by racial cross–identification. Central to the new generation's collective reconfiguration of standard English was an attempt at mimicking the speech patterns of African Americans—however exaggerated and distorted this co–opted idiom proved to be as filtered through the optic of racist misunderstanding. What studies like North's and Douglas's propose is that in the emergence of an American modernism, to echo Eric Sundquist's succinct summary, "African Americans appear[ed] as the answer to the search among Anglo-Americans for a national culture" (104). Or, as North himself articulates it, overall, "[t]he new voice that American culture acquired in the 1920s, the decade of jazz, stage musicals, talking pictures, and aesthetic modernism, was very largely a black one" (7).

North's assessment of American modernist literature specifically posits that the style's development depended on a racialized rebellion in language, whereby white writers, looking for linguistic expansion and struggling for self–definition against the authority of English Victorian culture, tried to speak in "black voices," appropriating African American cultural identity through a crude Negro dialect or romanticized representations of black American characters. Thus, Eliot (who sometimes signed letters "Tar Baby," and whom Ezra Pound nicknamed "de Possum," in part for his minstrel–like exaggeration of "black" identity) turned to dialect in his unpublished King Bolo poems and in *Sweeney Agonistes* (1923); H.D. attributed a kind of psychic liberation to the casual speech of the black cook Mandy in her novel *HERmione* (1927); and Gertrude Stein transferred the sexual politics of one of her own early relationships into the dialect of the black lovers Melanctha and Jeff in *Three Lives* (1909).

However, the language used in these instances, as Douglas notes, was both an exaggeration and a misunderstanding of the "real" language spoken by African Americans:

> Negro dialect, whether used by whites or blacks, was not the same thing as Black English; it was not a transcription of actual black speech. Black English is the term used by language scholars of today for the special form of English developed and spoken by blacks in slavery and post–slavery days, and it was a full and complete language in its own right, with its own grammatical laws and notions of expressiveness; it seems incorrect in other words, because outsiders do not know its rules. In contrast, the Negro dialect used by white and black artists in the nineteenth and early twentieth centuries represented a stereotypical and exaggerated take on the perceived "incorrectness" of black speech as judged solely by the criteria of Standard English. (369)

Though Douglas attributes the use of "Negro dialect" to both whites and blacks here, North suggests that, ironically, the racialized language favored by so many white writers was a linguistic mode that many African American writers of the 1920s sought to avoid. For black poets of that generation, "dialect [was] a 'chain' [. . .] a constant reminder of the literal unfreedom of slavery and of the political and cultural repression that followed emancipation. Both symbol and actuality, it stands for a most intimate invasion whereby the dominant actually attempts to create the thoughts of the subordinate by providing it speech" (North 11). Thus, the anxiety over dialect felt by young black moderns like Jean Toomer and Claude McKay was as central to their attempts to innovate American language and literature as its ease of use was to the white moderns. As North summarizes, "it is impossible to understand either modernism without reference to the other, without reference to the language they so uncomfortably shared, and to the political and cultural forces that were constricting that language at the very moment modern writers of both races were attempting in dramatically different ways to free it" (11).

Expanding on these notions of racially composite language and changing expressivities in the 1920s, Douglas compares the tendency toward "Americanizing" English among the moderns to the wholesale reconfiguration of Western music being fashioned at the same time via jazz. Just as white appropriation of black English and African American vernacular expression influenced the linguistic rebellion against standard English, so, too, did the syncopation and rhythmic play of the new black music inform new trends in American popular music. America's cultural self–definition in the 1920s, Douglas argues, thrived on the analogous processes of "ragging" (named for jazz's early precursor, ragtime) and "slanging," both of which distanced American expression from its European antecedents and were considerably indebted to a specifically African American vernacular culture:

> Black and white Americans have always remade language by letting verbs take over nouns, by putting the language on the run; they have always restyled Standard English, in other words, by something like a ragging process. Slanging and ragging in the 1920s, whether of classical music or Standard English or both, simply updated, accelerated, and made self–conscious the tactic. As the ragtime pianist varied and mocked his traditional left–hand bass march time with his iconoclastic right–hand treble syncopation, the speaker of the American language, white or black, played a conventional or verbal or grammatic usage off against an unconventional one. The American language gained its distinctive character by its awareness of, and opposition to, correct British Standard English; white slang was played against conventional middle–class Anglo-American speak, and the Negro version

of the language worked self–consciously against the white one. In both cases, the surprise came from the awareness of conventions being flouted or violated. (372–73)

While Douglas's linguistic metaphor for describing the influence of black aesthetics on American musical practice hinges on its cultural impact—on its capacity for iconoclasm and its disruptive engagement with tradition—this notion of jazz as language is ubiquitous, lasting, evident in examples ranging from Fisher's early comments in the *American Mercury* to Ellison's remarks at mid–century to innumerable assessments from musicians, critics, and writers since.

Of course, jazz, like any music, possesses its own syntax and grammar, expressive qualities that invite the comparison with language. To play up music's communicative properties and assert its connection to language is hardly novel. Consider, for example, John Milton's appeal in his early ode, "At a Solemn Musick" (1633), to the "Sphere–born harmonious sisters, Voice and Verse," those sibling muses of music and poetry, whom he implores to "Wed your divine sounds, and mixed power employ" (81, lines 2–3). And yet, this connection is forever amplified in the specific, contemporary case of jazz. Critics, creative writers, musicians themselves, all emphasize the way the music mimics language, effects story. For example, in his online *Jazz Improvisation Almanac*, educator Marc Sabatella emphasizes how jazz improvisation is comparable to learning the power of conversation in language:

> Improvisation in music is the act of deciding what to play on a moment to moment basis. An improvisation is a product of the musician as well as the music being performed. Each decision made during the course of improvisation is based partly on past experiences and partly on the current situation.
>
> In a sense, this is no different from ordinary conversation. You decide what to say immediately before saying it. What you say is based partly on your experiences and partly on the flow of the conversation. Your past experiences include your knowledge of language as well as conversations you have heard and taken part in. The current situation includes the subject of the conversation as well as your interaction with the other participants.

In a 1998 article for *Down Beat* magazine's "Woodshed" column—a monthly feature intended for apprentice musicians and jazz educators—Roger Freundlich also compares jazz improvisation to language use, advocating an improvisation exercise he calls "Talk/Play/Talk/Play":

> This exercise emphasizes the close relationship between musical phrasing and speech patterns. The linking of speech and playing processes automatically results in more vocal, natural and communicative musical phrasing.
>
> Parallels to this starter exercise can be found in certain kinds of blues. The student says a few words about any subject, followed by a short instrumental figure played on the instrument, followed by another few words and another short instrumental figure. (62)

Likewise, discussing influences on his playing style, trumpeter Miles Davis acknowledged not only musical figures like Frank Sinatra and Nat "King" Cole, but also the actor Orson Welles, for his speech patterns and conversational style: "I learned a lot about phrasing back then listening to the way Frank, Nat "King" Cole, and even Orson Welles phrased. I mean all those people are motherfuckers in the way they shape a musical line or sentence or phrase with their voice" (*Miles* 70). Similarly, commenting on the playing of fellow saxophonists Lester Young and Charlie Parker, Dexter Gordon once remarked that the pair were always "telling a story" in their improvisations: "That kind of musical philosophy is what I try to do, because telling a story is, I think, where it's at" (qtd in Breton i). Ajay Heble has even tried to ascribe a poetics to jazz performance, mapping changes in its musical vocabulary against tensions over anti–representationalism in cultural and linguistic theory. "By tracing salient developments in the history of jazz from swing to the present day," Heble writes, "we can observe a series of fundamental changes which have taken place both in the theory of the music and in the theory of language" (31). Hence, Heble reads Louis Armstrong's diatonic approach as symbolic language, Charlie Parker's chromaticism as play with Saussurean signifiers, Ornette Coleman's free jazz through Jacques Derrida's post–structuralist theory of *différance*.

Throughout his massive study of jazz improvisation, *Thinking in Jazz*, Paul Berliner also notes how metaphors of conversation and storytelling dominate many musicians' theories and explanations of their own improvisational practice. Quoting musician Arthur Rhames, for instance, Berliner suggests that the emphasis on individuality in jazz improvisation encourages each of its performers to fashion unique modes of musical expression, as singular as one's own idiosyncratic language use. In turn, "[b]ecause all artists speak with 'their own natural rhythm and sequential order,' it is possible to 'emulate a person whose speaking you like, using his same effect—how he comes into a sentence or the way he constructs his things'—but without saying 'the exact same thing'" (143). And, as Berliner notes, players frequently compare the shaping of solos to storytelling:

> [W]hen it comes time for Buster Williams to solo, he "wants to tell a story, and the best way to tell a story is to set it up." If someone who is "very excited about something that just happened" comes running to Williams "saying, 'Buster, blah-blah-blah-blah,' the first thing I'm going to say is, 'Look, wait a minute. Calm down and start from the beginning.'" Williams's plan is the same for solo work. "Start from the beginning," he advises. "It's also like playing a game of chess. There's the beginning game, the middle game, and then there's the end game. Miles [Davis] is a champion at doing that. So is [John Coltrane]. To accomplish this, the use of space is very important—sparseness and simplicity—maybe playing just short, meaningful phrases at first and building up the solo from there." (201)

Moreover, Berliner points to how jazz educator Paul Wertico

> advises his students that in initiating a solo they should think in terms of developing specific 'characters and a plot. . . . You introduce these little different [musical] things that can be brought back out later on; and the way you put them together makes a little story. That can be [on the scale of] a sentence or paragraph. . . . The real great cats can write novels.' (202)

In her study of jazz improvisation, *Saying Something,* Ingrid Monson relies on linguistic metaphors such as these, and expands on them through the use of African American cultural theory from W.E.B. Du Bois and Henry Louis Gates, along with the dialogical criticism of linguist and literary theorist M.M. Bakhtin. "By examining sociolinguistic literature on conversational interaction as well as literary perspectives on language," Monson explores "the structural similarities between conversation and musical performance and the relationships among the aesthetics of social interaction, musical interaction, and cultural sensibility" (8). Building on Bakhtin's assertion that language is invariably social and political, Monson considers how the "language" of jazz mediates social concerns through parody and double–voicedness. Reading jazz improvisation through Du Bois and Gates, Monson argues that these modes of resistance and critique in the music are influenced by similar discursive strategies from an African American expressive tradition. Jazz virtuosity as complex language redresses American social imbalances, proffering a new tongue that is difficult, exclusive, semantically complex. "In music," Monson writes

> it is particularly important to talk about the relationship of African American aesthetics to the 'dominant cultural body,' because music is an arena in which the taken-for-granted hegemonic presumptions about race have been turned upside down by the leadership of African American music and musicians in defining and influencing the shape of American popular music. (103)

This notion that the "language" of jazz is an unmistakably African American argot runs throughout commentary on the music from its practitioners and from black writers and critics. For instance, African American trombonist Curtis Fuller articulates his first hearing of the music as follows:

> Jazz was [. . .] the kind of expression coming out of the black community. When I discovered jazz, it was like going to some part of the world where I hadn't actually studied the language, but finding out that I could understand certain things immediately, that it spoke to me somehow. I knew that I would have to travel a long and rocky road in my endeavor to play jazz, but I felt like I understood the language. (qtd in Berliner 21)

Similarly, in his essay, "My Poetic Technique and the Humanization of the American Audience," poet Michael S. Harper offers an anecdote to express his faith in both a distinctly American linguistic identity, and a specifically African American one, both embodied by jazz:

> When I was in South Africa in 1977 on an American Specialist Program, all by myself, I landed in Johannesburg at about 2:30 A.M. I was carrying Sterling Brown's *Southern Road* and Robert Hayden's *Angle of Ascent* and some of my own books, one with Coltrane's image on the cover. I was first addressed in Afrikaans, but not being colored, I answered in American, "I'm from Brooklyn . . . you ever head of Jackie Robinson?" [. . .] When the driver, a Black South African, approached I got ready to board. I was first in line. Telling me to wait, the driver held up his hand to me, boarded all the White passengers, and drove off. I stood there taking names so to speak. When the driver returned, he apologized for not taking me in the van with the other passengers. He wanted to know where I came from and then he asked—"What language do you speak when the White people aren't around?" I said,

"English," and he said, "No, no." What language did I speak when the White people weren't around? The second time he asked I changed my response to "American." "Brother," he inquired, "When Blacks are among themselves, don't they speak *jazz?*" I nodded, *right on,* brother. (31–32, original emphasis)

Accordingly, writing about African American music in general in *The Power of Black Music,* Samuel Floyd complements Harper's anecdotal declaration and argues that black music (to which jazz is so central in the twentieth century) constitutes a socially binding force that allows for the communal articulation of African American people and an expressive archive of their shared history. As Floyd writes, "Through the energizing and renewing magic of myth and ritual, there emerged from the volatile cauldron of Call–Response a music charged with meanings centuries old— meanings to which the initiated, the knowledgeable, and the culturally sensitive responded in heightened communication" (227). Rich with communal history and shared meanings, the music does then, on many levels, comprise what Rudolph Fisher, speaking for twentieth–century African Americans in the *American Mercury,* called "our language."

This book builds on the various critical contexts outlined above: traditional aesthetic assessments of a modernist style; re-evaluations of that form according to issues of race and cultural difference; cultural theory that analyzes the political importance of African American expressivities; and musicological studies that read jazz improvisation through linguistic theory and a cultural materialist attention to history. In *Swinging the Vernacular,* I identify a strand of African American modernist literature influenced by jazz, manifest in the work of Langston Hughes, Ralph Ellison, Michael S. Harper, and Albert Murray. Looking at each of these writers through the specific aesthetic and social contexts of the contemporaneous jazz styles by which their work was shaped, I show how this black modernist literary style uses signal elements from the music like irony, stylistic revision, and dialogism to effect both a radical black political intervention in American culture, and a "traditionally" modernist brand of aesthetic innovation. In their social and aesthetic interventions, each of these writers embodies what Ann Douglas calls "mongrel modernism," namely the distinctly American twentieth–century literary style that thrives on the cultural hybridity unique to the United States. At its origins, this book is influenced by the work of scholars like Douglas and North, who foreground the importance of race in the formation of an American modernist tradition in the 1920s and the 1930s. However, though both Douglas and North argue that it is the cultural interaction of so–called "blackness" and "whiteness" that defines

American modernism, they limit their studies mainly to reading how this affects the work of white writers. One guiding question for this project, then, is to examine how African American writing—in its own unique way—embodies this cultural hybridity as well.

My conceptualization of America's cultural hybridity, though rooted in the work of Douglas and North, is extended by the work of M.M. Bakhtin, Homi Bhabha and Paul Gilroy, all of whom examine how the intersection of diverse social groups affects cultural heterogeneity. In Chapter One, I suggest that the hybridity that Douglas and North mark is akin to what Bakhtin, in "Discourse in the Novel," calls "organic hybridity," namely, that unavoidable (and perhaps unconscious) mutation that occurs in a language when speakers of that language from different worldviews interact (358–59). That is, the hybridity that Douglas and North trace in white American modernist writing is marked in many ways by a lack of awareness of processes already in motion. African American modernist literature, I argue, underscores those organic processes and also frequently effects what Bakhtin calls an "intentional hybridity," the act of speaking in a language shared by two worldviews but recognizably different in its signification for each of those worldviews (304–05). For Bakhtin, these moments afford a kind of discursive resistance in which an insubordinated group may speak back to the dominant faction through motivated critique in this double–voiced language. Bhabha and Gilroy complement this theoretical standpoint in their shared position that the cultural hegemony of "colonizer" over "colonized," or "white" over "black," unavoidably deteriorates in shared linguistic space and through cultural interaction. Methodologically, then, my work relies on the work of these scholars, as well as on important texts of literary theory, like Henry Louis Gates's *The Signifying Monkey,* along with Houston Baker's *Blues, Ideology, and Afro-American Literature,* and *Modernism and the Harlem Renaissance.* All elaborate a theory of African American literature and literary "tradition" through an understanding of black vernacular culture and its necessarily political underpinnings. Moreover, my work is also informed by those scholars noted above, namely Samuel Floyd, Paul Berliner, and Ingrid Monson, all of whom have written on the jazz aesthetic and have argued how the music's improvisational freeplay inherently mediates expressive interests and social concerns.

Indeed, jazz is able to effect this social negotiation because of its unique position as a liminal form of expressivity, an aesthetic mode that at times ritualizes its politics through the topsy–turviness of improvised performance. As Victor Turner argues in "Liminality and the Performative Genres," "performative genres, cultural performances, modes of exhibition or presentation—such as ritual, carnival, theater, and film—[often function] as commentaries and critiques on, or as celebrations of, different dimensions of human relatedness" (19). Of the performative genres that best define twentieth–century American culture, jazz musical performance is especially fitted to this role, embodying as it does what Turner calls "liminality," specifically, "a betwixt-and-between condition often involving seclusion from the everyday scene" (21). For much of the twentieth century, African American jazz thrived on a kind of "outsiderism," ostensibly removed from a white middle–class mainstream by the workings of American segregation, and sited instead within "liminal" spaces like the nightclub or the after–hours jam. However, despite their seeming remove from the mainstream, each of these spaces constitutes a site of public liminality, a place where the established social order comes into question through the performance of cultural "subjunctivity," Turner's term for the collective expression of "supposition, desire, hypothesis, possibility" (20). In sites of public liminality, Turner notes how "anything goes: taboos are lifted, fantasies are enacted, the low are exalted and the mighty abased" (21). These spaces and the ritualized performances they host may be, in Turner's words, "the venue[s] and occasion[s] for the most radical skepticism [. . .] about [a given culture's] cherished values and rules" (22). Thus, in the ritual of jazz performance, with the improviser's ludic articulation of individual possibility and his creative engagement with musical collectivity, we see, perhaps, a liminal critique of American democracy and the breakdown of its ideals.

I wish also to note here that, throughout this work, I envision American modernism as an expressive mode that emerges in the 1920s but continues as a distinct style throughout the twentieth century. My conceptualization of "modernism" as a stylistic mode that transcends its temporal origins is indebted to Houston Baker's notion of "renaissancism" from *Modernism and the Harlem Renaissance*. In that work, Baker formulates a vision of modernism marked by black cultural difference and recognizably African American discursive practices. Though he traces the origins of these praxes to Booker T. Washington's famous "Atlanta Compromise" speech of 1895 and argues they culminate in the 1920s with the flourishing of the Harlem Renaissance, ultimately Baker suggests that these modes echo throughout the twentieth century. I root my conceptualization of modernism in the 1920s, the decade that saw the emergence of a distinctly American modernist writing through the work of Anglo-Americans like T.S. Eliot and William Carlos Williams and African Americans like Langston Hughes and Jean Toomer, and the spread of jazz like wild fire on the American scene. The strand of black modernism in which I am specifically interested extends throughout the twentieth century, shifting in aesthetic form and political approach alongside contemporaneous changes in the sound and sensibility of jazz, that most modernist of musical forms itself. While some argue that jazz did not achieve a "modernist" phase until the birth of bebop (with its radical collage and concert–hall aspirations) in the 1940s, I will argue throughout this work that—to borrow from the name of the Lincoln Center Jazz Orchestra's 1998 summer tour—"All Jazz is Modern."

Finally, it is necessary to address the fact that the four writers I have chosen for this study are men. While this selection may at first seem to rehearse the decidedly masculinist bent to which jazz discourse and practice have been inclined throughout their histories, I do not mean to offer an unchecked replication of that problematic gendered legacy. Rather, I wish to call attention here to the way that male jazz musicians and critics have forcibly constructed jazz as the province of masculinity.[5] Historically, men have represented the music as an expressive space that privileges conventionally masculine notions of physical prowess and complex genius, without admitting the place of women or considering the discursive or performative natures of gender identity. Indeed, Eric Porter demonstrates how, from the early days of jazz in the opening decades of the twentieth century,

> men were thought to possess physical qualities that made them better suited for the music business. Members of the American jazz community believed that women did not have the strength to excel on horns and drums or in certain styles (stride, for instance) on the often–feminized piano. They believed, too, that success in music depended on the ability to negotiate continued absence from home and family responsibilities and the means to survive dangerous performance spaces without damage to one's body or reputation. (27–28)

In a more specific example of these gendering processes, Hazel Carby persuasively argues how Miles Davis, throughout his autobiography, suppresses the importance of women in his personal life as he simultaneously celebrates his relationships with other male musicians. Throughout, Davis diminishes the role his mother and various female partners played in his personal and creative development, even representing these women as potential impediments to musical success alongside other male geniuses. Effectively, then, Davis's self–representation, and the binary division on which it turns, affirms jazz music as a site of male expressive possibility, wholly removed from—and even threatened by—feminine influence (Carby 135–65).[6]

While Carby highlights how one notable male jazz musician negates female influences in the midst of his masculine self–construction, Farah

Jasmine Griffin discusses how critical and artistic communities at large encourage the music's gendered reception:

> For the most part, the major critics of jazz were men. This is probably why male instrumentalists have received so much attention. Also, there is a way that music subcultures, not unlike athletic ones, are like fraternities. Young men are encouraged to pick up instruments most often associated with jazz—the horns and the drums, even the piano. (120)[7]

Moreover, as Sherrie Tucker astutely notes, even attempts to redress the gender exclusivity of jazz fraternities run the risk of reaffirming discursive traps. That is, while critical attention to the category of "women in jazz" attempts to acknowledge female contributions to the music's history and practice, that act of categorization in turn positions improvising women as exceptional or supplementary to the otherwise male community in which they intervene. This naturalized vision of a stable male musical community is the product, Tucker suggests, of jazz discourse: "a curious mix of romance about modernist geniuses who appear to have no communities and nostalgic communities for whom playing jazz seems to achieve historical and social and political transcendence" (247). However, "[i]n each case," Tucker writes, "politics and power"—the politics and power at work in the erection of gender hierarchies, for instance—"disappear from jazz history" (247).

While interrogating jazz music's ostensibly masculine ethos allows us to see how men have forced the disappearance of gender politics from the music's history, we witness similar mechanisms at work if we reconsider gender's place in the broad categories of modernism and African American modernism. As Marianne DeKoven suggests: "Despite the powerful presence of women writers at the founding of Modernism and throughout its history, and despite the near–obsessive preoccupation with femininity in all modernist writing, the reactive misogyny so apparent in much male–authored Modernism continues in many quarters to produce a sense of Modernism as a masculinist movement" (176). According to DeKoven, the critical perception of Modernism as a male enterprise is bolstered by efforts like the "terse, classical masculinity" of Ezra Pound's prose in his vorticist manifesto, or Henry James's anxious suggestion in "The Future of the Novel" that "a debased, feminine/feminized popular culture" represents the "social and aesthetic deterioration of standards" (176–77). Similarly, Ann Douglas represents the emergence of an American modernist sensibility as a gendered transition, from a feminized, matriarchal Victorian culture to a matricidal twentieth–century culture. This shift depended, in part, on the aggressive rhetoric of male modernists' self–construction. For instance, as Douglas points out, Ernest Hemingway went from calling his mother "my best girl" in letters sent home from Milan in 1918, to dismissing her as loathsome a few years later, and suddenly affiliating himself with his father (220). Hemingway's turn is central to his own lengthy performance of the modern writer as masculine archetype, and contributes to the gendering of modernism more universally.

During the Harlem Renaissance, the older African American intellectuals who mentored writers like Langston Hughes, and who effectively shepherded a specifically black modernism into existence, also articulated and directed the emergence of a markedly new sensibility through gendered language. For example, as Martin Summers points out, Alain Locke described the African American literary tradition to younger writers in "language that evoked the idealized images of nineteenth–century manhood—the artist as a skilled laborer and as a lone individual on the frontier" (206). In doing so, Locke "was in the process of constructing a predominantly male 'tradition' of arts and letters in which to foreground the work of the younger artists. As such, his interpretation of black modernism and its predecessors contrived a hierarchy based on gender" (206). Moreover, as Carby argues, Du Bois, the most dominant intellectual influence on the writers of the Harlem Renaissance, cast his ongoing pursuit for racial uplift in decidedly masculine terms. In his most famous work, *The Souls of Black Folk*, Du Bois uses "an authorial persona who enacts the ideal qualities of intellectual and political leadership and black masculinity" (Carby 35). Ultimately, Du Bois

> acts as an embodiment of his own ideal of an intellectual and graduate of the humanistic education he advocates; second, he appears as a contestant for black leadership whose voice gains authority through the process of critiquing other male leaders; and, finally, he quite deliberately uses his own body as the site for an exposition of the qualities of black manhood. (Carby 35–36)

Thus, in positioning himself at the intersection of these varied registers of African American success—as the epitome of black intellectual achievement, political leadership, and masculinity simultaneously—Du Bois effectively elides the difference between the three categories. The effect is to suggest that the artistic and academic success on which the hope for African Americans turned, as Du Bois argued repeatedly, is by its very nature a masculine pursuit. Like Locke, then, Du Bois contributed to the gendering of black modernism, and more broadly, helped shape what Philip Brian Harper identifies as a "dominant view" in African American culture, that "prideful self–respect [is] the very essence of healthy African-American identity," and that "such identity [is] fundamentally weakened where masculinity appears to be compromised" (*Men* ix).

These various gender contexts inspire my selection of the writers studied in this book. My choice is governed by a desire to map what I see as a binding stylistic genealogy, rooted in the interwoven discourses of jazz, modernist literature, and masculinity. All four writers are recognizably committed to intervening in translatlantic modernism, injecting African American expressivity into the creative mode too often thought to be the natural territory of Eliot, Pound, Williams, and Stein. This shared goal seems unequivocally different from the projects of the many African American women writers whom I perceive to be among the most meaningful in their use of jazz and blues, including, but not limited to, Alice Walker, Toni Morrison, Gayl Jones, Sherley Anne Williams, Ntozake Shange, Thulani Davis, and Xam Wilson Cartier. The work of the four writers I cover in this book departs intellectually from Du Bois's famous formulation that "the problem of the Twentieth Century is the problem of the color line," and as such attempts to redress that problem in the arts by innovating modernist expressivity through the African American vernacular (Du Bois, *Souls* 5). The women writers listed here, however, seem more deconstructive in their approach, attempting to dismantle dominant artistic traditions—like existing perceptions of jazz or modernism—through experimentalism, in order to clear an aesthetic space in which the complexity of black female subjectivity may be articulated. Through these efforts, these women try to reveal, as Darlene Clark Hine articulates, that "[t]he history of the American Negro is more than a history of efforts as Du Bois put it 'to attain self–conscious manhood,' it is simultaneously a story of the development and preservation of a dynamic, multiconscious black womanhood" (338). Thus, my joining of these four male writers is not intended to suggest that men alone have a natural entitlement to jazz, or to modernist literature, but that these writers are integral to the way that jazz and modernist literature have been constructed in masculine terms. But that is not to say that gender issues go unacknowledged in the work of Hughes, Ellison, Harper, and Murray. Rather, as I show at various points in this book, these writers frequently engage (sometimes critically, sometimes not) with the construction of masculinity and the gendered divisions that dominate contemplations of jazz, both within the music community and without.

Chapter One
Langston Hughes and the First Book of Jazz

The foundations for a jazz–influenced strain of black literary modernism emerged almost as soon as the music itself made its passage from the cradle of the South to the urban bustle of New York and Chicago. Not long after Southern musicians like King Oliver, Louis Armstrong and Jelly Roll Morton landed in Northern cities, in the late 1910s and early 1920s, and began their wholesale revision of the American musical lexicon, an unassuming young African American poet named Langston Hughes began marking his own significant revision of the country's literature.[1] An unabashed admirer of the new music, Hughes saw literary potential in jazz's revolutionary aesthetic, in its combination of folk community with the attention to individual consciousness that had come to characterize literature in the inchoate century. If, as Virginia Woolf famously declared, "On or about December 1910, human character changed," then Hughes heard that transition in the jarring shifts and rhythmic traffic of jazz (4). Whereas white poets like Carl Sandburg and William Carlos Williams had already begun to borrow from the music in their attempts to step away from the orthodoxy of traditional English verse, Hughes recognized that liberatory potential and much more.

Jazz was key to Hughes's expression of the racial self–assertion that defined Harlem's developing New Negro spirit. Despite its thorough consumption by white listeners hungry for novelty as the 1910s gave way to the twenties, jazz was marked by unmistakably African American features.[2] The music had emerged from black communities, was descended from the sorrow songs and the blues. For Langston Hughes, then, to write poetry from jazz was to address the *zeitgeist*'s sudden changes while maintaining fidelity to a larger African American political project of race advancement. In doing so, in collections like *The Weary Blues* (1925) and *Fine Clothes to the Jew* (1927), Hughes revitalized American verse while he revolutionized African American letters, sounding a call to which his successors Ralph Ellison, Michael S. Harper, and Albert Murray would all respond in time.

Viewing the early work of Langston Hughes, one is less surprised to see that the poet was influenced so extensively by jazz, than that he was so alone among his African American contemporaries in his use of the music. Jazz is the most significant artistic form to have emerged from the cultural production of the United States during the twentieth century, and more specifically, it is likely the most influential contribution African Americans have made to their national culture and beyond.[3] The music is almost universally venerated by this point early in the twenty–first century. Jazz is both an object of popular reverence and a site of scholarly fascination. As Krin Gabbard writes, "Jazz has entered the mainstream of the academy," its arrival signified by "such peri–academic phenomena as the proliferation of jazz titles now being published by university presses, the birth of jazz repertory orchestras and the [. . .] jazz division at New York's Lincoln Center" ("Introduction" 1).[4]

And yet, this contemporary legitimization of jazz is a radical departure from the intolerance and contempt that characterized many early critical evaluations of the music during the formative years of Langston Hughes's literary career. White critics writing during the period of the music's birth in the 1910s and twenties proclaimed it, at times, an abomination, a violation of refined sensibilities. For example, a 1917 article from the *Times–Picayune* in New Orleans, the recognized city of the music's birth, defines jazz as an anti–artistic phenomenon that can only appeal to low aesthetics and bestial tastes. "To uncertain natures," the piece declares, "wild sound and meaningless noise have an exciting almost intoxicating effect, like crude colors and strong perfume, the sight of flesh or the sadistic pleasure in blood. To such as these, the jass [sic] is a delight" (qtd in Meltzer, *Reading* 52). Even those commentators willing to admit that jazz was an influential cultural form could be disparaging, unkind. Clive Bell, for instance, writing of the "jazz movement" in *The New Republic* in 1921, offered a similarly acerbic reaction, describing the art form as "irritating" (92).[5] "Impudence," he announces, "is its essence—impudence in quite natural and legitimate revolt against Nobility and Beauty: impudence which finds its technical equivalent in syncopation: impudence which rags" (Bell 93).

Though African Americans obviously did not share these disparaging appraisals of a music that was largely their creation, the assessment of jazz by Hughes's black intellectual contemporaries in this early period did not approach the unbridled acclaim that the music receives today. Rather, black critics avoided the scathing rhetoric of white commentary and abused jazz in a different way—through an undervaluing of its aesthetic importance. Jazz was suspiciously excluded from the unofficial race–advancement project promoted by the black intelligentsia in the 1920s, during the period that came to be known as the Harlem Renaissance.[6] Nathan Huggins notes that despite the fact that "Harlem intellectuals promoted Negro art, [. . .] except for Langston Hughes, none of them took jazz—the new music—seriously" (9–10). Similarly, Richard A. Long observes that "Nowhere in *Crisis*," the official magazine of the NAACP, "even during the high days of the jazz age, do we find [editor W.E.B.] Du Bois mentioning [early jazz musicians Louis] Armstrong, or [Duke] Ellington [. . . or] Fletcher Henderson" (130). From a periodical ostensibly committed to the advancement of African American achievements, the omission is glaring.[7]

The exclusion of jazz from the Renaissance intellectuals' design hinges on factors ranging from a desire to resist stereotypes circumscribed by primitivism and exoticism to a heightened class consciousness among 1920s African Americans. As well, the omission is informed by an over–appreciation of Eurocentric artistic product and an underrating of the African American vernacular tradition. The combination of these various aims and misconceptions caused black intellectuals other than Hughes to overlook the significant and lasting contribution to (African) American culture that the jazz musicians of Harlem were making under the guise of popular entertainment and without the pretense of overstated refinement. As Huggins summarizes, "The jazzmen were too busy creating a cultural renaissance to think about the implications of what they were doing" (11). David Meltzer adds: "Despite the early stereotype of jazz musicians as noble savages or simple–minded entertainers [. . . these musicians were involved] in the transmission of an intellectual activity as complex as theoretical physics, allied to a core of emotional power and intelligence" (4–5). The academic complexity of early jazz appears to have eluded the black intellectual mainstream during the 1920s, though. This is evident in Countee Cullen's 1926 *Opportunity* review of Hughes's *The Weary Blues;* Cullen calls Hughes's jazz poems from the collection "interlopers in the company of the truly beautiful poems in other sections of the book," and questions whether "jazz poems really belong to that dignified company, that select and austere circle of high literary expression which we call poetry" (3, 4).

Though the Renaissance defies conclusive categorization and was not a movement working from a decided manifesto or universally agreed–upon aims, it may be summarized in part by some widely accepted generalizations. Cary D. Wintz, for example, labels it "primarily a literary and intellectual movement," and "basically a psychology—a state of mind or an attitude—shared by a number of black writers and intellectuals who centered their activities around Harlem in the late 1920s and early 1930s. These men and women shared little but a consciousness that they were participants in a new awakening of black culture in the United States" (1–2). Similarly, Stephen Watson calls the Renaissance "the first self–conscious black literary constellation in American history," yet adds a historical caveat to allay any undue conclusions (9). "The Harlem Renaissance participants," Watson notes, "did not promote a consistent aesthetic or write in a recognizably 'Renaissance' style" (10).

And though the black intelligentsia who shaped the Renaissance did not form an explicitly named coalition and were by no means a homogeneous or uncontentious group, they undeniably shared some key tenets. One of these was the belief that an oppressed group could better its condition and bring about political and social change through artistic excellence. As Huggins reports, most Harlem intellectuals "saw art and letters as a bridge across the chasm between the races. Artists of both races [. . .] might meet on the common ground of shared beauty and artistic passion. It was thought that this alliance 'at the top' would be the agency to bring the races together over the fissures of ignorance, suspicion and fear" (5). The strategy was espoused in some form by all four of the men who comprised the Renaissance's quartet of unofficial intellectual leadership—namely, W.E.B. Du Bois, Charles S. Johnson, James Weldon Johnson, and Alain Locke.

Cary Wintz reports that as early as 1905 Du Bois was advocating the use of literature to better the Negro's condition by improving the opinion of African Americans in the white imagination. The forum in which Du Bois envisioned this reconfiguration taking place would be a literary "Negro Journal" that would offer depictions of black American life "on its beautiful and interesting side" (qtd in Wintz 143). Charles Johnson shared Du Bois's faith in the importance of black literary publications, but also put to work the notion of self–improvement through art in practical ways, like engineering the March 1924 Civic Club dinner to celebrate the publication of Jessie Fauset's novel, *There Is Confusion,* an occasion that brought together black writers like Fauset, Langston Hughes, and Countee Cullen and white writers like H.L. Mencken and Eugene O'Neill (Lewis 89–93). Likewise, in his 1922 preface to *The Book of American Negro Poetry,* James Weldon Johnson offered his variation on the theme, attesting that "nothing will do more to change the mental attitude and raise his status than a demonstration of intellectual parity by the Negro through the production of literature and art" (9). Four years later, Locke would project virtually the same sentiment in his anthology, *The New Negro,* claiming that the "immediate hope [for improving the conditions of African Americans] rests in the revaluation of white and black alike of the Negro in terms of his artistic endowments and cultural contributions, past and prospective" (15). However, despite this rhetoric of exaltation for the black arts, jazz music— already a product of popularity and influence by the 1920s—was ignored in this strategic cultural awakening.

Though the Harlem intellectuals appreciated jazz as background music for the Renaissance—ubiquitous as it was in Harlem nightclubs—and, per-haps more importantly, as potential fodder for more refined African Ameri-can artistic products, none of the quartet found the music worthy of acclaim on its own merits. Rather, they confined jazz to the province of the vernacu-lar and the folk, to those African American traditions that might prove the foundation on which the "real" Negro contributions to American art and culture might be built. Jazz could be valuable only as the basis for something more ambitious. James Weldon Johnson dramatized this notion in his 1913 novel, *The Autobiography of an Ex-Colored Man,* in his black protagonist's desire to take the ragtime music that had "originated in the questionable resorts about Memphis and St. Louis by Negro piano–players [. . .] guided by natural musical instinct and talent" and transform it into symphonic com-positions (447). Likewise, an essay, entitled, "Jazz at Home," by J.A. Rogers in Locke's *New Negro,* referred to the "vulgarities and crudities of the lowly origin" of jazz which, if superseded, might yield a "higher" musical form (221). Though Rogers could admit that jazz ranked "with the movie and the dollar as a foremost exponent of modern Americanism," his belief that the "true spirit of jazz is a joyous revolt from convention, custom, [and] author-ity" seems to have moved him to separate the music from the "high" arts (216–17).[8] Furthermore, Stephen Watson notes that "Du Bois did not entirely reject such African-American folk expression as the blues and the black dance, [but] he believed that they would assume more elevated 'artistic' forms as the race evolved. From his perspective, there was little place for Jelly Roll Morton or Bessie Smith, the blues or jazz [. . .] until these idioms had been transformed into 'serious' art" (94).

If jazz was perceived as occupying a place on the low end of the "evo-lutionary" scale of African American culture—that is, as a form that was itself crude but might be transformed into something refined—one chief reason was likely the music's unfortunate association with the primitivist commodification of black culture for white consumers. In the 1920s, white New Yorkers used jazz and black musical entertainment as controlled points of contact with the primitive and the exotic. For example, the strip of clubs on "133rd Street between Lenox and Seventh avenues" which "catered to a predominantly white trade" was nicknamed Jungle Alley (Watson 124). As Ann Douglas writes:

Jazz, like the dances it spawned, like its predecessor ragtime and its companion the blues, was the creation of America's Negro population, and white urban Americans wanted to go straight to the source to get more of it. [. . .] About 125 [Harlem] nightclubs, led by the Cotton Club and Connie's Inn, served up African-American music and dancing to the white patrons eager to enjoy a little regression back to jungle life. (74)

Nathan Huggins notes that "cabarets [were] decorated with tropical and jungle motifs," providing a "cheap safari" for white New Yorkers, a safe journey into a virtual heart of darkness where the "black savages were civilized—not head–hunters or cannibals" (89–90). And the music of perhaps the most famous band to emerge from the Renaissance—the Duke Ellington Orchestra—came to be known as the "jungle style," typified by "the beat of the rhythm and plaintive wail of the reeds, as well as [. . .] muted growls, dirty tones, and wah–wah lines in the brass" (Clar 304).

Accordingly, the "primal African–ness" of the music is repeatedly underscored in white writers' responses to jazz from the period. An infamous 1921 article by Anne Shaw Faulkner for *Ladies Home Journal* asks in its title, "Does Jazz Put the Sin in Syncopation?" and traces the music's genealogy back to "the accompaniment of the voodoo dancer stimulating the half–crazed barbarian to the vilest deeds" (16). Likewise, even though the music's incubation occurred unquestionably on American soil in the early years of the century, R.W.S. Mendl in a 1927 volume entitled *The Appeal of Jazz* refers to the music as a "strange, excitable visitor from another continent" (qtd in Meltzer, *Reading* 67). Mendl's label simultaneously inscribes jazz, and by extension its African American creators, as alien and animal.

White writer and Harlem Renaissance impresario Carl Van Vechten corroborates the primitive stereotype in his description of jazz performance in the opening section of the 1926 novel, *Nigger Heaven:*

Their knees clicked amorously. On all sides of the swaying couple, bodies in picturesque costumes rocked, black bodies, brown bodies, high yellows, a kaleidoscope of colour transfigured by the amber searchlight. [. . .] The drummer in complete abandon tossed his sticks in the air while he shook his head like a wild animal. [. . .] The banjos planked deleriously. The band snored and snorted and whistled and laughed like a hyena. (14)

Van Vechten's phantasmagoria emphasizes the wildness of the music and exoticizes the various colors of the men and women in attendance. In addition, it introduces another menacing trope that dominates early jazz discourse: the inexorable link between jazz music and exaggerated or immoral sexuality. As the "magic rhythm" of the music in Van Vechten's scene concludes, his character Ruby promises her companion, "Ah sho' will show you some lovin,' daddy" (15). Likewise, a "scrawny yellow girl in pink silk" suggestively sings: "Mah daddy rocks me with one steady roll;/Dere ain' no slippin' when he once takes hol'" (16).[9]

The eroticization of jazz turns up time and again in early texts covering jazz. Describing the broadcast radio performance of a "negro orchestra" in 1929, the Russian novelist Maxim Gorky writes: "All this insulting chaos of mad sounds is submitted to an imperceptible rhythm and after listening for one, two minutes to those wails, one begins unwillingly to imagine that this is an orchestra of maniacs, stricken with sexual mania and directed by a man–stallion who brandishes a huge genetic member" (119). Whereas Gorky's estimation of jazz confirms Frantz Fanon's later assertion in *Black Skin, White Masks,* that in the white imagination black males are invariably a figure of sexual potency (170), a 1927 *Variety* review of Duke Ellington's inaugural performance at Harlem's Cotton Club associates jazz with a fetishized representation of the black female body. The article, written by critic Abel Green, fixates predominantly not on the musicianship of Ellington's orchestra, but on the band's accompanying dancers. Sexual attraction informs the review:

> The almost Caucasian–hued high yaller gals look swell and uncork the meanest kind of cooching ever exhibited to a conglomerate mixed audience. One coocher, boyish bobbed hoyden, said to be especially imported from Chicago for her Annapolis proclivities who does the Harlem River Quiver like no self–respecting body of water. The teasin'est torso tossing yet, and how! (31)

"Harlem River Quiver," an early number that the Ellington band recorded for RCA Victor just two weeks after this review's publication, impressed itself on Green's imagination only in conjunction with the sexually uninhibited performance of the Cotton Club dancers. The review, like Gorky's description, reveals how the shock of an ostensibly exaggerated African American sensuality in jazz eclipses any genuine estimation of musicality for the white listener/spectator.

Undeniably, then, an unwillingness to pander to this voyeuristic economy and perpetuate the notion of the American black as the bestial, lustful Other helped precipitate the exclusion of jazz from the informal political agenda of the Harlem intellectuals.[10] Du Bois was especially ardent in his public contradiction of this persistent misrepresentation. He criticized Van Vechten's novel as an "affront to the hospitality of black folk," and a gross distortion of Harlem life in its depiction of "one damned orgy after another" (*"Nigger Heaven"* 516–17). Du Bois was similarly critical of work by black novelists like Rudolph Fisher and Claude McKay whom he felt ignored the "beauty" of black life and depicted the ghetto existence of the African American instead. Criticizing McKay's 1928 novel *Home to Harlem,* a book that notably features representations of Harlem's jazz–scored nightlife, Du Bois raged that the author had pandered to the "prurient demand on the part of white folk for a portrayal in Negroes of that utter licentiousness which conventional civilization holds white folk back from enjoying" ("Two Novels" 202). Ultimately, Du Bois frowned on any black literature that was potentially self–deprecating to the race as a whole, and argued that African American artists and writers needed always to represent black experience in "beautiful" terms.[11]

Though the Harlem intelligentsia were reluctant to endorse jazz within their race–advancement agenda, many white modernist writers in the United States looked to the music as one of the home–grown factors that defined the national scene and enabled the emergence of a distinctly American culture. Through depiction of jazz performances or mimesis of the music's stylistic properties, jazz figured into 1920s poems by "high" modernists like T.S. Eliot, William Carlos Williams, and Mina Loy, and by popular poets like Carl Sandburg and Vachel Lindsay.[12] Williams in particular argued through-out his career that jazz was emblematic of and crucial to the American idiom he championed. Defining that indigenous style in language and literature, the poet proclaimed in 1950: "We should have to insist that English prosody as established by English custom [. . .] is a purely arbitrary matter wholly unre-lated to our own [American] language or necessity" (qtd in Wagner 60).[13] Loy made similar connections between modernist poetics and the music. In her 1925 essay "Modern Poetry," she asserted that both American poetry and jazz reflected "the collective spirit of the modern world," an aggregate character that recognized itself in "the new music of unprecedented instru-ments" and in "the new poetry of unprecedented verse" (157). As Loy explained, the similarity between the two lay in the "fresh impetus" both had received from "contemporary life; they ha[d] both gained in precipitance of movement" (157). In her reading of jazz as one of the obvious products of the accelerated motion of modern life, Loy echoed Waldo Frank, who saw jazz as a cultural commodity that exemplified industrial urbanization:

> Jazz syncopates the lathe–lunge, jazz shatters the piston–thrust, jazz shreds the hum of wheels, jazz is the spark and sudden lilt centrifugal

to their incessant pulse. Jazz is a moment's gaiety, after which the spirit droops, cheated and unnurtured. The song is not an escape from the Machine to limpid depths of the soul. It is the Machine itself! [. . .] Its voice is the mimicry of our industrial havoc. (118–19)

In all of these readings of jazz, the music is ultra–modern art, the signal sound of the *zeitgeist*. It is not a folk product—as Harlem's Negro intelligentsia had asserted—that was important only as possible source material for future artistic landmarks.[14] While W.E.B. Du Bois, the Johnsons and Alain Locke saw potential in jazz but not artistic arrival, white modernists—perhaps overwhelmed by the sudden recognition of the rhythmic difference and improvisational nature of African American music with which they had been previously unfamiliar—heralded the music as a key signifier of contemporary life.[15]

By using jazz so extensively in his poetry, Langston Hughes thus seems especially prescient in his recognition of the music's importance to America's national culture, and akin to his white contemporaries in realizing the poetic importance of jazz. This connection between Hughes and white modernism is perhaps too often ignored in evaluations of the poet's career. Hughes has long been relegated to the province of "blackness," recognized for his place within the Harlem Renaissance, but under–appreciated as a key voice in American literature overall.[16] Though Hughes was indeed a poet who turned to "racial" themes throughout the 1920s and gave voice to African American causes, he did maintain aesthetic connections with white writers and recognized his place within a broader American literary tradition. As a high school student, for instance, Hughes was introduced to and influenced by moderns like Edgar Lee Masters, Edwin Arlington Robinson, Amy Lowell, Vachel Lindsay, and Carl Sandburg (Rampersad 28). Hughes himself admitted in his first autobiography, *The Big Sea*, that as a teenage apprentice he tried to write like Sandburg, whom he called "his guiding light" (29–30). Thus, from the beginning of his literary career, Hughes imagined himself within the general context of contemporary poetry, rather than only within African American expressive traditions. Unsurprisingly, then, his use of jazz seems to answer imperatives set by expatriate Ezra Pound, the outspoken patriarch of modernist poetry, in the 1915 preface to *Some Imagist Poets*. Among the "essentials of all great poetry," Pound includes:

1. To use the language of common speech [. . .] .
2. To create new rhythms—as the expression of new moods—and not to copy old rhythms, which merely echo old moods [. . .] . In poetry, a new cadence means a new idea.

> 3. To allow absolute freedom in the choice of subject. [. . .] We
>   believe passionately in the artistic value of modern life [...] . (135)

Hughes's verse responds to Pound's calls on all accounts.[17] In his literary
stylization of the blues, Hughes adopts the language of "common"—that
is, black vernacular—speech; the fragmented lining and irregular caesurae
of his jazz poems fashion new rhythms in their break from traditional English meter; his willingness to depict Harlem's rent parties and cabarets
reveals his faith in the aesthetic value of modern black urban life, as well as
his assertiveness against the strictures on representation maintained by
Harlem's intellectual leaders.

However, by emphasizing this connection between Hughes and "mainstream" modernism, I do not wish to downplay his relationship to a distinctly African American modernism. Rather, I wish to argue that Hughes
and African American modernism itself should occupy a more central place
in readings of American modernist literature based on the contention that
"black" and "white" cultures in the United States were inextricable in the
development of American modernism. In this, I want to build on the work
of scholars like North and Douglas, and develop their suggestion that American modernism is a distinctly "mongrel" tradition that reflects the exchange
of indigenous cultural influences in the United States.[18] Both North and
Douglas argue that black–white interaction in the United States is one of the
crucial facets, if not the defining condition, of modernist literature in America. Hughes is an especially critical figure in the development of American
"mongrel" modernism because his poetry forges a conscious stylistic kinship
with white "mainstream" modernists while it marks black cultural difference and furthers the political agenda of Harlem's cultural leaders. Moreover, the poet's use of jazz is vital to his importance in American modernism
because the music is especially key to that cultural evolution, just as significant a development as the iconoclastic efforts of white modernist artists. For
instance, as David Levering Lewis writes, "[t]he March 12, 1926, opening
of the Savoy [Ballroom in Harlem] shook America as profoundly in its own
way as the 1913 Armory Show had turned the world of mainstream art
inside out" (170). In this view, the hot jazz of Fletcher Henderson's Rainbow
Orchestra is as important to the definition of modernism as Marcel
Duchamp's (in)famous painting, "Nude Descending a Staircase." Lewis's
assessment puts jazz music among the cultural landmarks with which it
belongs—next to Surrealist art and Imagist poetry—rather than ignoring its
significance due to its African American popular culture origins. And yet,
though major studies like North's and Douglas's acknowledge the importance of cultural hybridity in the definition of American modernism, these

books are predominantly centered around (re)readings of white modernist literature, focusing primarily on previously unexplored "black" influences in the work of writers like Eliot, Williams, and Loy.[19] If American modernism is to be re-evaluated as a culturally hybrid phenomenon, then the work of black writers demands more consideration, especially in relation to a national modernist literature, and as more than just an "influence" on white cultural production.[20] Thus, the writers of the Harlem Renaissance need to be placed closer to the center of the field and recognized for their contributions to this hybridity.

My thinking in this regard departs from the work of Douglas and North, but is influenced considerably by theories of hybridity, as suggested by Homi Bhabha and Paul Gilroy, which seek to deconstruct longstanding discursive divisions between "colonizer" and "colonized" (in Bhabha's case), or between "black" and "white" (in Gilroy's). As Bhabha argues, the relationship between the colonizer and colonized in colonial states is always one of interdependence, and contact between the two unavoidably leads to the mutual construction of their subjectivities. Colonial cultures, then, are marked by a hybridity in which the division between the two ostensibly distinct cultural entities is collapsed, to be replaced by a blended third space that undermines the colonizer's anxious assertion of discreteness and domination. Thus, the complete division of colonizer and colonized in their shared cultural space is always an artificial separation of self and Other repeatedly erected and maintained by the former. As Bhabha writes, "the effect of colonial power [cannot be seen as . . .] the noisy command of colonialist authority or the silent repression of native traditions," but rather as "a *problematic* of colonial representation and individuation that reverses the effects of the colonialist disavowal, so that other 'denied' knowledges enter upon the dominant discourse and estrange the basis of its authority" (154, 156, original emphasis). Similarly, Paul Gilroy argues that African diasporic cultures have been inextricable from the development of Western modernity and that the Black Atlantic (as he terms the diaspora, to describe its intercontinental status) disrupts notions of fixed cultural differences maintained by both the discursive guardians of that Western intellectual tradition and its politically insubordinate others. As Gilroy observes, the "reflexive cultures and consciousness" of European settlers and the peoples they oppressed "were not, even in situations of the most extreme brutality, sealed off hermetically from one another," though that ostensibly "self-evident observation [. . . .] has been systematically obscured by commentators from all sides of political opinion" (2). To counter this persistent trend, Gilroy suggests an attention to "routes" rather than "roots" when examining the culture of the Black Atlantic and its relationship to the development of Western thought. In effect, then, scholars, in assuming the constructed-ness of absolute cultural difference, should turn to material histories, and the sometimes haphazard interactions that result, when considering moder-nity's complex problem of cultural formation (19).

I should be clear at this point that I am not trying to ignore the histor-ical specificities that inspired these two theoretical models by awkwardly superimposing the two frameworks onto the development of American lit-erary modernism, but I do find them enabling in their shared revelation of the ongoing constructedness of ethnic and/or racial cultural difference. This constructedness, as both theorists assert, is the superficial effect of either a power struggling to maintain itself or divided factions trying to defend sep-arations of self–other for nationalistic purposes in the cultural arena. Con-sequently, my view of Hughes as a "hybrid" modernist departs from the very valuable foundations Douglas and North have laid in their studies of American modernism, but is refined by the complications that Bhabha's and Gilroy's theories propose. While Douglas and North make efforts to demarcate racial influences and discrete cultural differences, I find it pro-ductive to keep in mind Bhabha and Gilroy's efforts to subvert assertions of absolute difference.

In addition, while I find Bhabha and Gilroy useful to my project for their theoretical propositions about hybrid subjectivity, with respect to lan-guage and literature I view American modernist hybridity as akin to what M.M. Bakhtin calls "organic hybridity," namely, that unavoidable (and perhaps unconscious) mutation that occurs in a language when speakers of that language from different worldviews interact.[21] As Bakhtin writes in "Discourse and the Novel":

> [U]nintentional, unconscious hybridization is one of the most important
> modes in the historical life and evolution of all languages. We may even
> say that language and languages change historically primarily by means
> of hybridization, by means of a mixing of various "languages" co-existing
> within the boundaries of a single dialect, a single national language, a sin-
> gle branch, a single group of a different branches [. . .]. (358–59)

Despite its unconscious nature, this process of organic hybridization can be, in Bakhtin's estimation, "profoundly productive [, . . .] pregnant with potential for new world views"—a process capable of producing a distinct "Americanness" in language that revolutionizes modernist letters (360). Indeed, the "hybridity" that Douglas and North trace in white American modernist writing is marked in many ways by a lack of awareness of those processes already in motion. That is, when writers like Stein, Eliot or

Williams mine from indigenous cultural materials (read, in part, African American expressivity), they are willfully unaware of the constant process of cultural definition that those forms already enact on American language and literature. Thus, as Aldon Nielson suggests, it is absurd to go back and read white American literature with an attention to the discrete black influences that impress on that "white" expressivity. Instead, one should be looking at American literature with the assumption that *all* of it constitutes a cross–racial and intertextual tradition already, marked by forms of expression that have always permeated socially constructed boundaries. However, in arguing as much, Nielson does not seek to neglect the material inequalities in power relations that inevitably affect language and expression, and, as a result, read American literary hybridity as a balanced process of cultural exchange that is identical for black and white writers. Rather, he concedes, "black and white writers can and often do mean differently when using the 'same' words and forms"—but even this concession to difference is ultimately complicated by the fact that "[American] languages [can] never be wholly pulled apart" (23).

In *The Signifying Monkey,* Henry Louis Gates takes up Bakhtin's notion of hybridity in language as he constructs a theoretical paradigm for reading African American literature based on expressive modes that he argues are unique to the black vernacular. The black literary tradition, Gates posits, is inherently intertextual and revels in the free play of signification. It is a tradition of repetition and revision, ever rehearsing and modifying both white texts and texts from its own tradition. As well, both the self–reflexivity of black literature and its intertextual relationship to white literature are informed by the oral/aural matrix of the African American vernacular. As Gates writes, "Free of the white person's gaze, black people created their own unique vernacular structures and relished in the double play that these forms bore to white forms. Repetition and revision are fundamental to black artistic forms, from painting and sculpture to music and language use" (xxiv). Gates argues that this constant intertextual play within the African American vernacular led to the formation of a black literary tradition that is "double–voiced," composed of "texts that talk to other texts," an expressive mode he calls Signifyin(g). This process, as Gates himself notes, is similar to the concept Bakhtin calls an "intentional hybrid" or a "double–voiced word" in language, in which "two points of view are not mixed, but set against each other dialogically" in a single utterance (360).

This notion of double–voicedness in African American literature is significant to the literary milieu of the Harlem Renaissance. As Nathan Huggins articulates, the challenge of the Harlem Renaissance writer was to create art that "attempts to speak with two voices, one from the stage of national culture and the other from the soul of ethnic experience" (195). The quintessential hybrid modernist, Langston Hughes addressed this challenge, and indeed, his use of jazz was essential to the formation of this double-voiced address, facilitating both his "national" articulation and the "ethnic" speech that was distinctly African American. Hughes recognized the inseparability of jazz from the race–advancement project championed by the intelligentsia. He could see that jazz had become ubiquitous beyond the boundaries of "Negro culture" in a short period of time. Its problematic association with primitivism and white specularity notwithstanding, the music was making an impact on American modern culture's definition-in-process. If the intent of the New Negro "movement" was to improve the state of African Americans by affirming the importance of black culture on the universal scene, then jazz seemed too consequential a product to ignore. As Hughes proclaimed in his famous essay, "The Negro Artist and the Racial Mountain," nothing was more indicative of black culture's aesthetic achievement in a world of white power than the new music: "[J]azz to me is one of the inherent expressions of Negro life in America: the eternal tom-tom beating in the Negro soul—the tom-tom of revolt against weariness in a white world, a world of subway trains and work, work, work; the tom-tom of joy and laughter, and pain swallowed in a smile" (58).

Hughes's jazz poems are so important to American modernism because they make use of the stylistic innovation within the "American idiom" that defined the white moderns while, at the same time, they enable the assertion of African American culture and racial pride imperative to the New Negro renaissance. In their use of jazz, white modernists too often fell into what Michael North calls "a pattern of rebellion through racial ventriloquism," distancing themselves from their English literary antecedents by adopting "black voices" (9). Jazz was attractive to these iconoclasts because it was both indigenous to the United States and radically removed from any artform that had emerged in periods past from across the Atlantic. Charles S. Johnson perceived this difference in a 1928 article in *The Carolina Magazine,* entitled "Jazz Poetry and the Blues." Distinguishing between "Negro" poems *about* African Americans (of which he considered Sandburg's jazz poems an example) and "Negro" poetry *by* African Americans, Johnson wrote that the latter was "the expression of something more than experimentation in a new technique. It mark[ed] the birth of a new racial consciousness and self conception" (17). That is, while white modernists looked to jazz as an enabling form in their modernization of American poetics, black poets like Hughes, whom Johnson quotes explicitly, might use jazz in that way *and* to assert racial pride. White modernists turned to jazz merely as a break from polite conventions; Hughes, by contrast, looked to jazz as a celebration of African American life.

Consider the difference, for example, between William Carlos Williams's "Shoot It Jimmy," a lyric from 1923's *Spring and All,* and Hughes's "Jazz Band in a Parisian Cabaret," from *The Weary Blues.* Williams uses jazz as the untutored idiom—nonstandard, musical slang— that enables a break from English verse, an insurrection conveyed through the speaker's brusque colloquialisms: "Our orchestra/is the cat's nuts—"; "That sheet stuff/'s a lot a cheese" (lines 1–2; lines 9–10). Ultimately, his engagement with jazz is superficial. Though Williams tries on some level— with the use of irregular rhythms and ragged caesurae—to simulate jazz rhythm, the poem is predominantly an epigrammatic experiment with the hipster parlance associated with jazz musicians. Williams uses the special- ized lingo of the jazz musician to make good on the "terrible honesty" Ann Douglas argues was crucial to communication among the moderns, the generation that "introduced into what was left of polite society the full spectrum of long-tabooed profanity" (54). Furthermore, beyond its break from conventional English verse, the poem is emblematic of another rebel- lious trend David Meltzer sees in American literature of the period, particu- larly by white male writers who "used the art of jazz as a tactic to shock the bourgeoisie and separate themselves from the cultural and social pressures of middle-class entrapment" ("Pre-ramble" 5).

Conversely, in "Jazz Band in a Parisian Cabaret," Hughes rejects this depiction of jazz as an impudent form that facilitates rebellion and a radical break from polite sensibilities, and instead celebrates the music as a liberat- ing idiom that allows for communication between African Americans and the world at large:

> Play that thing:
> jazz band!
> Play it for the lords and ladies,
> For the dukes and counts,
> For the whores and gigolos,
> For the American millionaires,
> And the school teachers
> Out for a spree.
> Play it,
> Jazz band!
> You that tune
> That laughs and cries at the same time.
> You know it.

> May I?
> May oui.
> Mein Gott!
> Parece una rumba.
> Play it, jazz band!
> You've got seven languages to speak in
> And then some,
> Even if you do come from Georgia.
>   Can I go home wid yuh, sweetie?
>   Sure.
>   (*Collected* 60)

Hughes contradicts Williams's simple depiction of jazz as a ragging of standard English. Where Williams emphasizes the music's ostensible capacity for insurrection, Hughes underscores its semantic complexity beyond that superficial boldness. Hughes admits that jazz may appear raw to the untrained observer, but he is quick to point out the short–sightedness of that reading. The jazz band may come from Georgia, but its music speaks seven languages and then some. The music as imagined by Hughes eschews rough rebellion and expresses a complex humanity that transcends stereotype.[22]

In addition, Hughes's celebratory use of jazz is emblematic of the "two–tiered mastery" of form and technique that Jon Michael Spencer argues is crucial to the "success" of African American modernism, especially in black music. In *The New Negroes and Their Music*, Spencer offers a re-evaluation of the Harlem Renaissance, contradicting earlier retrospective assessments, like those by Huggins and Lewis, which argue that the Renaissance was a failure as a concentrated "movement" intent on mixing politics and aesthetics. Challenging the notion that the Renaissance failed because it did not alleviate "the old problem of racism," Spencer contends that the New Negro "movement" was successful because it fulfilled its own most important goal: to "vindicate" the New Negro from the sentimental mythology of the Old Negro, which had endured under the influence of white discourses for too long (5–6).[23] Spencer purports that the unofficially accepted *modus operandi* for fulfilling this objective was what he calls a "two–tiered mastery" in the arts. Basing his concept on Alain Locke's statement that "[t]he artistic problem of the Young Negro has not been so much that of acquiring the outer mastery of form and technique, as that of achieving an inner mastery of mood and spirit" (qtd in Spencer 20), Spencer suggests that African American modernism, as it developed out of the New Negro renaissance, revises white artistic forms and techniques according to Negro "mood and spirit." That is, African American modernism is centered on artistic innovation through the injection of a recognizably black cultural difference.

Spencer derives his thinking here from Houston Baker's *Black Modernism and the Harlem Renaissance,* building on Baker's theory of "mastery of form" and "deformation of mastery." As Baker argues, "mastery of form" and "deformation of mastery" are the signal tropes that define African American modernist expressivity and cultural performance. Both concepts, he maintains, can be likened to the wearing of masks. Mastery of form is the assumption of a minstrel–type mask, a mask that conceals "real" black identity, and through which the African American cultural performer may speak to whites from a position of safety. On the other hand, deformation of mastery is the donning of a mask that distinguishes, that, in fact, *advertises* black difference as through vernacular performance.[24] In his notion of "two–tiered mastery," Spencer proposes that black music of the Harlem Renaissance constitutes a progression across the range marked by Baker's signal tropes. That is, the insertion of "black difference" into European and traditionally "white" cultural forms constitutes a move from "mastery of form" to "deformation of mastery" (Spencer 110). Spencer argues that the music of New Negro composers like R. Nathaniel Dett, who orchestrated Negro spirituals for "traditional" choral groups, and William Grant Still, who composed his *Afro-American Symphony* based on blues and jazz figures, enacts a "creative deformation" that—true to the aims of Harlem intellectuals—vindicated African Americans from the strictures of stereotype and the legacy of the Old Negro.[25]

Spencer centers his discussion of "two–tiered" mastery in New Negro music on major classical composers. Because his defense of the New Negro renaissance is founded on the contention that the "movement" realized its own objectives, Spencer's discussion of African American music focuses on composers championed by intellectuals like Locke and Johnson, rather than jazz bandleaders like Duke Ellington and Fletcher Henderson, or noted soloists like Louis Armstrong and James P. Johnson. As Spencer points out, the Negro intelligentsia who articulated this plan of racial vindication did not have faith themselves in "the popular music of the urban Negro" (read jazz) for accomplishing this aesthetic–political goal because the music "did not show the mastery of the resources of the modern orchestra" (22). This belief is governed by the misguided notion that jazz was a folk music—an expressive form marked by untutored spontaneity—and as such was wholly removed from the "higher" regimen of European classical music. I contend, however, that jazz fashioned a "mastery of form and technique" (to use Spencer's term) perhaps even more important than that

offered by the music of Dett or Still, because jazz established black difference in Western music through its influence on white classical composers.
Indeed, the aesthetics of jazz became the ideals to which those composers
aspired. As Nathan Huggins suggests, "It was as if black jazzmen, from the
very beginning, sensed that they were creating an art, and the whole world
would have to find them the reference point for critical judgment" (198).
Consider the list of significant white modernist composers inspired to
adopt jazz styles in their orchestral works, a group that includes Stravinsky,
Milhaud, Ravel, Satie, Debussy, and Gershwin. To exclude jazz from the
project of "racial vindication" for its superficial incongruities with classical
music was to ignore its larger musical significance. As Duke Ellington
expressed later in 1944:

> Jazz, swing, jive, and every other musical phenomenon of American musi-
> cal life are as much an art medium as are the most profound works of the
> famous classical composers. [. . . To] attempt to elevate the status of the
> jazz musician by forcing the level of his best work into comparisons with
> classical music is to deny him his rightful share of originality. (6)

I offer this defense of jazz *vis-à-vis* Spencer's re-evaluation of the
Harlem Renaissance in order to develop my contention that Hughes was
the quintessential *literary* New Negro modernist, according to the framework of "two–tiered mastery" Spencer defines in black music. Hughes is
perhaps not the most obvious New Negro writer to exemplify Spencer's
scheme; his contemporary, Countee Cullen, a poet who wrote sonnets (a
fixed "form and technique") about racial themes (thus capturing the Negro
"mood and spirit") may seem a more likely analogue to the African American classical composers Spencer celebrates. However, I wish to adopt in a
more meaningful way Spenser's valuable standards for re-evaluation of the
Renaissance to argue that Hughes, like the jazz musicians by whom he was
influenced, exemplifies African American modernism more significantly
because his music poems constitute mastery on a larger level. Hughes's
propensity for stylistic experimentation through mimesis of jazz represents
a mastery of literary form and techniques that were *in flux*. Thus, his kinship with white poets like Williams and Loy marks his relevance to the definition of a national modernism—in all that culture's chaos and
discordance—more strongly than Cullen's use of traditional literary forms.
If the goal of the New Negro movement was to vindicate African Americans from the fiction of the Old Negro via a revision of the arts, then
Hughes was surely one of the period's most successful practitioners for
being *so* modern in his poetics.

Moreover, one of the reasons I wish to emphasize Hughes's place among those traditionally exalted white modernist figures is to debunk the notion that Hughes was a "folk" poet, a simple writer who was driven by spontaneity and impulse rather than literary skill. Hughes's poetry is too often misinterpreted as unartistic, viewed as dissimilar from the intellectual experimentation of the white moderns. His stylistically complex work is as misunderstood as the music of those jazz contemporaries from whom he drew inspiration—those musicians whom David Meltzer argues were stereotyped as "noble savages or simple–minded entertainers" ("Pre-Ramble" 4). This misreading dominates contemporary reviews of Hughes's work and later evaluations. For example, the black American writer and NAACP secretary Jessie Fauset wrote in her ostensibly celebratory 1926 *Crisis* review of *The Weary Blues* that Hughes's "poems are warm, exotic and shot through with color. Never is he preoccupied with form. But this fault, if it is one, has its corresponding virtue, for it gives his verse, which almost always is imbued with the essence of poetry, the perfection of spontaneity" (239). A similar discourse of atavism and spontaneity informed early receptions of the same volume in the white press as well. Irvin Shapiro's 1926 *Washington Herald* review, for instance, described Hughes's poems as "rich, powerful and spontaneous," and suggested that "[t]here was authentic Negro rhythm running through his verse" (6D).

Furthermore, a fixation on blues "authenticity" and an untainted folk "blackness" carries over into later academic readings of Hughes's early poetry. Too often critics of the poet have missed the modernness of Hughes's work and instead have tried to place him in a folk context, viewing him next to the "black and unknown bards," to use James Weldon Johnson's words, who sang (and continue to sing) the blues within the collective anonymity of African American oral culture.[26] Nathan Huggins, for instance, in discussing Hughes's liberation from traditional verse forms, rehearses the primitivist myth that dictates those earlier reviews of the poet's work:

The acceptance of an intuitive truth and a spontaneous art freed [Hughes] from any commitment to a necessary form [. . .] . Any arrangement of words could be poetic if it captured the mystical essence of the human voice. The measure of rightness had more to do with the closeness to real human experience than it did with rules of verse or rhyme. Hughes never studied versification in any formal way [. . .] . Hughes believed the poet should not wrestle with rules of poetics; they distorted the freshness and trueness of the poet's vision. A poem was an instant life–song frozen into words. (221–22)

Huggins too easily collapses the transitional distance I wish to maintain between Hughes and the folk when he concludes that Hughes, in drawing on the vernacular (as in his blues poems), "was not writing to be approved as a literary poet" and "avoided the Scylla of formalism only to founder in the Charybdis of folk art" (226–27).

My underlying problem with these interpretations of Hughes's poetic practice is their misreading of the poet's relationship to the blues. I suggest, in contrast, that even though Hughes wrote poems in blues lyric form, the mere act of transforming that vernacular orature into a stylized literature—and thus transposing the source material of the folk into a new context—unavoidably constitutes an act of revision that privileges and asserts the poet's individual voice before the folk collective. This act corresponds with the process that Malcolm Bradbury and James McFarlane argue is central to a general modernist style: "[The Modernist artist] is perpetually engaged in a profound and ceaseless journey through the means and integrity of art. In this sense, Modernism is less a style than a search for a style in a highly individualistic sense" (29). Moreover, this process that Bradbury and McFarlane locate in all modernist art is especially prominent to the specifically African American modernist art of jazz.

Viewed in close context with jazz, Hughes's work clearly reveals the confluence of American "national" modernism and African American "ethnic" modernism that I am trying to establish. Steven Tracy implicitly asserts this when he compares Hughes to early jazz and "classic" blues composers like Andy Razaf, Clarence Williams, and W.C. Handy, "who drew upon their black folk roots but had a somewhat more distanced perspective on those roots" ("Tune" 74).[27] Specifically addressing the artistic similarities between Hughes and Handy, Tracy writes that "both were concerned with 'championing' the blues and with imposing some of their own ideas on the authentic folk material as well" (75). Indeed, the imposition of the individual as paradoxically part of, but more important than, the collective is one of jazz music's central stylistic traits, and one that had become a recognizable quality in the music during Hughes's early years as a jazz–inspired poet. The music's chief innovator in this regard was undoubtedly Louis Armstrong, the New Orleans–born trumpeter who is almost universally acknowledged as the first great soloist in the jazz pantheon. As Ted Gioia posits, Armstrong's 1923 recordings with the King Oliver Creole Jazz Band almost single–handedly ushered in the Age of the Soloist in jazz. Armstrong's playing in that ensemble, which specialized in the collective improvisation that defined early New Orleans jazz, reconfigured the jazz aesthetic through its inconcealable technical virtuosity. The trumpeter's solos placed new emphasis on the ability of the jazz musician to define him– or herself as an individual voice in the medium (Gioia 51–55). This new accent on individual style, I would argue, is the point at which jazz— and Hughes as a writer immersed in the jazz aesthetic—converges with the "mainstream" modernism of which Bradbury and McFarlane write.

To articulate my argument that Hughes's use of the blues exemplifies a jazz–influenced modernist act, I wish to compare what is perhaps Hughes's most famous blues–based poem, 1925's "The Weary Blues," with the blues–based recording that marked the apex of Armstrong's early individualistic style, "West End Blues," from 1928. Both works reveal the distancing of the solo voice from the folk that I maintain is crucial to the perception of Hughes as quintessential American modernist. In each, the relationship of the solo performance to the folk matrix from which the blues originates is one of intertextuality or inter- musicality, but not imitation. For example, in "The Weary Blues," Hughes immediately establishes this modernist distance by foreground- ing his own solo voice (through the use of the first person "I") as the channel through which the poem's blues singer will be heard. By prefac- ing the blues lyrics that follow with "I heard a Negro play" and "I heard that Negro sing, that old piano moan—," Hughes establishes an intertex- tual relationship between himself and the unnamed blues singer on whom the poem appears to focus (*Collected* 50, lines 3 and 18).[28] The blues that follows—of which Hughes provides two verses—is filtered through the voice of the poet's "I," and thus becomes a musico–textual quotation rather than an untouched expression of the anonymous blues- man's self. Armstrong's "West End Blues" features a similar filtering of the folk through the individual. Though the composition is ultimately a "simple" instrumental blues, the trumpeter's recording begins with a twelve–second *a capella* introduction, such that Armstrong's unique sound on trumpet frames the verse that follows. Similarly, on the record- ing's out–chorus, Armstrong scats the melodic figure around which the verse is based in his own singing voice before drawing the recording to a close with an improvised cadenza on trumpet. Thus, like Hughes's poem, which frames its blues with an assertion of the poet's "I" voice, Arm- strong's recording bookends its "simple" blues verse with dramatic affir- mations of the soloist's musical identity. I make this comparison here between these two seminal African American works of the 1920s not to assert a one-to-one relationship between the two—a move that would be obviously anachronistic—but to emphasize the stylistic debt I read in Hughes's work to the individualistic aesthetic that developed in jazz dur- ing the period. Moreover, I intend my readings of these two works to highlight the interconnectedness I perceive between jazz and the modernist "individualistic" search for style.

In addition, I read Hughes's more straightforward blues poems—that is, those composed in standard blues verse form—as being governed by the same jazz–inspired distance that I read in "The Weary Blues." Unlike other Hughes critics who divide the poet's music poems into two categories, "jazz" and "blues," based on the musical form that each piece resembles on the surface, I read all of Hughes's music poems as "jazz poems," that is, as poems composed according to a jazz aesthetic.[29] Even when the poet is writing lyrics that seem, at first glance, to be merely blues verses transposed to the printed page, I argue that his treatment of the material constitutes a jazz–inspired creative process. In this, I concur with Steven Tracy's reading of Hughes as a "literary–jazz improviser" (*Blues* 225). Moreover, even though jazz and blues seem to be (and indeed in salient ways *are*) discrete musical genres, the latter has its own place within the jazz tradition. A brief exploration of the various connotations of the musical term "blues" here may preclude complications and illuminate the distinctions I wish to establish.

"Blues" is a complicated musical category because, as Tracy notes, it simultaneously refers to "a number of separate entities—an emotion, a technique, a musical form, and a song lyric" (*Blues* 59). Similarly, Paul Oliver and Barry Kernfeld also acknowledge the complexity of the term: "There is no single definition of the term 'blues.' It may indicate a state of mind, describe a music that expresses that state of mind, define a form or structure for performing the music, or identify a manner of performance; it is frequently applied to performances and song types that have a number, if not all, of these characteristics" (121). Both definitions highlight how blues may be a feeling, a standard structural form, or a way of performing a musical composition. As Tracy notes, the term "blues" to describe a feeling is derived from "blue devils," "refers to a mood of despondency," and is not specific to the African American oral or musical traditions (*Blues* 59).[30] This aspect of the term is conveyed in lyrics like Bessie Smith's "Backwater Blues" from 1925:

> Backwater blues done cause me to pack my things and go
> Backwater blues done cause me to pack my things and go
> Cause my house fell down and I can't live there no more.

"Blues" as a structural form in African American music most commonly refers to an eight or twelve bar sequence, harmonically centered around the dominant, subdominant, and tonic of the song's key, usually with an AAB lyric. The "blues" as a musical technique, on the other hand, refers to a performance that incorporates any of the following characteristics: "rough" timbered notes, use of "the so–called blue notes achieved by microtonal flattening of the third and seventh [. . .] of the scale [. . . , b]ending of the notes [. . .] and unconventional techniques of sliding on guitar strings and striking adjacent notes on the piano not quite simultaneously to convey a passing note in imitation of the voice" (Oliver and Kernfeld 122). It is Miles Davis's use of these techniques, for example, that compels jazz biographer Jack Chambers to describe the trumpeter's 1963 recorded performance of Clarence Williams's vaudeville standard, "Baby Won't You Please Come Home," "as a languid ballad that shifts into a lilting blues" (2: 55).

The relationship between blues and jazz is both genealogical and symbiotic. The folk blues as a genre is definitely one of the forms out of which jazz developed, while at the same time, blues as song structure has always been a common framework for jazz improvisation.[31] Indeed, the blues, being such a ubiquitous form in African American music, lends itself well to informal jam sessions among musicians, and as such, has always been a proving ground for young improvisers. For example, jazz pianist Randy Weston comments: "What's the most important element of [jazz]? To play the blues—that's the way I was taught. Incidentally, that's the way our music is always taught, not from books, but aurally, by hanging out with other musicians. Playing the blues was always the test while I was young" (qtd in Lyons 213). As well, many musicians note how the blues—as form, as feeling—constitutes the expressive "heart" of jazz improvisation. For instance, bebop saxophonist Jackie McLean notes that "[t]he blues feeling is part of jazz," and avers, "as long as I play jazz I'll always have that blues feeling. That's for *sure*" (qtd in Wilmer, *People* 121, original emphasis). Pianist Red Garland adds, "When the house is getting cold, play some blues and you can bring it back to life" (qtd in Lyons 148).

In the 1920s, when Hughes began his career as a poet, the symbiosis of jazz and blues was more pronounced than in subsequent periods in the history of jazz. Jazz and blues have become mainly discrete genres of American music over the twentieth century, confined to different performance venues and distinct divisions of record labels. The two forms have developed in different ways: blues emphasizes harmonically "simple" structures and remains a more vocally centered music; jazz is largely a province of instrumental improvisation and ventures into more involved harmonic territory. The chief stars of blues music play the guitar and the harmonica; jazz champions pianists, saxophonists, and trumpet players. Yet in the 1920s, jazz and blues—the popular, urban blues of Harlem and Chicago, at least—were more inextricably linked. For instance, Louis Armstrong, the decade's most influential jazz musician, accompanied the period's most popular blues singer, Bessie Smith, on many of her most famous sides.[32] Likewise, blues compositions rank among ot only Armstrong's most famous 1920s recordings, but also those of his influential jazz contemporaries, Duke Ellington and Jelly Roll Morton.[33]

However, even though jazz and blues were closely linked as Hughes began his literary career, there was clearly a difference between the ways jazz and blues musicians approached the blues. As Steven Tracy writes, "From the beginning of jazz performing, it has been obvious that the jazz musician plays the blues differently from the blues musician" (*Blues* 245).[34] Ted Gioia concurs, using Bessie Smith's 1925 collaborations with Louis Armstrong on "St. Louis Blues" and "Reckless Blues" to develop his position: "[W]e can already hear the different aesthetic sensibilities that, even at this early date, were beginning to distinguish the jazz and blues idioms. Armstrong favors ornamentation and elaboration; Smith tends toward unadorned emotional directness" (19). Burton Peretti, noting the distance between jazz and blues, writes: "Many musicians who later became important early jazz musicians in New Orleans began their lives in the [Mississippi] Delta's plantations, the large riverside settlements worked by white farmers and black sharecroppers. The music these instrumentalists made, however, marked them as men who broke with tradition, as well as with the resolutely rural orientation of the Delta blues and the jook joint" (*Creation* 17). Jazz—especially after Armstrong's individualism—has always marked distance from the blues, using the form as a place from which improvisation departs on the way to transformation for each soloist. "The succession of forms that students learn commonly," to quote Paul Berliner, "begins with the blues, one of the most venerable vehicles in the jazz repertory" (76). Berliner's assertion recalls Randy Weston's statement that the blues constituted both the idiom through which he learned jazz and the form through which he was required to prove himself in playing with other musicians. Moreover, in discussing how jazz musicians play the blues to facilitate the development of their unique musical identities, Samuel A. Floyd, Jr. and Ingrid Monson both perceive the relationship as intertextual, informed by distinctly African American modes of cultural expression. In fact, both Floyd and Monson read the relationship between jazz and blues through Gates's literary theory of Signifyin(g).

Gates himself reads the same double–voicedness he outlines in black literature throughout African American music, especially jazz. He argues: "There are so many examples of Signifyin(g) in jazz that one could write a formal history of its development on this basis alone" (63). Gates adds: "Improvisation [. . . which is] so fundamental to the very idea of jazz, is 'nothing more' than repetition and revision. In this sort of revision, again where meaning is fixed, it is the realignment of the signifier that is the signal trait of expressive genius" (63–64). This is precisely the line of argument upon which Floyd and Monson draw when they comment on the relationship between jazz and the blues. Using Gates's theory as a point of departure, Floyd argues that Signifyin(g) is a dominant expressive mode in African American music:

> In African-American music, musical figures Signify by commenting on other musical figures, on themselves, on performances of other music, on other performances of the same piece, and on completely new works of music. Moreover, genres Signify on other genres—ragtime on European and early European and American dance music; blues on the ballad; the spiritual on the hymn; jazz on blues and ragtime [. . .] . (95)

Contemplating African American musical traditions broadly, Floyd structures his argument around Gates's theory and emphasizes the similarity of expression between the verbal play that Gates observes and the intermusicality in which Floyd is interested:

> [M]usical Signifyin(g) is troping: the transformation of preexisting musical material by trifling with it, teasing it, or censuring it. Musical Signifyin(g) is the rhetorical use of preexisting material as a means of demonstrating respect for or poking fun at a musical style, process, or practice through parody, pastiche, implication, indirection, humor, tone play or word play, the illusion of speech or narration, or other troping mechanisms. (8)

Writing specifically of the jazz idiom, Monson is likewise influenced by Gates's theory and documents the same process of repetition and revision in jazz. Jazz, Monson observes, revels in Signifyin(g)'s play and change; it is a logical extension of an African American musical tradition that turns on the "[t]ransformation of existing genres" (104).

Hughes's blues poems represent this same kind of genre transformation. Unlike critics who read Hughes's blues lyrics as a straightforward attempt to recreate the blues, I maintain that these poems constitute an act of Signifyin(g). Like the jazz soloist who absorbs other genres and stylistic motifs in his performance, Hughes repeats and revises the folk blues in a new context. This process is consistent with the trope of intertextuality that

Gates reads throughout the black literary tradition, but in its specific play with African American musical contexts, it is influenced by the specific acts of intermusical revision on which jazz thrives. Hughes's poetry stands at the crossroads of the African American literary and musical traditions that the above critics map; his work constitutes a literature informed by Signifyin(g)'s process of transformation as governed by the comprehensiveness of jazz. Hughes himself recognized how jazz was an inclusive music that incorporated and transformed other genres. In the 1955 children's book, *The First Book of Jazz,* he succinctly writes, "Jazz is *a way of playing* music even more than it is a composed music. Almost any music can become jazz if it is played with jazz treatment" (46, original emphasis). Similarly, in a contemporaneous *Chicago Defender* essay, "Jazz as Communication," Hughes writes metaphorically, "Jazz is a great big sea. It washes up all kinds of fish and shells and spume and waves with a steady old beat, or off–beat" (493).[35]

Thus, when Hughes writes in blues lyric form, he assumes the inclusivity befitting, in Tracy's words, "a literary–jazz improviser." He takes the blues—either the form or the techniques associated with the music, or both—as a jazz musician might, and incorporates them within his own expressive vocabulary. This is especially evident in the way that Hughes represents the aural performance of the blues singer in his blues poems. Often the poet simulates the unique phrasing and vocal techniques of those who sing the blues. Consider stanzas from "Gypsy Man" and "My Man," respectively, two of Hughes's "blues poems" from *Fine Clothes to the Jew.* In both, Hughes simulates blues vocal style through rhythmic play and repetition:

> Ma man's a gypsy
> Cause he never does come home.
> Ma man's a gypsy,—
> He never does come home.
> I'm gonna be a gypsy woman
> Fer I can't stay here alone.
>
> Once I was in Memphis,
> I mean Tennessee.
> Once I was in Memphis,
> Said Tennessee.
> But I had to leave cause
> Nobody there was good to me. (*Collected* 66, lines 1–13)

Again, in "My Man":

He kin play a banjo.
Lordy, he kin plunk, plunk, plunk.
He kin play a banjo.
I mean plunk, plunk . . . plunk, plunk.
He plays good when he's sober
An' better, better, better when he's drunk. (*Collected* 67, lines 8–13)

In these stanzas, Hughes masterfully suggests the rhythmic play of the blues singer, and, as well, recreates the improvised variations that blues vocalists often perform on the repeated A line in the music's ubiquitous AAB form. The poet's use of the dash, for example, in the third line of "Gypsy Man," typographically signifies a lingering on "gypsy's" second syllable, a tone that Hughes's singer carries across the expected division of the musical bar. This implication is reinforced, as well, by the dropping of "Cause" to start the stanza's fourth line—a beat filled by the holding of "gypsy." Similarly, in the fourth line of "My Man," Hughes uses an ellipsis to create a pause between the fourfold repetition of the word "plunk." Both typographical strategies simulate musical phrasing where it might otherwise seem impossible. Notice how the typographical riff occurs in both poems over the pair of poetic lines that constitutes the second A of the AAB stanza. In both instances, the typographical variation shows a deviation from the rhythm of the poem–song that Hughes sets up with a "straightforward" presentation of the A line to begin the stanza. Thus, Hughes establishes the rhythm of his poem with the first A of the AAB and then plays with the rhythm by either lingering over the implied beat (as in "Gypsy Man") or lagging behind it (as in "My Man"). The strategy simulates the common practice in African and African American musics of Signifyin(g) on the beat of the music: playing on top of or behind a sometimes unheard, but always felt, pulse that guides the performance. As Henry Louis Gates writes:

> Because the form is self–evident to the musician, both he and his well–trained audience are playing and listening with expectation. Signi-fyin(g) disappoints these expectations; caesuras, or breaks, achieve the same function. This form of disappointment creates a dialogue between what the listener expects and what the artist plays. Whereas younger, less mature musicians accentuate the beat, more accomplished musi-cians do not have to do so. They feel free to imply it. (*Signifying* 123)

In addition, while Hughes suggests musical variation in the AAB stanza with typography, he also performs improvisations on his song's lyrics with verbal variation. There are minor changes in the repeat of the A line in both poems. "Cause," as I noted above, is dropped in the repeat of "Gypsy Man"'s first stanza; "Said" replaces "I mean" in the repeat of that poem's second stanza. In "My Man," "I mean" replaces the exhortation "Lordy" in the A line's repeat. All of these subtle verbal variations constitute Hughes's willingness to recreate the blues singer's process in his written work. They represent the common blues practice of improvising on the repeat line in performance. On a connotative level, though, the verbal licks are also important because they collapse the space between the poet's verbal and musical intentions in their simultaneous play with meter and emphasis on speech. Throughout the poem, Hughes foregrounds language—what is "said," what he "means"—as his expressive idiom. He emphasizes the poem's position as a verbal performance, an expressive act that incorporates music *within* its literary–jazz solo—my term for the unique two–way Signifyin(g) relationship Hughes creates between music and text. Just as Floyd remarks that musical Signifyin(g) often includes the "illusion of speech or narration," Hughes highlights speech and narration in the lyrics of a poem that creates the "illusion" of musicality.

Moreover, as other Hughes critics have observed, the poet's blues lyrics also approximate the musical form through their lining and thematic organization. Dellita L. Martin, for example, addresses the former, and notes that Hughes's division of the standard three–line blues stanza in his poetry into a six–line stanza is innovative because it suggests the call-and-response expression common to blues performance. As Martin notes, blues is structured around call-and-response, such that "each vocal statement is balanced by an instrumental response" (152). Martin argues that in his six–line blues stanzas, Hughes recreates this antiphony by making each line in the standard AAB blues stanza enact both a call and a response. An example of this technique, she continues, occurs in "Suicide," also from *Fine Clothes to the Jew.* Consider that poem's first stanza:

> Ma sweet good man has
> Packed his trunk and left.
> Ma sweet good man has
> Packed his trunk and left.
> Nobody to love me:
> I'm gonna kill ma self. (*Collected* 82, lines 1–6)

As Martin points out, the arrangement of the lines creates three antiphonal pairs per stanza, each of which offers either the dialogical affirmation of an idea or its ironic contradiction. For example, the third pair in the above stanza constitutes a call-and-response that affirms the despondency of the poem's singer. The repeated pair with which the stanza begins, on the other hand, is an ironic call-and-response in which the singer reveals the cause of that despondency: her otherwise "sweet good man" has gone and done something awful. The technique replicates a facet of blues performance that might otherwise have seemed impossible to duplicate, yet at the same time, it facilitates the development of the lyric in its literary context: the oscillating relationship between each pair of lines creates thematic interest in its tension (Martin 152). Steven Tracy shares Martin's assessment of Hughes's use of the "half–line" in writing down the blues and notes that it seems an obvious attempt to "bring more of the oral performance, the rhythms of the music and voice, into his poetry" (*Blues* 154). As well, Tracy observes that "[a]lthough Hughes imitated an oral nuance [with the technique], the effect is amplified on the printed page, where the suspension of the line is both auditory *and* visual. This is a perfect example of a literary use that coincides with an oral characteristic" (156, original emphasis).

David Chinitz reads Hughes's blues poems with a similar attention to how the poet replicates blues characteristics through literary style. Chinitz argues that Hughes's creation of ostensibly incongruent stanzas in his blues poems "authentically" replicates the free–associative thematic organization of a blue singer's spontaneous performance.[36] An example of the technique, which Chinitz cites, is Hughes's "Young Gal's Blues" (1927):

> I'm gonna walk to de graveyard
> 'Hind ma friend Miss Cora Lee.
> Gonna walk to de graveyard
> 'Hind ma friend Miss Cora Lee.
> Cause when I'm dead some
> Body'll have to walk behind me.
>
> I'm goin' to the po' house
> To see ma old Aunt Clew.
> Goin' to the po' house
> To see ma old Aunt Clew.
> When I'm old an' ugly
> I'll want to see somebody, too.
>
> The po' house is lonely
> An' the grave is cold.
> O, the po' house is lonely,
> The graveyard grave is cold.
> But I'd rather be dead than

To be ugly an' old.

When love is gone what
Can a young gal do?
When love is gone, O,
What can a young gal do?
Keep on a-lovin' me, daddy,
Cause I don't want to be blue. (*Collected* 123)

As Chinitz maintains, Hughes balances between literariness and faithfulness to his oral sources by closing the lyric with the seemingly incongruent final stanza. Whereas the first three stanzas reveal a thematic consistency that, by Chinitz's estimation, "would be remarkable in an improvised folk composition," the inclusion of the fourth stanza, which collapses that thematic development, simulates the organization one would expect from a spontaneous blues performance where emotional mood would be more likely to govern structure (Chinitz 180). As Chinitz concludes, the composition of the fourth stanza "sacrifices what would have been a most un–folkish tidiness by having the girl step outside the apparent parameters of the poem to elaborate on her fear of loneliness. The structural superfluity of the fourth stanza, in other words, is functional" (180).

However, to read Hughes's poetry as only an "authentic" folk literature is to place him on an earlier point on the quasi–temporal plane of black expressivity that spans the period from slavery's orature to postmodern African American literature. Critics who read Hughes as folk poet misinterpret his unique jazz–inspired innovations within the Signifyin(g) tradition that Gates outlines in *The Signifying Monkey*. Hughes is not a bluesman standing at a mythical site of black expressive origins—an anonymous folk voice singing at the crossroads of Africa and America—but rather, a jazzman who signifies on that tradition with an all–encompassing intertextual/intermusical approach. Hughes himself asserted this distance when speaking about his writing: "I'm not a Southerner. I never worked on a levee. I hardly ever saw a cotton field except from the highway" ("Communication" 492). Strictly urban and modern, Hughes's creative expression does not conform to the folk blues aesthetic, which Houston Baker defines:

Rather than a rigidly personalized form, the blues offer a phylogenetic recapitulation—a nonlinear, freely associative, nonsequential meditation—of species experience. What emerges is not a filled subject, but an anonymous (nameless) voice issuing from the black (w)hole. The blues singer's signatory coda is always *atopic,* placeless: "If anybody ask you who sang this song / Tell 'em X done been here and gone." (*Blues* 5)

Hughes's work is not lodged deeply and anonymously within what Baker calls the "matrix" of the folk blues. Rather, the poet's use of the blues is emblematic of a recurring process in African American literature that Gates notes—namely, the use of "anonymous" vernacular material to assert one's literary distinctiveness:

> The concern to be original is so frequently expressed in black letters that it deserves a full–length study. Reacting to the questionable allegations made against their capacity to be original, black writers have often assumed a position of extreme negation, in which they claim for themselves no black literary antecedents whatsoever, or else claim for themselves an anonymity of origins as Topsy did when she said she "jes' grew." This second position, curiously enough, often stresses the anonymous origins and influence of the Afro-American vernacular tradition, as figured in the spirituals, the blues, and vernacular secular folk poetry as that found in the toasts of the Signifying Monkey, as if group influence, unnamed, is more enabling than would be the claim of descent through a line of precursors or even from one black precursor. This is originality at its extremes, a nameless progeniture [. . .] . (*Signifying* 114)

For Hughes, this relationship to the vernacular was enabling on a number of levels. To work out of African American musical forms allowed him a way to celebrate the lifestyle and traditions of the black folk he loved. Moreover, the innovation of writing American literature through jazz allowed space for the originality—at its extremes—that the period demanded: amidst American literature's becoming modern, while the *New Negro* was in vogue.

Hughes's music poetry is especially important in its innovations on one of the signal tropes Gates locates in the Signifyin(g) tradition: the preservation of orality in the black written word. By continually invoking the meter of the blues and the rhythms of jazz, Hughes imprinted his work with a signature African American difference, an oral quality that modified what Gates calls the Trope of the Talking Book. As Gates writes,

> the curious tension between the black vernacular and the literate white text, the spoken and the written word, between the oral and the printed forms of literary discourse, has been represented and thematized in

black letters at least since slaves and ex-slaves met the challenge of the
Enlightenment to their humanity by literally writing themselves into
being through carefully crafted representations in language of the black
self. (*Signifying* 131)

Gates defines the Trope of the Talking Book as the result of this tension, as
the ongoing attempt by black American writers to represent the "black
self" in literature by representing black cultural difference through echoes
of black orality.

Hughes reiterates this trope throughout many of his early poems,
repeatedly depicting the black subject as a vocal entity, as in "The Negro
Speaks of Rivers" or in "I, Too," in which the poem's black speaker, a
self–professed "darker brother" argues, "I, too, sing America" (*Collected*
46, lines 1–2)."[37] And yet, Hughes also innovated the Trope of the Talking
Book by expressing his idea of the "black self" through literary representations of new African American musical forms—jazz and classic blues—
rather than only through approximations of the spoken word. Consider, for
example, "Negro Dancers" from *The Weary Blues*:

> "Me an' ma baby's
> Got two mo' ways,
> Two mo' ways to do de Charleston!
>   Da, da.
>   Da, da, da!
> Two mo' ways to do de Charleston!"
>
> Soft light on the tables,
> Music gay,
> Brown–skin steppers
> In a cabaret.
>
> White folks, laugh!
> White folks, pray!
>
> "Me an' ma baby's
> Got two mo' ways
> Two mo' ways to do de Charleston!" (*Collected* 44)

In the poem, Hughes represents the black subject's voice on one level
through elision—the dropped "d" on "and," the silenced "re" on
"more"—a technique for representing African American speech that Gates

himself plays with by bracketing the final "g" on Signifyin(g). Moreover, though, Hughes implies music with the repeated riff, "Me an' my baby's/Got two mo' ways/To do the Charleston," and through the use of the staccato "nonsense" syllable, "Da," which signifies with its tonal power more than its visual imprint. This latter technique is an example of a specific characteristic that Clyde Taylor locates at the intersection of musical and verbal expression in the African diaspora, namely, the use of "intonationality" to express meaning:

> A tolerance for semantic ambiguity, already supported by an African tendency toward indirection in speech, found wider use on the new scene. Semantic ambiguity made for a kind of speech as music. At the core of the play and experimentation characteristic of the new linguistic situation was the lost mythological significance, delving into the surviving communications matrix and finding there a laboratory made up of music, vocalizations, and non–semantic speech. (4)

Among the representative examples of this process in the specific musical language of jazz, Taylor includes Adelaide Hall's wordless vocal *obbligatos* in Duke Ellington's "Creole Love Call," the recurring cry of the playful lyrics "Salt Peanuts" in Dizzy Gillespie's bebop anthem of the same name, and Aminata Moseka's extended vocalizations in Max Roach's "Freedom Now Suite." Taylor's observations reinforce Gates's theory of Signifyin(g) on two important levels: in his emphasis on West African syncretisms in African American expressivity, and also in his foregrounding of a uniquely black freeplay of signifiers.[38] The intersection of these two critics is vital for reading Hughes, highlighting the importance of the poet's use of "non–semantic" syllables to signify black musical sound.

Hughes also signifies the black musical voice through typography and stanzaic organization. Whereas the first stanza of "Negro Dancers"—in which the subject sings about dance—is presented in quotation marks, the second stanza is not. Instead, the second stanza is presented in a self–consciously poetic rhyme that expresses the observation of the poem's dancing/singing subjects from without. The specularity of this "poetic" voice is then juxtaposed against the third stanza, "White folks, laugh!/White folks, pray!," an ambiguous pair of lines that functions both as an imperative directed at whites in attendance (who are themselves not represented as speaking subjects in the poem) and as an inscription of that white gaze. The poem then returns to a reiteration of the vocal riff with which it began, presented once again in quotation marks to signify orality. In all, the poem's combination of white speechlessness, white specularity, and black vocality and motion creates a version of the Signifyin(g) black difference that Gates locates within the Trope of the Talking Book, and which Taylor calls "into-nationality." The black subject is distinguished through speech, song, and dance, all of which are located within a jazz–specific context: the Charleston in a cabaret, amidst the "non–semantic" sound of African American music.

In two other early poems from *The Weary Blues,* "Saturday Night" and "Harlem Night Club," Hughes suggests musical accompaniment by juxtaposing verbal signification against both typographical play and non–semantic syllables within a fixed rhyme scheme. In "Saturday Night," Hughes establishes a steady ABCB rhyme scheme in the poem's first twelve lines before blasting into a non–semantic riff within that rhyme over the following four lines:

> Play it once.
> O, play some more.
> Charlie is a gambler
> An' Sadie is a whore.
> A glass o' whiskey
> An' a glass o' gin:
> Strut, Mr. Charlie,
> Till de dawn comes in.
> Pawn yo' gold watch
> An' diamond ring.
> Git a quart of licker,
> Let's shake dat thing!
> Skee-de-dad! De-dad!
> Doo-doo-doo!
> Won't be nothin' left
> When de worms git through. (*Collected* 88, lines 1–16)

The use of the non–semantic words in lines 13 and 14 against the verbal signification in lines 15 and 16 sets up a musical–verbal antiphony in the rhyme between the two pairs. The poem then continues with a four–line break from the rhyme before returning to the fixed structure and closing with a similar juxtaposition of language and non–semantic sound:

> An' you's a long time
> Dead
> When you is
> Dead, too.

So beat dat drum, boy!
Shout dat song:
Shake 'em up an' shake 'em up
All night long.
   Hey! Hey!
   Ho . . . Hum!
   Do it, Mr. Charlie,
   Till de red dawn come. (*Collected* 88, lines 17–28)

Again, in the poem's final quartet, the non–semantic interjections in the opening pair of lines constitute a musical call to which the poem's verbal coda in the final two responds through rhyme. As well, Hughes punctuates the non–semantic lines in the closing quartet with exclamation marks—a typographical touch he uses in the earlier non–semantic riff as well—which implies sound (a change in volume perhaps) in its visual suggestion of intonational variation.

In "Harlem Night Club," Hughes eschews the use of non–semantic tones, but he does once again use typographical variation to suggest musical performance. In both the poem's first and fifth stanzas, Hughes uses unorthodox typography to imply the aural within the visual:

Sleek black boys in a cabaret.
Jazz-band, jazz-band,—
Play, plAY, PLAY!
Tomorrow. . . . who knows?
Dance today! (*Collected* 90, lines 1–5)

and

Jazz-boys, jazz-boys,—
Play, plAY, PLAY!
Tomorrow. . . . is darkness.
Joy today! (*Collected* 90, lines 22–25)

In the first stanza, Hughes once again uses the suggestion of music to create the Signifyin(g) difference of black vocality. The poem begins with a specular acknowledgment of its black subjects—the "sleek black boys" of the Harlem night club jazz band—and then directs an imperative at the those musicians: an order that *becomes* the signification of the musical sound midway through, with the crescendo of Hughes's typographical play. As the black musicians are acknowledged by the poem's unnamed initial speaker, they immediately become speaking subjects of a musical language that is foregrounded typographically in high caps. Their music becomes the discernible signifier of black presence.

Thus, while Hughes's contemporaries, like Zora Neale Hurston and Jean Toomer, revisited the Trope of the Talking Book, as Gates notes, by representing their Signifyin(g) black difference through the use of black vernacular speech and a privileging of the oral voice, Hughes commonly sounded his difference through the aural filter of jazz and the composition of verse governed by a jazz aesthetic. The overall effect of this is the foundation of the strain of black modernism that I chart throughout this book. Keeping in mind Hughes's pioneering techniques in the development of a jazz–influenced black modernism, and playfully acknowledging both Gates's Trope of the Talking Book and Hughes's own famous children's volume, I want to distinguish the poet's Signifyin(g) innovations on orality as The First Book of Jazz. The First Book of Jazz marks the unique intersection of modernist literary technique and African American sound that dominates Hughes's oeuvre and is the inheritance of Ralph Ellison, Michael S. Harper and Albert Murray. It is a crossroads of expressivity from which Hughes worked throughout his career, from his early jazz poems into the later bebop–influenced work I discuss in Chapter Two.

The technique that perhaps best embodies Hughes's place at the crossroads of literary modernism and African American expressivity is his use of multivocality. In many of the poet's jazz–inspired works he juxtaposes diverse voices. This strategy constitutes a response to what Richard Sheppard calls "the crisis of language" in modernism, in ways similar to those offered by the poet's "mainstream" contemporaries Pound, Eliot, and Williams.[39] At the same time, though, Hughes's multivocal expression corresponds with the creative community central to jazz, a musical form that turns on the ability of performers to respond to each other within the group. In Hughes's jazz poems, diverse voices frequently overlap, such that at times the transition from one speaker to another becomes all but indistinguishable. Note, for instance, that in "Saturday Night" and "Harlem Night Club," the identity of the speaker—or singer, player—is not clear at all moments in either poem's sequence. The ambiguous unity that ensues from this chaotic representation is commonplace in much modernist poetry. Eliot's *The Waste Land* is likely the best example in its various moments of paradoxically fragmented unity and intertextual collage. Indeed, as James McFarlane notes, a bringing–together of fragments is perhaps the signal characteristic of modernist writing:

> [T]he defining thing in the Modernist mode is not so much that things
> fall *apart* but that they fall *together* [. . .] . In Modernism, the centre is

seen exerting not a centrifugal but a centripetal force; and the consequence is not disintegration but (as it were) superintegration. The
threat to (conventional) order comes not from the break–down of a
planetary system but from the repudiation of a filing system, where
order derives as much from keeping separate as from holding together [
. . .] . (92, original emphasis)

However, this impulse to layer modes of expression on top of one
another is, of course, not specific to Western literature in the early twentieth century. As Samuel Floyd documents, African American music is also
dominated by an aesthetic that favors the juxtaposition of diverse voices
within group performance. Floyd calls this characteristic "the heterogeneous sound ideal," taking the term that black composer Olly Wilson uses
to describe a similar expressive mode in West African music. Describing the
African musical process that Floyd regards as a source for black American
musical expression, Wilson writes that the "heterogeneous sound ideal"
results from "the timbral mosaic created by the interaction between lead
voice, chorus, rattle, metallic gong, hand clapping, various wind or string
instruments, and drums, which exist in greater or lesser degrees of complexity in almost all African ensemble music" (331). As Floyd summarizes,
"[w]hat Wilson is referring to here is, of course, Africans' overwhelming
preference for timbres that contrast rather than blend and their adoration
of the resulting 'tonal mosaic' as ideal for their culture" (28).

Floyd traces the continuity of this aesthetic into jazz music. He suggests, for example, that the music of the Duke Ellington Orchestra, the
greatest jazz ensemble to emerge from the Harlem Renaissance, perfectly
embodies the "heterogeneous sound ideal" and the "tonal mosaic" as it
endures in musical modernism:

Duke Ellington fully embraced [the heterogeneous sound ideal] in an
unsurpassed orchestral palette, with not only the instruments themselves providing timbral contrasts, but each of the musicians providing
even more such contrast within the confines of his individual instrument. It is well known that Ellington selected his sidemen for stylistic
and tonal *difference.* He surely recognized that *Signifyin(g) difference*
powerfully enhances the heterogeneous effect. (114, original emphasis)

Ingrid Monson also notes the importance of heterogeneity to the jazz
aesthetic. Monson documents how jazz thrives on the tension between
each individual performer's unique voice and a commitment to group
expression:

There is an inherent tension within the jazz ensemble between the individual and the group. On the one hand, the aesthetic of the music is
centered on the inventiveness and uniqueness of individual solo expression; on the other, climactic moments of musical expression require the
cohesiveness and participation of the entire ensemble. In an improvisational music, such as jazz, the interaction between group and individual
greatly affects the ultimate composition and development of the music.
(*Saying* 66–67)

Building on the African American musical aesthetic that both Floyd and Monson describe, Hughes imbues his poems with a multivocality that captures jazz
music's "creation by committee" while it keeps pace with the stylistic
"falling–together" that McFarlane locates throughout modernist literature.[40]

For instance, in "The Cat and the Saxophone (2 A.M.)," from *The
Weary Blues,* Hughes presents a jazz–centered vignette that captures
diverse oral and musical voices in juxtaposition, recalling techniques used
by white modernists while remaining faithful to African American musical
form:[41]

EVERYBODY
Half–pint,—
Gin?
No, make it
LOVES MY BABY
corn. You like
liquor,
don't you, honey?
BUT MY BABY
Sure. Kiss me,
DON'T LOVE NOBODY
daddy.
BUT ME.
Say!
EVERYBODY
Yes?
WANTS MY BABY
I'm your
BUT MY BABY
sweetie, ain't I?
DON'T WANT NOBODY
Sure.

BUT
Then let's
ME,
do it!
SWEET ME.
Charleston,
mamma!
!
(*Collected* 89)

The poem presents three distinct voices: a pair of speakers in a cabaret, and a musical performance that intersects with the pair's conversation. For the musical voice, Hughes uses an actual jazz number, Spencer Williams's "Everybody Loves My Baby" from 1924.[42] By using the lyrics of a popular tune that had recent currency, Hughes is able to suggest music within the borders of language. Though he eschews use of musical syllables in this poem, his use of Williams's lyrics would no doubt evoke the song's melody for readers familiar with jazz. Thus, the poem not only mimics the structural organization of jazz performance in its simultaneous representation of different voices, but also implies the sound of the music in its allusion to an actual song. Moreover, while the poem's musical reference invokes The First Book of Jazz's Signifyin(g) sound, the piece also signifies on Eliot's disorienting intertextuality in its repetition and revision of a memorable section from the poet's masterwork. In both its tavern setting and its juxtaposition of that milieu's "common" conversation with aural interference from outside the dialogue, "The Cat and the Saxophone (2 A.M.)" is reminiscent of lines 139–72 of Eliot's *The Waste Land*. In that segment, which closes the long poem's second section, "A Game of Chess," Eliot repeatedly interrupts the conversation in a public house with the bartender's insistent call for closing time, an ominous, recurring cry in high caps. As the section concludes, the voices merge with each other in an incoherent series of farewells before dissolving into an echo of Ophelia's mad song from *Hamlet*:

Well, if Albert won't leave you alone, there it is, I said,
What you get married for if you don't want children?
HURRY UP PLEASE ITS TIME
Well, that Sunday Albert was home, they had a hot gammon,
And they asked me in to dinner, to get the beauty of it hot—
HURRY UP PLEASE ITS TIME
HURRY UP PLEASE ITS TIME
Goonight Bill. Goonight Lou. Goonight May. Goonight.

Ta ta. Goonight. Goonight.
Good night, ladies, good night, sweet ladies, good night, good night.
(lines 163–72)

Hughes's poem avoids the self–consciously literary climax to which Eliot's section builds, and instead closes with the amalgamation of the musical and oral voices. The lovers in Hughes's poem take to the dance floor with the cry of "Charleston, Mamma!" and in that song–like interjection become fused in a moment of performance with the jazz music. This is exemplified by the double exclamation marks Hughes uses to bracket the musical and oral dialogues. In all, the communal performance of dance and song is a stark contrast to Eliot's move to the lone voice of Ophelia in the Shakespeare allusion. Whereas Eliot builds to a privileging of the literate, Hughes champions sound, motion, and community. His gesture is emblematic of "the curious tension between the black vernacular and the literate white text" that Gates notes throughout African American literature (131).[43]

Thus, in his early jazz poetry, Hughes asserted his place among his so–called mainstream modernist contemporaries by actively contributing to American literature's invigoration of English poetics through experimentation, while at the same time he added to the political project of the New Negro Renaissance by celebrating black experience and stressing the aesthetic importance of African American cultural forms. However, despite the social commentary and stylistic innovations yielded by this early work, Hughes's poetry was still potentially problematic for Harlem's political agenda in its play with the cult of primitivism's iconography. Hughes's Signifyin(g) on jazz cabaret life, for example, could be precarious for the ease with which it might be co-opted by a dominant racist mindset that might find affirmation of its atavistic distortions in the poet's representation of black Americans as distinctive through their speech, song, and dance. This was certainly a problem of black culture's commodification during the Jazz Age—a problem shared by Hughes's contemporaries in jazz, like Duke Ellington and Louis Armstrong, who struggled to maintain ironic distance from the primitivist economy while they recorded songs like "Jungle Nights in Harlem" and "King of the Zulus," respectively. This tension was one that jazz music's next generation of innovators—the bebop musicians of the 1940s—was determined to resolve, through their radical overhaul of the music's stylistics, a paradigm shift that was to prove consequential for Langston Hughes and his inheritors in the development of an African American jazz literary modernism.

Chapter Two:

Thriving on a Riff: Bebop and Langston Hughes's *Montage of a Dream Deferred*

Throughout the 1920s and thirties, jazz stars had enabled their music's passage into American popular culture by playing to and *with* white ideas of "blackness." In performance, the music's early innovators had, like Langston Hughes in his poetry, played with "mastery of form"—one of the two signal tropes of African American modernism as defined by Houston Baker, outlined in Chapter One. Repeatedly these artists had "masked" their genius within the expectations of popular entertainment as descended from minstrelsy. This ensured that jazz maintained an air of familiarity for white consumers despite the potentially alienating effects of its radical newness. Louis Armstrong, for instance, tempered his innovative trumpet style with an affable onstage demeanor, a savvy revision in some ways of the Old Negro stereotype. Before a crowd Armstrong could become Pops or Satchmo, a joking presence who dazzled audiences with down–home wit and folksy charm. Likewise, Duke Ellington, whose compositions have since established him as a major force in twentieth–century music, marketed his orchestra's sound as "jungle" music to great success during the Harlem Renaissance. The Ellington band could simulate the primitive pulse of the "dark continent" with syncopated drums and roaring horns, but Ellington's stage presence as a debonair, new aristocrat offset any potential discomfort for white listeners.

However, though the strategic intelligence exhibited by jazz musicians in cultural performance throughout the twenties and thirties facilitated the music's entry into the mainstream, as jazz reached the apex of its early popularity in the thirties and forties, many of the music's black practitioners found themselves increasingly disenfranchised from the economic returns that jazz's popularity now afforded.[1] By the late thirties, jazz had become America's popular music, the soundtrack to which the country's youth lindy–hopped and fell in love. And with white America's increasing accept-ance of the music after its initial splash between the 1910s and twenties, white musicians had become increasingly involved on the jazz scene. Unsur-prisingly perhaps, it had been a group of white musicians—the Original Dixieland Jazz Band—who in 1917 was the first group to have their sound transferred to record.[2] By the height of the Swing Era, this initial invest-ment by record companies had matured exponentially, such that by the 1930s, the high–profile and best–marketed stars of jazz records and radio were white bandleaders: Benny Goodman, Glenn Miller, the Dorsey Broth-ers, Artie Shaw.[3] Jazz had not, however, become a completely "whitened" product of mainstream interests; some black performers—like Armstrong, Ellington, and Count Basie, who had emerged out of Kansas City in the early thirties—continued to enjoy success. But the prosperity commanded by those artists was small compared to that garnered by their white coun-terparts. White bands enjoyed larger marketing budgets and higher–profile bookings than black groups. As well, white bandleaders and prominent soloists ascended beyond the localized environment of the cabaret; they were darlings of the national entertainment scene, starring in Hollywood films and moving in social circles with America's biggest celebrities.[4] Elling-ton and Basie may have been titled Duke and Count respectively, but it was Goodman whom media and record buyers crowned "the King of Swing."[5]

These imbalances proved the catalyst for innovations in the jazz idiom by young black musicians in the 1940s. If the movement of jazz from the "fringes" into "mainstream" American culture had initially required the music's players to make ostensible concessions that masked self–empowerment, the music's new generation was less guarded in its poli-tics. These soloists, led by alto saxophonist Charlie Parker and trumpeter Dizzy Gillespie, were disillusioned, weary at the way African American innovation had been exploited by a white market within the strictures of segregation. As Scott DeVeaux writes, by the 1940s, "competition stiffened [in the music industry] and the underlying inequities of race were felt with renewed force. Entrenched patterns of segregation, both in the music indus-try and in society at large, automatically gave white musicians a nearly insuperable advantage in the mainstream market, blunting black ambition and forcing it into new channels" (*Birth* 27).[6] Parker and company were talented improvisers laboring within the few black big bands the flooded swing scene was able to sustain. These musicians were aware of the ceiling over their current market potential. With the marquee of popular music bearing so many white names already, where was the hope for great success among aspiring black musicians? How many more black big bands could swing's popularity support when those groups run by Ellington or Basie or Cab Calloway were already in danger of being crowded out by so many high–profile white dance bands? In the face of these concerns, the young jazz musicians of the 1940s began to reimagine the sound of jazz. While they worked as sidemen, young players like Parker and Gillespie, as well as drummer Kenny Clarke, pianist Thelonious Monk, and bassist Oscar Pettiford, convened in after–hours jam sessions and collectively began a wholesale reassessment of the jazz vocabulary. It was an ongoing experiment that gave birth to what was undoubtedly the greatest paradigm shift in the music's history: modern jazz or bebop. As DeVeaux argues, "Bebop was [. . .] an attempt to reconstitute jazz—or more precisely, the specialized idiom of the improvising virtuoso—in such a way as to give its black creators the greatest professional autonomy *within* the marketplace" (*Birth* 27, original emphasis).

The location at which these jam sessions most often took place was Minton's Playhouse, a club in Harlem "started in 1938 by Henry Minton, a tenor saxophonist and the first black delegate to Local 802 of the musicians' union," and managed by a former bandleader named Teddy Hill (DeVeaux, *Birth* 219).[7] Minton's was frequented by Parker and company and offered a warm atmosphere for musicians to gather.[8] It

> offered a kind of sanctuary [. . . and] was intended primarily for the use of professional musicians. Because of Minton's connections to the union, musicians could sit in without fear of being fined by the union delegate for playing without pay. Unlike many other jam session spots, the self–described "Showplace of Harlem" was a legitimate nightclub, staying open only until the official curfew of 4 A.M. It was ideal for musicians working with a big band at a theater like the Apollo or the Paramount, as they could drop by after their job was through for the night (which might be as early as eleven o'clock). It was also popular with out-of-work musicians [. . .] Everybody was welcome on Monday night, the traditional night off—dubbed "Celebrity Night" because Hill invited the entire cast of the Apollo Theatre for a buffet dinner. As always, the evening culminated in a jam session. (DeVeaux, *Birth* 219)

Minton's was an important venue because it allowed young black musicians a place to play away from the expectations of audiences, white or black. It was a gathering place that facilitated the exchange of musical ideas without the need to perform under the burden of mainstream audience expectations.

Because the club became a favorite meeting place of the circle of improvisers who revolutionized the music over the course of the decade, it has become a site of fabled activity in jazz historical discourse. Too often, perhaps, the end–result of the jams at Minton's has overshadowed the process that took place there over time. As Amiri Baraka notes:[9]

> By now it is almost impossible to find out just what did go on at Minton's during the early 40's. There are so many conflicting stories, many by people who have no way of knowing. But in my adolescence the myth went something like this: "Around 1942, after classical jazz had made its conquests, a small group used to get together every night in a Harlem club called Minton's Playhouse. It was made up of several young colored boys who, unlike their fellow musicians, no longer felt at home in the atmosphere of 'swing music.' It was becoming urgent to get a little air in a richly decked out palace that was soon going to be a prison. [. . .] The bebop style was in the process of being born."
>
> It sounds almost like the beginnings of modern American writing among the emigrés of Paris. But this is the legend which filled most of my adolescence. However, as Thelonious Monk put it, "It's true modern jazz probably began to get popular there, but some of these histories and articles put what happened over the course of ten years into one year. They put people all together in one time and place. I've seen practically everybody at Minton's, but they were just there playing. They weren't giving lectures." (*Black Music* 21–22)

While Baraka's essay highlights the misguided reduction that surrounds narratives of bebop's birth, it also underscores one of the key unifying characteristics among the bebop generation: restlessness with the older modes of cultural performance that had previously defined the place of the African American artist on the national scene.[10] Baraka continues:

> Bop also carried with it a distinct element of social protest, not only in the sense that it was music that seemed antagonistically nonconformist, but also that the musicians who played it were loudly outspoken about who they thought they were. "If you don't like it, don't listen," was the attitude, which seems to me now as rational as you can get. These musicians seemed no longer to want to be thought of merely as "performers," in the old Cotton Club–yellow hiney sense, but as musicians. (23)

Thus, the musicians defining bebop derived their musical innovations from political and economic motivations.

Racial politics were also key to the developments at Minton's Playhouse. The younger generation projected a fervent militancy in the face of white mistreatment. They were quick to criticize earlier jazz musicians who had assumed the role of entertainer to carve out a niche in a market governed by white expectations. Armstrong was an easy target; his mother–wit signifying on the Old Negro may have seemed disconcertingly close to a mere reiteration of minstrelsy's gross exaggerations of blackness. Gillespie later admitted to being one such critic:

> I criticized Louis for [. . .] his "plantation image." We didn't appreciate that about Louis Armstrong, and if anybody asked me about a certain public image of him, handkerchief over his head, grinning in the face of white racism, I never hesitated to say I didn't like it. I didn't want the white man to expect me to allow the same things Louis Armstrong did. (*To Be* 295–96)

Similarly, Miles Davis, another musician to come up out of the bebop school, writes of Armstrong in his autobiography: "I loved the way Louis played trumpet, man, but I hated the way he had to grin in order to get over with some tired white folks. Man, I just hated when I saw him doing that, because Louis was hip, had a consciousness about black people, was a real nice man" (313).[11] In contrast to Armstrong's agreeable performance, many beboppers did little to make themselves accessible as entertainers, opting instead for a studied coolness onstage. By the 1950s, Miles Davis took this aesthetic of indifference to extremes, often improvising solos with his back to the audience. Yet the stage presence of the beboppers was not so much governed by contempt as by the belief that they need not entertain, that the music they were playing was "serious"—as complex as anything heard in a concert hall. And indeed it was in the complexity of the new music that beboppers uttered their greatest social commentary.

Bebop's major innovation was a rethinking of the relationship of "acceptable" melodic notes to a song's harmonic sequence. As Ted Gioia writes, "bop harmonic thinking revolutionized the flow of the melodic line in jazz. One recalls Parker's alleged statement that an improviser should be able to use any note against any chord—it was simply a matter of placing it in the right *context*" (203, original emphasis). Whereas the playing of Armstrong and company had been largely diatonic, always sticking close to the dominant of each chord in the sequence, the music of Parker and cohorts ventured into radical chromaticism, with an emphasis on "unorthodox" melodic substitutions over each song's harmonies. Indeed, many bebop compositions "simply followed, more or less, the conventional progressions of prewar standards" (Gioia 203). For example, Parker's bop anthem, "Ornithology," is a reinvention of Morgan Harris's "How High the Moon"; and his "Anthropology" follows—as so many bop tunes do—the chord progression of Gershwin's "I Got Rhythm."[12]

In using these earlier sources, bebop musicians adopted a version of the modernist aesthetic that James McFarlane identifies as a falling–together of older materials, the gathering of diverse fragments in collage (92). Eric Lott adds that bebop is "one of the great modernisms," its "incorporation of elements of the popular (Bird was fond of quoting the 'Woody Woodpecker' theme) reminds one of Joyce or Mahler" (462). In addition, bebop's play with the popular songs of Tin Pan Alley embodies Henry Louis Gates's theory of Signifyin(g) pushed to its limits. The reworking of songs that were so embedded within white America's cultural fabric is an example of the process of revision that Gates finds central to African American expressivity. The gesture is a manifestation of Signifyin(g)'s political–aesthetic strategy, always repeating and revising texts from without. Bebop enabled Signifyin(g)'s directive of "redress[ing] an imbalance of power, to clear a space, rhetorically" (Gates, *Signifying* 124).[13] As Lott suggests, "writing new melodies for Broadway tunes was [. . .] an intervention into the dominant popular culture of the period—in tunes such as [Tadd Dameron's] 'Hot House' [which reworked Cole Porter's 'What Is This Thing Called Love?' there was] a kind of ritual dismemberment" (462).

Furthermore, if jazz improvisation is, as Gates himself notes, "nothing more" than Signifyin(g) repetition and revision, then bebop allowed for heightened Signifyin(g) by opening space for more improvisation, through a reconfiguration of the jazz group's standard size. At swing's apex, big bands ruled the jazz world. Accordingly, there was less room for stretching out musically in that context; prewritten arrangements were necessary to prevent group performances from getting chaotic and unwieldy. Perhaps initially governed by the intimacy of Minton's jam sessions, bebop favored fewer players on the bandstand. Quintets and quartets became the norm among the new generation's groups, with a standard rhythm section of bass, drums, and piano usually augmented by one or two horns. The result of this reconfiguration was more freedom for all members in the group throughout the performance; improvisation need no longer be confined to assigned solo breaks within a band's stock arrangement. Thus, bebop was more interactive; the soloist was forced to play off of the contributions of his or her bandmates at all times.

In addition to this increased participation, bebop's young lions also raised the demands on individual improvisers in the moment of solo performance. "It was a soloist's music," Lott observes, "despite the democratic ethos of jazz (in which soloists assume a momentary universality in a highly mutual context), and particularly of bop (its dependence on unison riffs, the extreme sympathy required between players to negotiate the rhythms)" (462). Not only was bop based around patterns of harmonic conception that were novel in jazz, but these labyrinthine turns through difficult chord substitutions were made quickly. The beboppers' assault on both the musical and cultural status quo was fostered through virtuosity. Swing had become a site of too–easy accessibility, and its lengthy development had settled into a tradition of standard forms that could be learned. The beboppers countered this by making jazz exclusive again from within.[14] As Gillespie remarked in a 1952 article in *Down Beat* magazine, "when we first began to jam at Minton's [. . .] cats would show up who couldn't blow at all but would take six or seven choruses to prove it. So on afternoons before a session, Monk and I began to work out some complex variations on chords and the like and we used them at night to scare away the no–talent guys" (qtd in Hentoff, "Crazy" 14). Curiously—or not, since this interview was published in a magazine popular with white jazz fans—Gillespie speaks of the exclusivity of bop here in terms of talent, not race. His comments do not explicitly acknowledge the widely accepted notion that bebop's experimentation was motivated by racial concerns.[15] Indeed, given that so many bebop musicians later hired white musicians in their bands, it is unlikely that the music was created purely out of racial conflict.[16] An examination of the social conditions under which bebop developed suggests, nonetheless, that the music likely was, in some ways, a response to white institutionalized racism. Certainly, scrutiny of its stylistic qualities shows bebop's place within a distinctly African American musical continuum.

Many commentators on bebop's history in fact highlight the music's inextricable link with social conditions for African Americans in the 1940s. Amiri Baraka, for example, suggests that the beboppers' self–imposed exile from the mainstream in jazz was moved by their realization that even after involvement in another World War and despite recurring attempts to adapt to the dominant culture's social ideals, African Americans were still not welcome in white society. Baraka proposes that bebop's aesthetic was an assertion of non–conforming blackness that countered failed attempts by African Americans to assimilate into the mainstream (185–86).[17] Eric Lott proposes a similar narrative of bebop as militant action and reads the music's birth alongside various contemporaneous events that were significant to a new aggressive push by African Americans for civil rights in the 1940s: the contribution of thousands of black auto workers in the UAW's efforts to unionize the Ford Motor Corporation; the desegregation of defense plants under the leadership of A. Phillip Randolph; the founding of the Congress of Racial Equality in 1942; riots in Los Angeles, Detroit, New York, and other cities (Lott 457–58). The beboppers' radical break from older conventions signified an aesthetic realization of a generational combativeness off the bandstand. "Brilliantly outside," Lott writes, "bebop was intimately if indirectly related to the militancy of the moment. Militancy and music were undergirded by the same social facts; the music attempted to resolve at the level of style what the militancy fought out in the streets. If bebop did not offer a call to arms [. . .] it at least acknowledged that the call had been made (459).[18] The musicians creating bebop were engaged in a cultural performance with significant social implications. Their music's "relationship to earlier styles was one of calculated hostility," moved by a conscious distancing "from both the black middle class and the white consensus," a gesture which "gave aesthetic self–assertion political force and value" (Lott 462). Integral to this aesthetic militancy was the personal style many of the musicians adopted—berets, cigarette holders, zoot suits, goatees—flamboyant uniforms that further marked their separation from the mainstream.[19]

Frank Kofsky also contextualizes bebop's birth out of adverse social conditions for African Americans, and argues that the music's break from popular styles was a clarion call for advanced civil rights protest. Kofsky too locates bebop within the co-optation of African American sound by white musicians and maintains that "bebop [. . .] was a manifesto of rebellious black musicians unwilling to submit to further exploitation" (57).[20] His reading of bebop as a proactive aesthetic movement—committed to the assertion of African American racial pride and advancement within a larger push for social reform—is corroborated somewhat by the following interview with Dizzy Gillespie and Kenny Clarke, included in Gillespie's memoirs:

> *But were you making any statement about the world around you?*
> KC: "Yeah, in a way. The idea was to wake up, look around you, there's something to do. And this was just a part of it, an integral part of our cultural aspect. And somebody'd say, 'Yeah, that Dizzy, man, sure gave us the word.' Things like that."
>
> *What was the word?*
> KC: "Wake up."
>
> *"Bebop" was later publicized as a "fighting" word. Was this a "fighting" music?*
> KC: "No, no, by all means no!"
> DG: "It was a love music. [. . .]"

Did this music have anything special to say to black people?

DG: "Yeah, get the fuck outta the way [. . .] ."

KC: "Yeah, like I said it was teaching them. I mean people who you idolize. It was nice when you'd see a brother, ballplayer on the field, and you knew that he'd just finished college. You'd have a certain amount of respect for him. [. . .] There was a message in our music. Whatever you go into, go into it *intelligently.* As simple as that. (142, original emphasis)

Moreover, while the interview with Clarke and Gillespie highlights bebop's position as an aesthetic change that asserted African American racial pride, it also foregrounds the music's position as a response to adverse economic conditions like Kofsky argues. Responding to the question, "What kind of statement, if any, were you making about the social scene around you?" Clarke answers, "It was an economic thing because we were already together socially" (qtd in Gillespie 142).

Scott DeVeaux constructs his narrative of the music's origins through economic circumstances. Unlike his predecessors, DeVeaux downplays the role of the bebop musicians as "high modernist" virtuosi or altruistic defenders of an aesthetic blackness. Instead, he underscores their position as working musicians trying to carve out a marketable niche for themselves in a business that was sagging under the deluge of swing big bands. As DeVeaux writes, the beboppers' "reaction to the Swing Era, to both its music and its business arrangements, was not revulsion that art and commerce had promiscuously been allowed to mix, but frustration that things could no longer be made to work to their advantage" (*Birth* 170). Ultimately, though, DeVeaux does not completely dismiss the importance of race to bebop's birth. Rather, he encompasses race into his complicated consideration of the music's social history. Though DeVeaux argues that "bebop cannot be easily tied to a conscious expression of separatist sentiment," he also recognizes that "it was nevertheless rooted deeply in the uncomfortable realities of race in America" (169). "Without the omnipresent pressure of racial hostility," he concludes, "musicians of such divergent talents and temperaments might not have found themselves forced into the same narrow space, and they would not have had the same incentives to forge a new path" (169). Even with his complication of a unilateral narration of bebop's social history through race, DeVeaux's musical analysis of the style highlights the many qualities in the music that establish its place within an African American musical tradition: its use of Signifyin(g), its emphasis on complicated rhythms, and its break from "conventional" musical notation by "playing in the cracks."

Likewise, in his discussion of bebop's musical aesthetics in *The Power of Black Music,* Samuel Floyd emphasizes the style's place within a black musical continuum. Floyd argues that bebop's innovators "changed the course" of jazz by "returning to and embracing elements of African-American myth and ritual" (136). As Floyd shows, bebop advertised its place in an African American musical genealogy by returning to the blues, and by increasing both the importance of Signifyin(g) and the prominence of the drums in jazz. Beboppers frequently used the blues as a harmonic foundation for improvisation, and favored "a melodic angularity in which the blue note of the fifth degree was established as an important melodic–harmonic device" (138).[21] And coming out of informal jam sessions, in which musicians commonly vaunted their talents to each other, the "bebop cauldron was a hotbed of epic toasts and of the cutting contests in which these toasts thrived" (138).[22] The music's heightening of Signifyin(g) dialogues between musicians looked back "to the game rivalry and rhyming contests of Afro-America [. . .] and of Africa and to the band battles of early jazz in New Orleans, Chicago, and New York" (139). In addition, bebop—which changed the role of the drummer from time–keeper to rhythmic contributor in a group dialogue—"returned," as Floyd summarizes, "the percussive sounds of ring culture to their original place of importance" (138). The primacy of the drum in bop evoked the cultural memory of antebellum early African American ritual, when the sounds created from the body—rhythm, voice—were the center of musical expression.[23]

Thus, even conceding to DeVeaux's suggestion that the *causes* that led to bebop's birth were not purely racial, the *effects* of the music undoubtedly addressed issues of race. In the music's departure from the white mainstream, in its foregrounding of signature qualities from the black musical tradition, bebop advertised African American cultural difference. The style moved jazz performance away from "mastery of form" and toward a "deformation of mastery," the second signal trope that Houston Baker argues defines African American modernism. "Deformation of mastery," Baker proposes, also constitutes the wearing of a mask, but one that "distinguishes rather than conceals" (*Modernism* 51). Whereas "mastery of form" constitutes a disguising of "real blackness" (in masks that bear the "nonsense" of minstrelsy), "deformation of mastery" announces black difference in proud display. It is a strategy that, in Baker's metaphorical language, protects black "indigenous" territory from outside intrusion by producing sounds that "appear monstrous and deformed *only* to the intruder"—and thus, in the case of bebop, guarding the sanctity of black jazz from the intervention of an exploitative and racist economy (*Modernism* 51–52, original emphasis). The previous generation of jazz musicians had deployed "mastery of form" in performative personae that contrasted with (or even distracted from) the deformative qualities of their innovative music. The new generation, on the other hand, bridged this divide between persona and expression by integrating deformative sound and presentation more thoroughly. In all, the bebop musicians of the 1940s celebrated "blackness" in a more comprehensive cultural performance that had vast stylistic implications for the jazz–influenced black modernist literature, as made evident in the later poetry of Langston Hughes and the fiction of Ralph Ellison.

Just as Langston Hughes had assertively maintained the political–aesthetic importance of jazz in the 1920s, when he argued forcefully for its recognition in "The Negro Artist and the Racial Mountain," the poet also called attention to the social relevance of bebop's new sound. Hughes articulates this awareness in "Bop," one of many humorous commentary pieces written for the *Chicago Defender* that featured the naively wise Everyman, Jess B. Semple, or simply, "Simple." In the short narrative, Hughes expresses a familiarity with the new musical developments: the determined stylistic break of bop from earlier jazz forms; the importance of race and economics to bebop's birth; and the position of bop as a politically charged aesthetic correlative to the widespread angst and militancy of young African Americans after the Second World War. As the story begins, Jess and his perennial straight man, the often unnamed narrator of the Simple stories, are together on Simple's stoop and overhear the sounds of a Dizzy Gillespie record coming from an apartment upstairs. When the narrator remarks that Gillespie's "nonsense" vocalizations ("Ool-ya-koo;" "Ba-Ba-Re-Bop!"; "Be-Bop!"; "Mop!") sound very much like Cab Calloway's famous scat lyrics of the 1930s ("Hi-de-*hie*-de-ho!"), Simple immediately disagrees and asserts a difference between the two performers' work.[24] As well, Simple corrects the narrator's use of the term, "Re-Bop," to describe the music of Gillespie and company, arguing that "Be-Bop" is the proper term for the new style.[25] When the narrator asks what the difference is between "*Re* and *Be*," the following exchange ensues:

> "A lot," said Simple. "Re-Bop was an imitation like most of the white boys play. Be-Bop is the real thing like the colored boys play."
> "You bring race into everything," I said, "even music."
> "It is in everything," said Simple. (56)

Thus, Hughes neatly articulates the ruptures in style that bebop effected from the swing of earlier jazz musicians like Calloway, and he also emphasizes the importance of race to the development of Parker and company's new paradigm—specifically the racially informed economics of appropriation that wrested financial reward from black musicians in the Swing Era.

Furthermore, Hughes dismisses the narrator's charge that Gillespie's vocalizations constitute "nonsense" and ascribes a political–semantic value to them as he explains their emergence out of institutionalized racism. The music, Simple proposes, comes "[f]rom the police beating Negroes' heads. [. . .] Every time a cop hits a Negro with his billy club, that old club says, 'BOP! BOP! . . . BE-BOP! . . . MOP! . . . BOP!'" (57). Bebop, Simple continues, reconfigures the sound of that mistreatment and transforms it into a musical protest, loaded with anger:

> " . . . *A dark man shall see dark days.* Bop comes out of them dark days. That's why real Bop is mad, wild, frantic, crazy—and not to be dug unless you've seen dark days, too. Folks who ain't suffered much cannot play Bop, neither appreciate it. They think Bop is nonsense— like you. They think it's just *crazy* crazy. They do not know Bop is also MAD CRAZY, SAD CRAZY, FRANTIC WILD CRAZY—beat out of somebody's head! That's what Bop is. Them young colored kids who started it, they know what Bop is." (58, original emphasis)

In these comments, Hughes, speaking through Simple, recognizes a lasting revolutionary principle in jazz, a process of angry rejuvenation that bebop had enacted, and which allowed jazz to remain a "tom-tom of revolt" even after early forms had been thoroughly consumed by the mainstream.

That process of angry rejuvenation certainly influences Hughes's later jazz work. Indeed, bebop's politicized reconstruction of jazz dominates Hughes's 1951 extended poem, *Montage of a Dream Deferred,* a sequence composed with attention to the disillusionment of Harlem blacks after the optimism of the New Negro movement had dwindled. However, as Hughes summarizes in the poem's introductory note, it was not just the *causes* of bebop that suited his agenda in *Montage* but the music's stylistic *effects* as well:

> [T]his poem on contemporary Harlem, like be-bop, is marked by conflicting changes, sudden nuances, sharp and impudent interjections, broken rhythms, and passages sometimes in the manner of the jam session, sometimes the popular song, punctuated by the riffs, runs, breaks, and disc-tortions of the music of a *community in transition.* (*Collected* 387, my emphasis)

Bebop was at times a discordant music, given to unorthodox exposition in its emphasis on reconfiguring well–worn jazz structures. Its fragmented

composition, its heightened accent on multivocality, and its jarring rhythmic assertion (recall Kenny Clarke dropping "bombs" on the drums
around the melodic statements of his bandmates) suited Hughes's goal: to
depict a weary Harlem in the wake of the Renaissance's ostensible diminu-
tion after the Depression and the riot of 1943.[26]

This mix of bebop aesthetics and social commentary is evident from
the sequence's opening lyric, "Dream Boogie"[27]:

Good morning, daddy!
Ain't you heard
The boogie-woogie rumble
Of a dream deferred?

Listen closely:
You'll hear their feet
Beating out and beating out a—

> *You think*
> *It's a happy beat?*

Listen to it closely:
Ain't you heard
something underneath
like a—

> *What did I say?*

Sure,
I'm happy!
Take it away!

> *Hey, pop!*
> *Re-bop!*
> *Mop!*

> *Y-e-a-h!*
(*Collected* 388)

The piece rehearses one of the conflicts that define much of Hughes's early
jazz poetry, namely the tension between the ostensible lightheartedness of
jazz and the underlying emotional core that the music inherits from the

blues: "laughing to keep from crying," or as Hughes himself puts it, "pain swallowed in a smile." The brightness of the lyric's initial address, "Good morning, daddy!" is quickly subverted by the lines that follow in the first stanza, an acknowledgment of solemnity in the "rumble" of a "dream deferred." The dream to which the line refers is superficially the failed promise of Harlem's flowering in the 1920s, though Hughes might just as well be imagining Harlem as symbolic of an historical series of failed promises for African Americans: Emancipation, Reconstruction, Double V. The deferral of these dreams' realization is the thematic center around which *Montage of a Dream Deferred* revolves, as mentioned in the work's title. It is also the subject of one of the sequence's best known lyrics, "Harlem [2]":

What happens to a dream deferred?

Does it dry up
like a raisin in the sun?
Or fester like a sore—
And then run?
Does it stink like rotten meat?
Or crust and sugar over—
like a syrupy sweet?

Maybe it just sags
like a heavy load.

Or does it explode?[28]
(*Collected* 426)

Thus, in "Dream Boogie," Hughes conveys the double–nature of jazz expression—its ability to articulate solemn themes through upbeat sound—in his attribution of a "boogie-woogie rumble" to the disillusionment and frustration that he will explore throughout *Montage* in lyrics such as "Harlem [2]." "Boogie-woogie," a jazz piano idiom featuring a recurring *ostinato* of rolling eighth–notes in the bass under improvised figures in the treble, is a form that thrives on "terrifying speed and accuracy" and generates, in jazz critic Len Lyons's words, "instantaneous excitement" in its audience (32). In naming it the initial sound of Harlem's deferred dream in *Montage,* Hughes summarizes the fundamental irony of jazz's double–nature. The poet further underscores this irony with his return to the deferred dream in "Harlem [2]," describing the failed promise of the past with images of decomposition that emphasize the severity of the "boogie-woogie rumble" through synaesthetic juxtaposition. Moreover, by beginning the sequence with an evocation of the boogie-woogie style, Hughes captures bebop's ability to balance revolution and historical comprehensiveness. Bop is ordered around fragmented referencing of other styles—as with Monk's forays into stride piano, Bird's blowing the blues, Dizzy's turn to Cuban rhythms—and Hughes uses that piecemeal composition as a guiding metaphor for black community in *Montage*. He writes of new transitions and change, but his poetic voice makes frequent fragmented calls to the past.

A second type of fragmentary expression that Hughes transfers from bop in "Dream Boogie" is disjunctive exposition.[29] Bebop soloists were given to disruptive breaks in the articulation of their melodic lines, abruptly shifting from one statement to another, ignoring the diatonic composition that characterized earlier jazz improvisation. As Scott DeVeaux writes:

> Fats Waller (who died in 1943) is said to have complained to unnamed musical tormentors at Minton's, "Stop that crazy boppin' and a-stoppin' and play that jive like the rest of us guys!" The bopping is inseparable from the stopping—the artful disruption of the natural expectation of continuity. [. . .] Parker's rhetoric [. . .] allows for irony, the juxtaposition of the unexpected. It may simply be a matter of ingeniously asymmetric phrasing. Or it may involve the juxtaposition of different *kinds* of rhetoric. At one point in [his 1943 recording of] "Sweet Georgia Brown," after another superbly executed phrase, Parker lands on the tonic. [. . .] Four bars of tonic harmony follow. Rather than generating momentum by superimposing harmonic movement over this passage, as he does in other choruses, Parker momentarily celebrates being stuck: he thickens his tone slightly and plays a brief Swing Era–type riff figure. On other occasions he is likely to suddenly shift to a blues mode, with all the idiomatic pitch bending and rhythmic "playing in the cracks," or he may quote from the vast store of popular songs in his memory. (*Birth* 267–68, original emphasis)

In "Dream Boogie," Hughes generates a similar ironic quality by repeatedly disrupting the poem's semantic flow. Note how the thought that closes stanza two ("You'll hear their feet / Beating out and beating out a—") is interrupted by the indented idea that constitutes the third stanza: *"You think / It's a happy beat?"* Similarly, Hughes builds grammatical expectation at the close of stanza four by formulating a simile ("something underneath / like a—"), only to subvert those expectations by again interrupting his own thought with another indented stanza break: *"What did I say?"* These two gestures approximate what DeVeaux calls the "dialogic" quality of bebop improvisation, ever articulating conflicting rhetorics within one soloist's extended statement (*Birth* 267).

DeVeaux's notion of the "dialogical" is of course indebted to M.M. Bakhtin, who conceived language as "ideologically saturated," and argued that literary writing, which frequently juxtaposes different forms of language, marks a "struggle among socio–linguistic points of view" (271, 273). Literary language, with its admission of various types of expression, creates dialogues between varying languages and their accompanying worldviews. This construction of language as a site of contestation between ideological points of view finds a musical analogue in bebop, which thrives on the juxtaposition of musical rhetorics and styles. This stylistic quality is especially key to the bop–derived political aesthetic adopted by Hughes.

Whereas Hughes uses bop fragmentation to structure a chiefly oral dialogue in "Dream Boogie" (note the nods to spoken address in the first voice's "Good morning, Daddy," and the second's, "*What did I say?*"), elsewhere in the sequence he uses the technique to juxtapose an African American oral rhetoric against the written word of white power. In doing so, Hughes again recalls the cultural hybridity that defines his earlier work—that is, a recognition of his own interstitial place between black oral–musical and Western written traditions—while he explores the paradoxes and damaging contradictions that characterize the intersection of white–imagined laws and black material reality. This occurs in "Children's Rhymes," for instance, a segment in which Hughes again uses indentation and italics to create ruptures in his verbal address. The lyric is a fragmented dialogue between an adult voice observing children at play and a collective voice that echoes the children's speech. Throughout, Hughes corrupts narrative flow by repeatedly sliding into one voice or another, representing these breaks through an alternating pattern of indented and non–indented, italicized and non–italicized, stanzas:

> When I was a chile we used to play,
> "One—two—buckle my shoe!"
> and things like that. But now, Lord,
> listen at them little varmints!
>
> > *By what sends*
> > *the white kids*
> > *I ain't sent:*
> > *I know I can't*
> > *be President.*

There is two thousand children
in this block, I do believe!

> *What don't bug*
> *them white kids*
> *sure bugs me:*
> *We knows everybody*
> *ain't free!*

Some of these young ones is cert'ly bad—
One batted a hard ball right through my window
and my gold fish et the glass. (*Collected* 390, lines 1–19)

Hughes lets the tension between these two sides of an African American oral dialogue develop throughout the first five stanzas, but as the lyric moves to its sixth stanza—to another return to the children's voice in italics—the poet compounds the ruptures of his dialogue by introducing a new rhetoric to his shifting expression, the voice of the white written word via the Pledge of Allegiance:

> *What's written down*
> *for white folks*
> *ain't for us a-tall:*
> *"Liberty and Justice—*
> *Huh—For All."* (*Collected* 390, lines 20–24)

The insertion of the quotation from the Pledge through the black children's voice intensifies the disjunction of the lyric exponentially; the fragmented exchange between different voices in the black community is suddenly engaged in a dialogue with the words of white nationalism and government. The move makes good on bebop's jarring aesthetic as it halts the expectation of continued exchange between the lyric's two black voices. At the same time it evokes the social significance of bop's disjunction. Parker's ironic play with fragmentation, for example, is not disjunction for its own sake. Rather, the improviser's sudden shifts into different statements constitute a constant Signifyin(g) play with both "black" and "white" musical rhetorics. His unexpected insertion of blues or earlier jazz styles into solos could constitute either homage to or parody of African American traditions; his evocation of popular songs from the mainstream constitutes a formal reordering of white utterance.

Hughes also emphasizes bebop's social importance by juxtaposing his ambivalent nationalistic "riff" against a crescendo of bop syllables as the segment comes to a close:

> *Oop-pop-a-da!*
> *Skee! Daddle-de-do!*
> *Be-bop!*
>
> Salt' peanuts!
>
> De-dop! (*Collected* 390, lines 25–29)

The insertion of the bebop quotation against nationalistic rhetoric constitutes a Signifyin(g) call-and-response. The "nonsense" of the Pledge (underscored by both the speakers' acknowledgment of that text's irrelevance to non–whites and their interruptive "Huh") yields to the semantics of the new music here, which ultimately wield more significance and meaning for the poem's black characters. The idealism of nationalistic discourse means little to African Americans, Hughes argues, so in exchange the poet cuts to an alternate rhetoric, bebop—the supposed "nonsense" that, as Simple argues in "Bop," actually speaks against racial inequities. Bebop, Hughes suggests, is inextricably linked to the social reality of urban African Americans. Moreover, in his presentation of the bop lyrics in both italics and regular typeface, Hughes collapses the distance between the segment's competing black voices by blending their distinguishing typographical features in his musical expression. Bop organizes diverse rhetorics in its dialogical organization and at times unifies these disparate voices, as Hughes does here, to mark the community underlying their ostensible division.

While Hughes takes pains to transfer bebop's disjunctive exposition to individual moments within *Montage,* he also organizes the entire long poem around that fragmentary aesthetic. As Hughes himself says in the introduction, the poem operates at times in "the manner of the jam session," and accordingly, *Montage* presents that setting's unanticipated turns and impromptu shifts in tone writ large. Through these sundry turns and shifts the poem offers a variation on bebop's own Signifyin(g) history of black music, incorporating fragments of various African American musical forms in an extended collage. Blues, boogie-woogie, and gospel, for example, are all represented in quotation. Of these three styles, boogie-woogie is given the most attention, appearing in six segments: "Dream Boogie," "Easy Boogie," "Boogie 1 A.M.," "Lady's Boogie," "Nightmare Boogie," and "Dream Boogie: Variation." As Steven Tracy notes, these pieces "have in common much more than the 'boogie' of their titles." Rather, they "comprise an intricate series of interwoven 'improvisations' over a set boogie-woogie rhythm, with Hughes modulating and modifying rhythm, words, imagery, moods, and themes" (*Blues* 225). The tension between boogie-woogie's steady bass–clef rhythm and its treble–clef improvisations is readily observable in "Dream Boogie," reprinted above. Note how Hughes suggests the pulse of the music with the strong cadence of the opening stanza, only to "improvise" on that rhythm with the disruptive variations that follow. Blues as a musical form appears most overtly through "Blues at Dawn," in which Hughes makes a brief return to the AAB verse form that dominated his early output. In the segment, the poet uses the same techniques of verbal and rhythmic variation that enabled him to suggest sound in those previous poems:

> I don't dare start thinking in the morning.
> I don't dare start thinking in the morning.
>> If I thought thoughts in bed,
>> Them thoughts would bust my head—
> So I don't dare start thinking in the morning.
>
> I don't dare remember in the morning
> Don't dare remember in the morning.
>> If I recall the day before,
>> I wouldn't get up no more—
> So I don't dare remember in the morning.
>> (*Collected* 420)

The insertion of this traditional blues verse in *Montage* with the new "blues" form of boogie-woogie—generally based around the same I-IV-V harmonic sequence—simulates bebop's composite musical history, a discourse Hughes extends in other directions with echoes of spirituals and gospel in "Mystery":

> *Jesus, lover of my soul!*
>
> Hail, Mary, mother of God!
>
> *Let me to thy bosom fly!*
>
> Amen! Hallelujah!
>
> *Swing low, sweet chariot,*
> *Coming for to carry me home.*
>> (*Collected* 416, lines 5–10)

And though Hughes alludes to these different forms of black music, he emphasizes their place within a specifically bebop musical context by returning continually to echoes of Gillespie–esque vocalization: "De-dop!" "re-bop," "oop pop-a-da," "ool-ya-koo," "pop-a-da." These bop syllables are ubiquitous throughout *Montage,* even appearing disruptively in poems that do not seem to signify music otherwise. They form an insistent *obbligato* that underscores the specific jazz idiom out of which Hughes is working.

Furthermore, though the sound of music reverberates loudly throughout *Montage,* the poem's disjunctive exposition extends beyond the borders of musical representation, incorporating spoken and written–word expressivity in its fragmentary cut-and-mix. Hughes is ever mindful of his position as a literary–jazz improviser, riffing intermittently on verbal forms as he crafts his music–influenced solo. "Children's Rhymes," discussed above, is one obvious example, collapsing as it does the ludic speech of young blacks against signature bebop sounds. In "Sliver of Sermon" and "Testimonial," Hughes turns his ears to other black spoken forms and records echoes of religious declaration:

> When pimps out of loneliness cry:
> *Great God!*
> Whores in final weariness say:
> *Great God!*
> *Oh, God!*
> *My God!*
>
> Great
> God!
> (*Collected* 417)

and

> If I just had a piano,
> if I just had a organ,
> if I just had a drum,
> how I could praise my Lord!
>
> But I don't need no piano,
> neither organ
> nor drum
> for to praise my Lord!
> (*Collected* 417)

The two segments form a verbal counterpart to "Mystery," complementing and standing in tension with the sounds of black music from that earlier segment. In addition, Hughes also nods to the significance of black oral communication in "Joe Louis [1]," paying tribute to the revered African American boxing champion who was the subject of so much verbal myth–making in black urban sectors:

> They worshipped Joe.
> A school teacher
> whose hair was gray
> said:
>> *Joe has sense enough to know*
>> *He is a god.*
>> *So many gods don't know.*
>
> "They say" . . ."They say" . . ."They say" . . .
> But the gossips had no
> "They say"
> to latch onto
> for Joe.
>   (*Collected* 423)

Evoking the black spoken word in its myriad forms throughout *Montage*, Hughes assembles an assortment of meaningful fragments, clipped monologues, and dialogues from all areas of an African American community that reveal the poet's appreciation for the vitality of black spoken address in his ongoing jazz collage.

Hughes also plays with written forms of address throughout *Montage*, constantly creating tension between the written and the oral–musical. The poet juxtaposes these various forms in the above–noted "Children's Rhymes," for example, in which the white written and black spoken words comprise two sides of a contest resolved through the music of the piece's bebop coda. Similarly, in "Ballad of the Landlord," Hughes again criticizes black–white power imbalances in metaphorical terms, by examining the inequities evident in the ongoing conflict between white written and black spoken expression:

> Landlord, landlord,
> My roof has sprung a leak.
> Don't you 'member I told you about it
> Way last week?

Landlord, landlord,
These steps is broken down.
When you come up yourself
It's a wonder you don't fall down.

Ten Bucks you say I owe you?
Ten Bucks you say is due?
Well, that's Ten Bucks more'n I'll pay you
Till you fix this house up new.

What? You gonna get eviction orders?
You gonna cut off my heat?
You gonna take my furniture and
Throw it in the street?

Um-huh! You talking high and mighty.
Talk on—till you get through.
You ain't gonna be able to say a word
If I land my fist on you.

Police! Police!
Come and get this man!
He's trying to ruin the government
And overturn the land!

Copper's whistle!
Patrol bell!
Arrest.

Precinct Station.
Iron cell.
Headlines in press:

MAN THREATENS LANDLORD
*
* *

TENANT HELD NO BAIL
*
* *

JUDGE GIVES NEGRO 90 DAYS IN COUNTY JAIL
                              (*Collected* 403)

The segment is a savvy commentary on how white written forms of address supersede black spoken voices amidst American institutionalized racism. As in other dialogic segments in *Montage,* Hughes sets up conflict between two voices—one, that of the ill–treated black tenant, and the other, that of the unfeeling white landlord, represented by italics. Through the segment's first five stanzas though, the latter is represented merely by absence, signified by the black speaker's rejoinders to unheard conversation ("Ten Bucks you say I owe you?" "You gonna cut off my heat?"). The move privileges the black spoken voice, as does Hughes's attempt to represent African American speech through colloquial language and elision ("Don't you 'member [. . .] " "Um-huh! You talking high and mighty"). However, as the conflict that Hughes dramatizes in the segment comes to its physical realization with the black speaker's threat of violence to the white landlord, the poet shifts first to the voice of the latter, before evoking the "sounds" of white institutional power, the "Copper's whistle," and the "Patrol bell." The usurpation of the segment's black voice reaches its climax in the newspaper headlines that close the piece. The three headlines recast the narrative of the poem. They are examples of the omnipotence of the white written word, mediating the entire episode and effectively disempowering the black tenant, wronged all along.

Hughes explores a similar tension between black orality and white literacy in the widely anthologized "Theme for English B," a monologue that dramatizes an African American student's ambivalence over being asked by a white instructor to define himself through writing. The poem's imperative recalls Henry Louis Gates's argument that, throughout history, white Europeans and their descendants have ordered the black subject to measure her "humanity, [her] capacity for progress, and [her] very place in the great chain of being" through writing ("Writing" 9). The pretense of "Theme for English B" is that the piece itself constitutes the speaker's effort for the assignment, a construction Hughes plays with to ironic effect throughout. The segment's voice is somewhat informal, given to the casual manner of conversation. Hughes sets this suggested orality in constant tension with the expectation of "formal literacy" that the assignment would command, and riffs on the incongruity of the black spoken voice with white written conventions:

The instructor said,

> *Go home and write*
> *a page tonight.*
> *And let that page come out of you—*
> *Then, it will be true.*

I wonder if it's that simple?
I am twenty–two, colored, born in Winston–Salem.
I went to school there, then Durham, then here
to this college on the hill above Harlem.
I am the only colored student in my class.
The steps from the hill lead down into Harlem,
through a park, then I cross St. Nicholas,
Eighth Avenue, Seventh, and I come to the Y,
the Harlem Branch Y, where I take the elevator
up to my room, sit down, and write this page:

It's not easy to know what is true for you or me
at twenty–two, my age. But I guess I'm what
I feel and see and hear, Harlem, I hear you:
hear you, hear me—we two—you, me, talk on this page.
(I hear New York, too.) Me—who?
Well, I like to eat, sleep, drink, and be in love.
I like to work, read, learn, and understand life.
I like a pipe for a Christmas present,
or records—Bessie, bop, or Bach.
I guess being colored doesn't make me *not* like
the same things other folks like who are other races.
So will my page be colored that I write?
Being me, it will not be white.
But it will be
a part of you, instructor.
You are white—
yet a part of me, as I am a part of you.
That's American.
Sometimes perhaps you don't want to be a part of me.
Nor do I often want to be a part of you.
But we are, that's true!
As I learn from you,
I guess you learn from me—
although you're older—and white—
and somewhat more free.

This is my page for English B.

                              (*Collected* 409–10)

In negotiating this tension between black orality and white literacy in the segment, Hughes offers a frank acknowledgment of his own cultural hybridity. As the speaker comments on the importance of black sound to black presence, "I guess I'm what / I feel and see and hear, Harlem [. . .] .," and then as he questions what renders his own presence unique, his stream of thought carries him to an admission of music's importance: "I like a pipe for a Christmas present, / or records—Bessie, bop, or Bach." However, as the speaker admits which records are personally meaningful to him, he realizes his own composite identity: he is a black man who appreciates the work of Bach, a European classical composer, as well as African American music by the beboppers and Bessie Smith. Both African American identity and American identity, Hughes argues here, are much more complex than traditional binaries allow for. Blackness and whiteness are not mutually exclusive in America's cultural mix. Speaking reflexively, Hughes's speaker notes this in his theme, acknowledging that even a page composed by an African American man bears something of his white instructor. And as the speaker notes in his penultimate statement, that white "something" likely carries more weight than black expression itself. In the realm of white text, and in a society governed by the power of such, the instructor undoubtedly is "somewhat more free."

While Hughes openly acknowledges America's racialized power imbalances in *Montage* and notes how those inequities are mitigated by the veneration of the white word, he also subverts the power of that discourse by fragmenting it within his recognizably jazz–motivated poem. Indeed, segments like "Children's Rhymes," "The Ballad of the Landlord," and "Theme for English B," feature individual moments of white "triumph" through written discourse, but their placement within Hughes's extended jazz statement reconfigures their power. Hughes quotes from or acknowledges the power of white written discourse to signify on it and to displace that authority by subsuming it within a larger literary performance governed by bebop's black aesthetic. Even though Hughes gives momentary voice to the power of white written discourse—as in the segments noted above—the poet constantly returns to the sound of bebop through his recurring *obbligatos,* or to the structure of bebop in his own verbal variation on one of the music's ubiquitous attributes: the riff.

The riff—a short melodic figure which may be repeated as is or varied according to harmonic progressions—is one of the oldest and longest–enduring characteristics of jazz performance. As J. Bradford Robinson writes:

> The riff is thought to derive from the repetitive call-and-response pat-
> terns of West African music, and appeared prominent in black-American
> music from the earliest times. It was an important element in New
> Orleans marching band music (where the word "riff" apparently origi-
> nated), and from there entered jazz, where by the mid–1920s it was
> firmly established in background ensemble playing and as the basis for
> solo improvisation. (1047)

The riff was especially key to the Southwest tradition of big band jazz that
came to national attention in the 1930s, with the success of groups led by
Bennie Moten and Count Basie. By the height of the Swing Era, bandleaders frequently turned to "riff tunes," which featured the fashioning of
short, infectious figures into song melodies.[30] Because of the popularity of
the "riff tune" and the wholesale incorporation of the riff into mainstream
jazz of the Swing Era, the beboppers' relationship to the tradition is
ambivalent, ironic. Parker and company were occasionally given to riff
tunes of their own, even in anthems like Gillespie's "Salt Peanuts," or
Parker's "Now's the Time," but their use of the riff in solo improvisations
was often laden with Signifyin(g) play that subverted the unambiguous sim-
plicity of riffing among the mainstream swing bands. Consider, for
instance, Parker's fondness for a parodic signature riff culled from the
"Woody Woodpecker" theme, or Gillespie's preference for (in Scott
DeVeaux's words) "witty, punning riff figures," which move jazz critic
Francis Davis to write that the trumpeter's solos had a "rich sarcasm about
them" (DeVeaux, *Birth* 269; Davis 15).[31] The bebop riff need not always be
a vehicle for parody, though, but rather could be implemented as homage
as well, as with Charlie Parker's incorporating stylistic gestures from the
solos of tenor sax legend Lester Young, or even with younger boppers like
trumpeter Clifford Brown borrowing phrases from Gillespie. If bebop was
jazz pushed to Signifyin(g) extremes, then the riff proved one of the key figures in its vocabulary.[32]

　　Hughes offers his own verbal take on the Signifyin(g) riff throughout
Montage, repeating the key phrase and dominant metaphor, "a dream
deferred," intact or with subtle variation in a number of segments. After
the initial invocation of the riff, "the boogie-woogie rumble / of a dream
deferred," in the opening "Dream Boogie," Hughes returns to the figure in
various forms in nine subsequent segments. These variations range from the
plaintive query, "Why should it be *my* dream / deferred," in "Tell Me," to
the statement of the poem's title, "Montage of a dream deferred," in
"Deferred" and "Dime," to a complete restatement of the initial figure,
"The boogie-woogie rumble / Of a dream deferred," in "Boogie: 1 A.M."

(*Collected* 396; 414, 420; 411). In both "Harlem [2]" and "Good Morning," presented in succession in *Montage,* Hughes asks, "What happens to a dream deferred?" while in the closing segment, "Island [2]," Hughes turns to a collective voice to state, "*Dream within a dream, / Our dream deferred*" (*Collected* 426–27; 429). Ultimately, the constant return to the riff further incorporates jazz style in the poem and complements the recurring invocation of bebop vocalizations throughout. The vocabulary and structural organization of bop improvisation is constantly at the fore, as is the ironic play with semantics at which Parker and Gillespie were so adept. Hughes tries to subvert the deferral of African American dreams by reminding his reader of them with such insistence.

Thus, in his experimentation with bebop throughout *Montage,* Hughes was able to negotiate the social and aesthetic interests that had characterized his earlier work, and help mend a cleft that had developed between those poetic interests in the 1930s. After his initial success in the 1920s, Hughes gradually turned away for a time from the representations of black cultural life and the explorations with black music that dominate *The Weary Blues* and *Fine Clothes to the Jew.* Instead, Hughes became an overtly political voice throughout the thirties, moving away from poetry that had a less overt political texture (in its Signifyin(g) play with white forms), and moving toward verse that was inarguably frank in its engagement with social issues. This change in style was perhaps motivated by the poet's growing interest in Marxism, and was evident as early as 1931, in the controversial long poem "Advertisement for the Waldorf-Astoria," which comments wryly on the disparity between the grandeur of the newly opened New York hotel and the mean poverty elsewhere in New York:

> LISTEN, HUNGRY ONES!
> Look! See what *Vanity Fair* says about the
>   new Waldorf-Astoria:
>   "All the luxuries of private home. . . ."
> Now, won't that be charming when the last flop-house
>   has turned you down this winter? (*Collected* 143–44, lines 3–8)

Hughes brought a similar unflinching voice to "Goodbye Christ" (1932), in which he champions Marxism over Christianity, crying:

> Goodbye,
> Christ Jesus Lord God Jehova,
> Beat it on away from here now.
> Make way for a new guy with no religion at all—

A real guy named
Marx Communist Lenin Peasant Stalin Worker ME—
                    (*Collected* 166, lines 17–22)

By the late 1930s and into the forties, Hughes made occasional returns to black music in later blues poems like "Barefoot Blues" and "Life is Fine," but it was not until *Montage* that the poet reconciled these discrete elements, blending overt social commentary with the celebration of African American cultural life.

Aside from offering political commentary through bebop's disjunctive exposition and heightened sense of Signifyin(g), Hughes also brings the frankness of his 1930s poems to *Montage of a Dream Deferred*. In "Flatted Fifths," for example, the poet pays tribute to the disillusioned artists of the bebop movement, acknowledging their disenfranchisement after the Second World War, their tenuous relationship with American consumerism, and their unsettling attraction to narcotics:

Little cullud boys with beards
re-bop be-bop mop and stop.

Little cullud boys with fears,
frantic, kick their draftee years
into flatted fifths and flatter beers
that at a sudden change become
sparkling Oriental wines
rich and strange
silken bathrobes with gold twines
and Heilbroner, Crawford,
Nat-undreamed-of-Lewis combines
in silver thread and diamond notes
on trade–marks inside
Howard coats.

Little cullud boys in berets
        oop pop-a-da
horse a fantasy of days
        ool-ya-koo
and dig all plays.
                    (*Collected* 404)

The momentary financial triumph of the "frantic" bebop boys—evident in the sudden appearance of silk and gold finery—is precarious, Hughes seems to suggest, ever in threat of descending into the fantasy of "horse"—heroin. The segment's title, which evokes one of the signature melodic motifs of bop, the flatted fifth note of the scale, even seems governed by the same pessimistic sense of irony, punning as it does on a common measurement (a fifth of a gallon) for alcohol sales. Hughes's frank acknowledgment of drugs in both the bebop lifestyle, and more generally in the African American urban landscape, occurs as well in "Gauge," a four-line segment composed only of slang terms—including the title—for marijuana:

> Hemp . . .
> A stick . . .
> A roach . . .
> Straw . . .
>
> (*Collected* 406)

A similar candor dictates "Cafe: 3 A.M.," in which Hughes criticizes the insidious and predatory nature of city police looking to arrest New York gays:[33]

> Detectives from the vice squad
> with weary sadistic eyes
> spotting fairies.
>> *Degenerates,*
>> some folks say.
>
> But God, Nature,
> or somebody,
> made them that way.
>
> Police lady or Lesbian
> over there?
>> *Where?*
>> (*Collected* 406)

This frankness occurs as well in "Not a Movie," in which Hughes writes in detail about a near-lynching in the South:

> Well, they rocked him with road-apples
> because he tried to vote
> and whipped his head with clubs
> and he crawled on his knees to his house

and he got the midnight train
and he crossed that Dixie line
now he's livin'
on a 133rd.

He didn't stop in Washington
and he didn't stop in Baltimore
neither in Newark on the way.
Six knots was on his head
but, thank God, he wasn't dead!
And there ain't no Ku Klux
on a 133rd.

(*Collected* 396)

Thus, the bebop aesthetic fashioned a way for Hughes to articulate a more complex version of his own black modernism in *Montage of a Dream Deferred:* stylistically experimental, openly political, and yet rich with the folk–derived expressivity that the poet espoused throughout his career. The ultimate effect of this blend was a work that was as quintessentially modernist as any other in American poetry. As Steven Tracy notes, its stylistic experimentation compares with other disjunctive sequences like Pound's *Cantos* or Robert Lowell's long poems—or with Williams's *Paterson,* I would add (*Blues* 225–26). At the same time, *Montage* is unarguably and *self–reflexively* indicative of the cultural hybridity that defines American modernism. Furthermore, the poem embodies Houston Baker's definition of a specifically African American modernism in its social relevance. *Montage of a Dream Deferred,* like the bebop music by which it was influenced, offers a manifestation of Baker's "deformation of mastery." The poem advertises its black difference through its adoption of key structural components from Gillespie and Parker's new African American music: fragmentary composition, discursive subversion, the Signifyin(g) riff. As Ralph Ellison would soon reveal, with the publication of his novel *Invisible Man,* all of these components could have necessarily important aesthetic and social effects in black American fiction, as well.

Chapter Three:
Riffing on the Lower Frequencies: Dialogism, Intertextuality, and Bebop in Ralph Ellison's *Invisible Man*

If Langston Hughes's jazz poetry constitutes what I call the First Book of Jazz—that is, the foundation for a jazz–influenced African American modernist literature—then Ralph Ellison's 1952 novel *Invisible Man* is surely that First Book's most significant addendum. The novel expands on Hughes's stylistic innovations, emphasizing musical sound as a meaningful signifier of black identity, and perhaps more importantly, further investigating the possibilities of bebop's "politics of style." Despite later registering ambivalence about bebop—calling it, for instance, a "revolutionary rumpus sounding like a series of flubbed notes" in 1958 ("Golden Age" 241)— Ellison saw the form develop first–hand in New York in the early 1940s, and integrated the most salient characteristics of the new style into his fiction.[1] Bebop, I argue, is the form of jazz that Ellison's novel most resembles. It is bebop's political style, its emphasis on assertive performance and its disruption of mainstream aesthetics through the celebration of a performed blackness, that is the most decisive source for the novel's intertextual network and complex design.[2] Influenced by the landmark musical innovations Parker and company had inaugurated, Ellison's *Invisible Man* is a Signifyin(g) masterpiece. Moreover, on a personal, creative level for Ellison, the novel marked the emergence of a signature style after early experimentation with various forms during his apprenticeship in the 1930s and forties.

Like Hughes's work from the 1920s and into the thirties, Ellison's early stories are divided in character. His fiction before *Invisible Man* is dominated by two clear stylistic threads: a hard–boiled social realism that dramatizes the young writer's interest in class politics, and a playful "residual orality" that explores the African American folk forms so central to his later work. His social realism was influenced personally and politically by his association with Richard Wright and his sympathies with leftist thought. While in New York in the summer of 1936, after his junior year of college at the Tuskegee Institute, Ellison met and befriended Wright, who first encouraged Ellison's writing by assigning him a book review later published in the Fall 1937 issue of *New Challenge*.[3] Until that point, Ellison had seriously pursued music and sculpture. He had received a scholarship to study music composition at Tuskegee with William L. Dawson, and after withdrawing from Tuskegee before his senior year, he spent much of 1936 studying sculpture in Harlem with Richmond Barthé.[4] With Wright's urging, though, Ellison, the aspiring musician and artist, became serious about writing and buoyed by the publication of his *New Challenge* review, contributed a story for the magazine's Winter 1937 issue. The piece was entitled "Hymie's Bull," and was based on his experience hoboing on freight trains. The story made it as far as the galleys for publication before being dropped for work by other writers.

Though Ellison later denied having ever written "Marxist" fiction, "Hymie's Bull" is obviously informed by the leftist associations the writer had at the time of its composition.[5] His friend and unofficial mentor, Wright was a vocal member of the Communist Party; Hughes, whom Ellison also met and befriended in Harlem around that time, was openly sympathetic to Marxist thought and was in the midst of composing his most "openly" political verse; Ellison himself attended Party gatherings that "were attended by such exempla of radical American letters as Granville Hicks, Isador Scheider, Kenneth Fearing, Clifford Odets, William Rollins, Jr., and Malcolm Cowley" (O'Meally, *Craft* 37). Furthermore, as Robert O'Meally suggests, Ellison's early book reviews—of which he contributed more than twenty between 1937 and 1944 to radical publications like *New Challenge, Direction, Negro Quarterly,* and *New Masses*—were dominated by the conviction that "the literature of black Americans (the subject of about half of his reviews in the thirties and forties) was [. . .] an emerging national literature that should serve to heighten the revolutionary consciousness of the black populace. The black writer should not instill in his audience, mere 'race consciousness,' however, but awareness of class" (*Craft* 38).

In "Hymie's Bull," Ellison puts this politically inspired theory of literature into effect, dramatizing his dual interest in issues of race and class. The narrative depicts police violence against train–riding vagrants during the Depression; the "bull" of the title is slang for a constable, a brutal figure whom a white vagrant named Hymie murders at the story's climax. Ellison tells the story through an unnamed black narrator, a blunt world–weary voice who relates the action in prose that seems almost parodically Hemingway–esque in its unaffected attention to human cruelty:[6]

> Bulls are pretty bad people to meet if you're a bum. They have head–whipping down to a science and they're always ready to go into action. They know all the places to hit a guy to change a bone into jelly, and they seem to feel just the place to kick you to make your backbone feel like it's going to fold up like the old cellophane drinking cups we used to use when were kids. Once a bull hit me across the bridge of my nose and I felt like I was coming apart like a cigarette floating in a urinal. (83)

Indeed, the likeness to Hemingway's laconic toughness is undoubtedly not coincidental. Ellison had begun reading the older writer's work in *Esquire* magazine in barbershops as a college student (Ellison, "Completion" 807). Moreover, as he became interested in writing fiction as an adult, he read Hemingway's work with renewed interest, closely observing the way the older writer structured sentences and organized narrative. For a time, Ellison even copied Hemingway's fiction in longhand "to get a feel for his language" (O'Meally, *Craft* 32).

Its somewhat exaggerated hard–boiled voice notwithstanding, Ellison's narration in "Hymie's Bull" offers a straightforward articulation of the writer's political interests at the time. The striking violence of the above passage, for instance, is central to Ellison's class concerns, as it reveals America's inhumanity toward its underprivileged. As the story continues, Ellison explores the implications of race within that system of injustice. The narrator notes that whenever a freight–train officer is murdered on a run, the authorities immediately take vengeance on black vagrants. "Most of the time," Ellison's speaker comments, "they don't care who did it, because the main thing is to make some black boy pay for it" (83). It is no wonder, then, that as the story concludes the narrator and the nine other black vagrants with whom he is traveling flee the train for fear of police retribution.

A similarly realistic narrative style and studied attention to race and class inform two other early stories of Ellison's from the late 1930s: "I Did Not Learn Their Names" and "The Black Ball."[7] Like "Hymie's Bull," these stories also feature anonymous, first–person narrators who disclose the action in a predominantly humorless tone. (Indeed, in reading these early realist stories, one sees few, if any, signs of the ironic play that Ellison uses so adroitly throughout *Invisible Man*.) "I Did Not Learn Their

Names" recalls the freight–train setting of the earlier story. The piece is a short vignette in which Ellison dramatizes how class struggles unite the impoverished across racial lines. In the story, the black narrator realizes the shortsightedness of his own blind contempt for whites when an elderly white vagrant couple on a freight train treats him with compassion and offers him food to eat. With "The Black Ball," Ellison departs from his freight train setting, but once more rehearses this narrative pattern of destitute or working–class peoples of differing races forging community according to their economic mistreatment. The story's black narrator, a caretaker humiliated by his condescending white employer, comes to an epiphany about the humanity of the white working class through an encounter with a white Communist trying to enlist him in the Party. Initially, the narrator resists the Communist's solicitations to join a worker's union, but reconsiders the invitation when the white man reveals extreme burns on his hands, explaining that he received the scars from a lynch mob in the South after testifying to the innocence of a black friend accused of rape. In this trio of early stories, Ellison is largely unambiguous as he uses narrative to sketch the contours of his political thought; the stories turn on solemn, unequivocal social commentary. They are certainly the work of the young ideologue who closed a 1937 letter to Wright with the enthusiastic pun, "Workers of the World Must Write!!!!" (qtd in Callahan, "Introduction," *Flying Home* xiv). Conversely, the other main strand that defines Ellison's pre–*Invisible Man* fiction is less overt in its political commentary and certainly more motivated by an interest in the stylistic potential of black vernacular forms.

In this second stylistic category, found in his 1940s' work, Ellison's stories stray somewhat from his social realism and begin to exhibit a distinct residual orality. They embody Bernard W. Bell's argument that African American letters are often marked by the "residue" of black culture's oral foundations, by the appearance of oral modes of expression that were formed in the past but are still active in the cultural processes of the present. Residually oral cultures return time and again, as Bell suggests, to the interplay or dialectic between the sound of the spoken word and the sight of the written one (20–21). Much as Hughes had composed a residually oral literature in his poetry through constant negotiation between representations of sound and a commitment to the visual text of the written word, Ellison performs similar stylistic gestures in a trio of early stories that center on the boy characters Buster and Riley. In "Afternoon" (1940), "Mister Toussan" (1941), and "That I Had the Wings" (1943), Ellison represents versions of the African American rhetorical rituals that Henry Louis Gates identifies as the core of the Signifyin(g) expressive matrix. In each of the stories, Ellison dramatizes how his two young protagonists negotiate their budding awareness of social injustices through Signifyin(g) play and oral contests.

Various modes of African American oral expression dominate the Buster and Riley stories. The epigraph to "Mister Toussan," for instance, is, by Ellison's own identification, a "[r]hyme used as a prologue to Negro slave stories":

> *Once upon a time*
> *The goose drink wine*
> *Monkey chew tobacco*
> *And he spit white lime* (22)[8]

As well, Ellison's boy protagonists are frequently given to verbal toasts, bursts of song, and hyperbolic play with language. Musing on the question, "What would you do if you had wings?" in one of the dialogues in "Mister Toussan," the boys challenge each other in a series of dynamic toasts:

> "Shucks, I'd outfly an eagle. I wouldn't stop flying till I was a million, billion, trillion, zillion miles away from this ole town."
> "Where'd you go, man?"
> "Up north, maybe to Chicago."
> "Man, if I had wings I wouldn't ever settle down."
> "Me neither. Heck, with wings you could go anywhere, even up to the sun if it wasn't too hot . . ."
> " . . . I'd go to New York . . ."
> "Even around the stars . . ."
> "Or Dee-troit, Michigan . . ."
> "Hell, you could git some cheese off the moon and some milk from the Milky Way . . ."
> "Or anywhere else colored is free . . ."
> "I'd bet I'd loop-the-loop . . ."
> "And parachute . . ."
> "I'd land in Africa and git me some diamonds . . ."
> "Yeah, and them cannibals would eat the hell outa you, too," said Riley. (24–25)

Other moments of oral play and verbal contest include Riley's response to the question of his father's meanness in "Afternoon"—"My ole man's so mean he hates hisself!" (43)—or the boys' delight in the following folk lyric in the same story:

'*If it hadn't a been*
for the referee
Jack Johnson woulda killed
Jim Jeffrie' (44, original emphasis)[9]

As this last example reveals, the boys are certainly prone to Signifyin(g) games when extolling the virtues of African American heroes: Jack Johnson, Joe Louis, or Louis Armstrong (who they argue is so good on trumpet that he can play a high *p*).

Of all the characteristic African American modes of oral expression in which the boys engage, call-and-response most significantly defines the tenor of their interaction. For example, when Riley offhandedly chants from an African American animal fable, "*Well I met Mister Rabbit down by the pea vine . . .*" in "Afternoon," Buster immediately returns:

"*An' I asked him where's he gwine*
Well, he said, Just kiss my behind
And he skipped on down the pea vine." (36, original emphasis)

The call-and-response patterns through which the boys communicate are important on a number of levels: for one, as in the above example, they constitute an act of play through which Buster and Riley may complement or contest each other's imaginations; however, these expressive moments also allow the boys to assert their communion as they negotiate various unsettling social pressures amidst their coming of age. In "Mister Toussan," for example, the boys engage in a call-and-response pattern about Toussaint L'Ouverture, the famed Haitian revolutionary who triumphed over Napoleon's army, and whom Buster has just learned about in school. For Buster and Riley, the expressive revelry over Mister Toussan's military bravado assuages the physical hurt that begins the story, when the two boys are chased from a white man's yard and called "little nigguhs" for trying to eat the fruit from his cherry tree. As the narrative progresses, the boys erupt into an antiphonal feverpitch that is part sermon, part secular verse in its signifying on Toussan's exploits:

"Really, man, she said that Toussan and his men got up on one of them African mountains and shot down them peckerwood soldiers fass as they'd try to come up . . ."
"Why good-God-a-mighty!" yelled Riley.
"Oh boy, they shot 'em down!" chanted Buster.
"Tell me about it, man!"

"And they throwed 'em off the mountain . . ."

" . . . Goool-leee! . . ."

" . . . And Toussan drove 'em cross the sand . . ."

" . . . Yeah! And what was they wearing, Buster? . . ."

"Man, they had on red uniforms and blue hats all trimmed with gold and they had some swords all shining, what they called sweet blades of Damascus . . ."

"Sweet blades of Damascus! . . ."

" . . . They really had 'em," chanted Buster.

"And what kinda guns?"

"Big, black cannon!"

"And where did ole what you call 'im run them guys . . . ?"

"His name was Toussan."

"Toozan! Just like Tarzan . . ."

"Not Taar-zan, dummy, Toou-zan!"

"Toussan! And where'd ole Toussan run 'em?"

"Down to the water, man . . ."

" . . . To the river water . . ."

" . . . Where some great big ole boats was waiting for 'em . . ."

" . . . Go on, Buster!"

"An' Toussan shot into them boats . . ."

" . . . He shot into 'em . . ."

" . . . shot into them boats . . ."

"Jesus! . . ."

" . . . with his great big cannons . . ." (26–27)

In this exchange, the boys affirm their shared position against the power imbalances that antagonize them. And in making call-and-response so central to the characterization of Buster and Riley's friendship, Ellison himself dramatizes the pivotal place of African American expressive forms in the definition of black community.

This expressive register of community marks an early debt to the African American vernacular forms—including the blues and jazz—that will later define *Invisible Man*. The antiphonal play of his boy protagonists embodies the effects of call-and-response that Barbara E. Bowen reads in the blues: "For the blues singer, the importance of the call-and-response pattern is its continual affirmation of collective voice. As antiphonal phrases repeat and respond to each other, the singers are assenting to membership in a group and affirming that their experience is shared" (189). In the case of the "Mister Toussan" call-and-response pattern, the boys exult in a shared historical dialogue that overturns the present day's defeat; both

Buster and Riley are united in the connection they forge with L'Ouverture's victories of the past.

Ellison's use of oral modes in the Buster and Riley stories, and his recognition of those modes as important to the assertion of African American community, was undoubtedly influenced by his tenure between 1938 and 1942 with the Works Progress Administration's Federal Writers Project, specifically his time spent collecting folklore in Harlem as part of New York's "Living Lore Unit." As Robert O'Meally notes, this project affirmed the vitality of "traditional" African American oral expressivity for Ellison; through the experience he recognized that the games, tales, toasts, and songs he was collecting (and which would figure so strongly in his fiction over the next decade) were elements of a vernacular matrix that was very much alive in contemporary black America (*Craft* 34).[10] Ellison himself later averred that "the WPA provided an important surge to Afro-American cultural activity," maintaining that the project was important for its preservation of communal black expressivity and its "resuscitation and transformation of that very vital artistic impulse that is abiding among Afro-Americans" ("Remembering" 664–65). Moreover, on a more personal level, Ellison declared that undertakings like the Living Lore Project were important because they allowed "many Negroes," himself included, "to achieve their identities as artists" ("Remembering" 665). His own work for the WPA, interviewing subjects and transcribing oral expression, "sharpened [his] ear," which was well–trained musically already, "for idiosyncrasies of speech and gave him practice in getting particular speech patterns onto paper" (O'Meally, *Craft* 34). This training proved indispensable for Ellison in his transition from musician to writer, a move imbued with modernist literary sensibilities. Ellison later acknowledged as much himself, citing the interdependence of his training as a young writer on the WPA and his personal interest in modernist fiction. For instance, Ellison connected James Joyce's attempts at capturing the vitality of Irish speech and song in *Finnegan's Wake* with his own use of black oral expression as a model for African American prose ("Indivisible" 390). Speaking more specifically about his own work on the WPA, he recalled that he was successful in capturing the sound of African American expression "on paper by using a kind of Hemingway typography, by using the repetition" ("Indivisible" 390).[11]

This last statement suggests how it was through a commitment to writing more recognizably "African American" material in the Buster and Riley stories that Ellison eventually located his work within an American hybrid modernist literary tradition. That is, though his earlier social realist stories seemed to bridge the superficial division between black and white in

American literature through their thematic privileging of class–based coalitions across racial lines and in their obvious stylistic debt to white writers like Ernest Hemingway and John Steinbeck, ultimately their awkward imitation of those antecedents appeared too much like caricature.[12] Though Ellison's stilted use of Hemingway's hard–boiled stoicism and Steinbeck's sentimental realism did constitute a cross–racial literary influence, the move was devoid of any of the signature qualities I am identifying within an African American literary hybridity: irony, dialogism, Signifyin(g). Even homage, certainly a key characteristic in some hybrid utterances within African American modernism, seems missing in those earliest stories. The young Ellison does not seem self–conscious enough in the work to mark any sense of tribute in his borrowings from others.

In the Buster and Riley stories, on the other hand, Ellison's development toward a hybrid modernist style is quite recognizable. The stories embody Gates's Signifyin(g) model in their revision of "white" form(s) with a signal African American difference. The characterization of Ellison's boy protagonists, for example, nods to Mark Twain's Huck and Tom in its attention to the boys' rebelliousness and their simultaneous sense of wonder and dissatisfaction as they become aware of the strictures in place against them. As well, as Robert O'Meally observes, the ongoing conflict between the boys and their parents, who "uphold their community's traditional (and usually conservative) values," recalls the tension between Huck and Tom and the parental proprietors of manners and conventions in Twain's fiction, proprietors such as Aunt Polly, Miss Watson, and the Widow Douglas (*Craft* 60).[13] Ellison himself acknowledges that Twain figured significantly in his consideration of the American literary imagination en route to *Invisible Man,* especially through Twain's formulation of the possibilities of the vernacular tradition, and his treatment of "the Negro and his status" as a metonym for American "moral concern" ("Art of Fiction" 223). However, Ellison was also admittedly frustrated by the lack of humanity, the minstrel–like artificiality, Twain engendered in his African American characters. Thus, Ellison's evocation of Twain's work in the Buster and Riley stories is emblematic of the ambivalence intrinsic to Gates's notions of motivated Signifyin(g) and double–voicedness. The intertextual relationship of Ellison's work to Twain's here is simultaneously an homage and a revision with a signal black difference—namely, a more mature and detailed realization of African American character and cultural life. Similar, but less obvious, is Ellison's revision of Hemingway in the Buster and Riley stories. Recall that Ellison himself acknowledged that his process of capturing black oral expressivity in written literature was indebted to his knowledge of Hemingway's typographical style and sense of dialogue. Thus, in writing these stories which center so thoroughly on the transmission of black voice in written form, Ellison effectively revises the emphasis on dialogue made famous by Hemingway, a writer whose work Ellison was so influenced by that he apprenticed himself by writing it out by hand. The stories maintain their signal black difference, though, in their attention to the African American voice and black cultural life, "the dramatic and symbolic possibilities" of which, Ellison observed, Hemingway had too often ignored ("Twentieth–Century Fiction" 86).

The suggestions of hybridity that I read in Ellison's Buster and Riley stories are validated by the writer's own commentary on American aesthetics in various essays. For example, in "Twentieth–Century Fiction and the Black Mask of Humanity" (1946; published 1953), Ellison argues against what he terms, "the segregation of the word." Here Ellison criticizes white writers' ongoing refusals to admit African Americans into their work. Even though black characters are at times physically present as characters in white fiction, Ellison notes that the image presented is too often one "drained of humanity" (82). For Ellison, this is problematic because American literature by necessity should work to *define* the character of American society. The shortcomings of white American writers in characterizing African Americans are thus perilous because they distort an American reality that is significantly defined by the presence and cultural influence of blacks. Ellison expands on this argument in "Brave Words for a Startling Occasion," his 1953 acceptance speech for the National Book Award. Here he suggests that "[f]or the novelist, Proteus stands for both America and the instance of illusion through which all men must fight to achieve reality" (154):

> Our task then is always to challenge the apparent forms of reality—that is, the fixed manners and values of the few—and to struggle with it until it reveals its mad, vari–implicated chaos, its false faces, and on until it surrenders its insight, its truth. *We are fortunate as American writers in that with our variety of racial and national traditions, idioms and manners, we are yet one. On its profoundest level American experience is of a whole. Its truth lies in its diversity* [. . .] . ("Brave Words" 154, my emphasis)

Moreover, in other work, Ellison articulates this conception of American culture not just through abstracted notions of American diversity, but through specific discussions of the culture's cross–racial influences. In "The World and the Jug" (1963–64), Ellison responds to white intellectual Irving Howe's criticism that he had turned his back on the influence of his black antecedent Richard Wright. Speaking biographically and remarking in retrospect on white writers' influence on the development of his own literary consciousness, Ellison writes:

> Howe seems to see segregation as an opaque steel jug with the Negroes inside waiting for some black messiah to come along and blow the cork. Wright is his hero and he sticks with him loyally. But if we are in a jug it is transparent, not opaque, and one is allowed not only to see outside but to read what is going on out there, and to make identifications as to values and human quality. So in Macon County, Alabama, I read Marx, Freud, T.S. Eliot, Pound, Gertrude Stein and Hemingway. Books which seldom, if ever, mentioned Negroes were to release me from whatever "segregated" idea I might have had of my human possibilities. I was freed not by propagandists or by the example of Wright [. . .] but by composers, novelists, and poets who spoke to me of more interesting and freer ways of life. ("World" 163–64)

However, Ellison's own conception of hybridity in American culture as articulated in his non–fiction is not so rudimentary as to be reduced to the belief that his antecedents were absolutely "white," or that the influence he drew from them is clearly demarcated along racial lines. Rather, while Ellison hints at what Bakhtin calls "intentional hybridity" by acknowledging his indebtedness to white writers, elsewhere he suggests Bakhtin's "organic hybridity" in his argument that expressive connections between ostensibly "white" and "black" forms are ubiquitous in American culture. For Ellison, these connections are especially recognizable in the rhythmic experimentation and allusiveness that runs through modernist literature and music. Commenting on Eliot's *The Waste Land* in "Hidden Name and Complex Fate" (1964), for instance, Ellison recalls that as a younger reader he observed that "[s]omehow [the poem's] rhythms were often closer to those of jazz than were those of the Negro poets, and even though [he] could not understand then, its range of allusion was as mixed and as varied as that of Louis Armstrong" (203).

This hybrid connectedness between supposedly white and black modernist forms comes to a creative realization in his 1944 story, "Flying Home," the piece that most anticipates the style of *Invisible Man*. The story centers on an encounter between an African American Air Force pilot who has crashed his plane (one of the famed "Tuskegee Airmen"), and an older, rural African American man named Jefferson. As Robert O'Meally notes, "Flying Home" employs a number of "conventional" modernist techniques—"surrealism, multiple perspectives, stream of consciousness—to reveal a world tempestuous and out of focus" (*Craft* 2). As well, it is akin to Eliot's *The Waste Land* with, in Ellison's words, "its discontinuities, its changes of pace and its hidden system of organization" (Ellison, "Hidden" 203)—all qualities that rendered that poem, by Ellison's estimation, like Louis Armstrong's "two hundred choruses on the theme of 'Chinatown'" (qtd in Callahan, "Introduction," *Flying Home* xvi). Indeed, if it were Armstrong who most clearly embodied modernist expressivity in African American music with his early translation of the black musical vernacular into individualistic breaks and riffs, then Ellison responds to those innovations—along with Eliot's—in "Flying Home" by reconfiguring black oral forms in modernist literary collage. His injection of black oral folktales (as told through the character of Jefferson) within the frame of the narrative invokes Eliot's earlier intertextuality and recalls Armstrong's modernist use of the black vernacular matrix in music (and by extension, Hughes's work from that same expressive core in literature).[14]

It is the character of Jefferson's oral narrative in "Flying Home" that complicates the piece's narrative trajectory, creating a dense story-within-a-story structure.[15] On one level, the relationship between Ellison's modernist narrative—that of the pilot Todd's crash—and Jefferson's folktale is similar to the jazz–intertextuality that Hughes creates in "The Weary Blues." Jefferson's tale is framed by Todd's story, and is thus mediated by the pilot's post–New Negro sensibility. While Jefferson tells his fantastical story about becoming an angel and being reprimanded by a white St. Peter for overstepping his place as a black and speeding about with his new–found wings, Ellison interrupts the folktale narrative with Todd's modernist stream of consciousness: "This is a new turn, Todd thought. What's he driving at?" and "He's mocking me, Todd thought angrily. He thinks it's a joke" ("Flying" 158). At the same time, though, Ellison's story intensifies the complexity of folk–modernist interaction through the surreal connections it proposes between Jefferson's cautionary fantasy and the framing story of Todd's own fall. The pilot's plane has crashed, the reader learns, because of interference caused by a passing buzzard (a "jimcrow" as Jefferson deems it). The detail breaks down the distance between the "realistic" story of the present and the fantastical narrative that Jefferson relates. It recalls similar blurring of boundaries in jazz performance: Armstrong may be asserting a kind of distance by quoting from the blues matrix in "West End Blues," for example, yet at the same time he plays *within* the blues form as he improvises on his AAB verse.

In addition, if the stylistic strategies Ellison employs in "Flying Home" suggest the influence of jazz, then the allusion in the story's title confirms that relationship. Given the tenuous position of blacks in America's war–time efforts, as represented through the pilot Todd's experience, Ellison likely intended the title to evoke the popular jazz dance hit of the same name, recorded by black vibraharpist Lionel Hampton and his big band in 1942. The song, a riff–tune composed by Charlie Christian, was a major commercial success, a record that allowed the Hampton band to "[break] into the national ranks" and achieve exposure beyond the African American "race records" market (DeVeaux, *Birth* 149). Moreover, with its infectious swing melody and hopeful title, the tune was not only a number that tapped into the whimsical fancy of record buyers, but also a necessarily optimistic statement in the country's popular culture: a hopeful call to America's stranded sons on the front lines overseas. As Robert O'Meally suggests, "Flying Home" is among those jazz recordings that "outflagwaves them all," a soundtrack that "evokes America at least as much as a Sousa march in a Fourth of July parade or even the fife and drums of 'Yankee Doodle Dandy'" ("Nation" 118). Thus, Ellison's evocation of the song, in a story that explores the political limitations imposed on African Americans during the Second World War, resonates with irony and anticipates the jazz–based political modernism that he was to explore more fully in *Invisible Man*. The irony of the story's title is even more meaningful considering Hampton's position in jazz music: the vibraharpist was one of two African American musicians (along with pianist Teddy Wilson) to break the "segregation of the bandstand" in swing, when Benny Goodman hired him to join his quartet and big band in the mid–1930s. As Scott DeVeaux recalls, though, the celebrated hiring of Hampton and Wilson was tempered with sensitivity to Jim Crow ideals; the two "were billed not as regular members of the band, but as 'guest artists' [. . .] a ruse that apparently satisfied conservative sponsors and audiences" (*Birth* 255). Hampton's situation in the swing market confirms the political commentary that Ellison proposes in "Flying Home": the inclusion of African Americans on the national scene never transcends the figurehead; blacks may occupy a place at the expressive center of American life, but their social, economic, and physical mobility are always subject to restrictions.

Of all of Ellison's pre–*Invisible Man* stories, then, "Flying Home" best exemplifies the writer's inchoate hybrid modernism and most anticipates the full realization of the jazz–based aesthetic that was to define his 1952 novel. The story shows Ellison's developing awareness of jazz's potential to negotiate the various thematic strands that dominated his consciousness as a young writer: a commitment to political expression, the exploration of modernist sensibilities, and a stylistic experimentation with African American cultural forms. Indeed, the development of Ellison's work from "Hymie's Bull" to "Flying Home" is comparable to the progression that pianist Walter Bishop, Jr. argues is central to excellence in jazz performance:

> It all goes from imitation to assimilation to innovation. You move from
> the imitation stage to the assimilation stage when you take little bits of

things from different people and weld them into an identifiable style—
creating your own style. Once you've created your own sound and you
have a good sense of the history of the music, then you think of where
the music hasn't gone and where it can go—and that's innovation. (qtd
in Berliner 120)

Throughout the 1930s and forties, Ellison moves through this pattern, imi-
tating social realists, assimilating the techniques of other writers in his turn
to local thematic material, eventually pushing himself toward change in his
own individual style. "Flying Home" is the first substantial sign of the
writer's potential to be the next significant "literary–jazz improviser" after
Langston Hughes. *Invisible Man* is the moment of innovative performance
that realizes that promise.

   Invisible Man constitutes both a large–scale realization of Ellison's
personal bop aesthetic and a significant contribution to jazz–influenced
modernism with its improvisations on the (African) American novel. Other
American novels had offered representations of jazz on more sordid or
superficial levels in the past: as a cultural emblem of Harlem's "hedonistic"
night life in Van Vechten's *Nigger Heaven,* for example, or as background
music to social activity among the Long Island upper class in F. Scott
Fitzgerald's *The Great Gatsby.* Black American novelists had looked to jazz
before Ellison, yet they too were largely given to perfunctory considerations
of the music's importance and aesthetic potential. Jazz seems merely an
incidental local detail in Claude McKay's *Home to Harlem,* for instance;
and though a working musician is the voice of reason in Hughes's *Not
Without Laughter,* from 1930, ultimately the poet pays only passing attention in this early novel to the myriad aesthetic and social connotations the
music brings to his poetry. Ellison's *Invisible Man,* on the other hand, is a
jazz–modernist masterpiece. The book negotiates aesthetic achievement
and social commentary within a dizzying literary solo, an act of inspired
social play befitting the new politics of Parker and Gillespie's generation.

   The novel begins with an allusion to music that invokes the sound of
jazz early on. Jazz frames the narrative from the prologue onward, when
Ellison's "invisible" protagonist expresses his affinity for Louis Armstrong,
heard in an early recording, "(What Did I Do to Be So) Black and Blue?"
As Larry Neal astutely notes, the "universe" of Ellison's novel is "introduced to us through the music of Louis Armstrong, whose music then
forms the overall structure for the novel. If that is the case, the subsequent
narrative and all of the action which follows can be read as one long [. . .]
solo" ("Zoot" 116). The Armstrong allusion is also significant for the
implications it bears on the novel's representation of black subjectivity.

Using the reference to Armstrong, Ellison associates the black subject (as represented in his unnamed, "unseen" Everyman narrator) with jazz music (represented by the ur-jazzman, Armstrong). The novel's speaker is, by his own admission, unrepresented in the material world. He is rendered metaphorically invisible throughout the narrative that follows by the power imbalances that impede his progress, by a persistent willingness among his white counterparts to impose their own preconstructed understandings of black identity on his person. As he says in the book's opening exposition:

> I am invisible, understand, simply because people refuse to see me. Like the bodiless heads you see sometimes in circus sideshows, it as though I have been surrounded by mirrors of hard, distorting glass. When they approach me they see only my surroundings, themselves, or figments of their imagination—indeed, everything and anything except me. (3)

Because of this, Ellison's narrator attempts to locate his identity through black sound, through the ironic lyrics and stylistic virtuosity of Armstrong's famous lament.[16] The "sound" of black jazz redresses the imbalances of power that impinge on the African American subject's materiality; the music's Signifyin(g) impulses rewrite "the received order," working to "clear a space, rhetorically" that the black subject may inhabit (Gates, *Signifying* 124). And though the turn to Armstrong, who is without question the representative jazzman of the music's pre–bop beginnings, may seem contradictory to the bebop influence I argue is so central to Ellison's aesthetic, the move, in fact, allies the Invisible Man's narrative with the jazz form specific to his generation by establishing bop's Signifyin(g) effects early on. That is, though bebop's practitioners wished to establish themselves as distinct from earlier players like Armstrong, they were not so naive as to believe that their new music was free from the influence of their most dominant antecedent and his contemporaries. This creative lineage is evident in the mentor role that swing tenor–sax legend Coleman Hawkins played to Minton's young iconoclasts, or in the famous quip by Miles Davis—arguably the most influential of Parker and Gillespie's disciples— that the entire history of jazz could be summarized in four words, "Louis Armstrong Charlie Parker."

Indeed, the allusion to Armstrong's records marks the ambivalent, intensified Signifyin(g) that is central to bebop and that prevails throughout the rest of the novel. The reference to "Black and Blue" establishes the productive tension between the novel's protagonist and the older African American cultural traditions that dominate the narrative. Yes, Ellison's narrator sympathizes with early jazz music as he negotiates his own tenuous identity, but it is an uneasy identification. The ties that bind the narrator to Armstrong are dubious, based on material and discursive constraints that the narrator wishes to resist, and a strategy of cultural performance that he hopes to avoid. As the Invisible Man admits, his attraction to Armstrong's music is based on a kinship of transparency: "Perhaps I like Louis Armstrong because he's made poetry out of being invisible. [. . .] And my own grasp of invisibility aids me to understand his music" (8). Despite this ostensible endorsement, the protagonist betrays dissatisfaction with his own invisibility elsewhere in the prologue, such as when he relates a moment of violence that transpires after accidentally bumping into a "tall blond man" on the street. As the Invisible Man discloses, he is spurred to violence in the moment, beating the blond man viciously and threatening him with a knife, after the other cursed him for the chance collision. The intensity of the narrator's reaction in the anecdote seems governed by a yearning to register an individual, material presence, to make the other man take notice.

The narrator's apparent desire to assert his presence also marks the transition he wishes to make from past strategies of African American cultural performance. In this, I am suggesting that the trajectory of the narrator's individual self–determination resembles the distinction I make in Chapter Two, between early jazz performance as "mastery of form" and bebop as heightened "deformation of mastery." Indeed, the Invisible Man's explanation of his affinity for Armstrong's music suggests Houston Baker's notion of "mastery of form." It recalls Baker's metaphor of masking, specifically in his explication of the trope as a performance from behind the obscuring presence of the minstrel mask. Ellison's description of Armstrong's creative exploitation of invisibility recalls this "mastery of form." Both suggest a performance in which the black subject represents itself through voice and sound against the tension of a concealing exterior. As Baker writes,

> [A]n Afro-American spokesperson who wished to engage in a masterful and empowering play within the minstrel spirit house needed the uncanny ability to manipulate bizarre phonic legacies. For he or she had the task of transforming the mask and its sounds into negotiable discursive currency. In effect, the task was the production of a manual of black speaking, a book of speaking *back and black*. (*Modernism* 24, original emphasis)

In early jazz, Armstrong embodies this task. As Laurence Bergreen notes, the musician revived the kind of routines that had thrived in minstrelsy, as on his 1926 record "King of the Zulus," which breaks in mid–musical performance for a comedy routine about a barbecue, culminating with Clarence Babcock cracking in a West Indian accent, *"Mahn, I come from Jamaica and I don't mean to interrupt the partee but one of me countrymen tell me there's a chittlin' rag going on heah!"* "These stereotypical images," Bergreen suggests, "were vivid presences in Louis's imagination, but he conjured them with a sardonic wit suggesting that he had moved into new musical and social realms" (288). Given this reading of Armstrong's work, Ellison's description of the trumpeter's talent for "poetry" underscores the strategy that Baker identifies as a "primary move in Afro-American discursive modernism" (*Modernism* 17). However, Ellison does not mark this kinship between the Invisible Man and Armstrong to offer an unchallenged endorsement of the musician's style of performativity. Rather, the move seems instead to map the discursive history from which the protagonist strives to depart as the narrative develops, a departure first suggested in the act of physical assertion he relates in the anecdote about the tall blond man.[17]

The Invisible Man is not always overt in his rejection of "mastery of form," but he is consistently overcome by uneasiness whenever he describes acts of African American performance that resemble that mode. This is first evident early in the novel when the narrator relates the dying words of his paternal grandfather, a speech that haunts him ever after:

> On his deathbed he called my father to him and said, "Son, after I'm gone I want you to keep up the fight. I never told you, but our life is a war and I have been a traitor all my born days, a spy in the enemy's country ever since I give up my gun back in the Reconstruction. Live with your head in the lion's mouth. I want you to overcome 'em with yeses, undermine 'em with grins, agree 'em to death and destruction, let 'em swoller you till they vomit or bust wide open." (16)

As the Invisible Man recalls, his grandfather's paradoxical advocacy of, and regret over, masked performance haunts him throughout his adolescence, especially as he finds himself performing variations on the accommodating strategy to succeed academically and socially. His recollection of his success at the performance leaves him anxious, detached from the core of his "true self": "The old man's words were like a curse. On my graduation day I delivered an oration in which I showed that humility was the secret, indeed, the very essence of progress. (Not that I believed this—how could I, remembering my grandfather?—I only believed that it worked.)" (17). Unsurprisingly, then, as the novel progresses, the narrator projects this uneasiness onto other black characters, whenever he witnesses them performing for white audiences. For example, when he hears Jim True-blood, a black sharecropper who has fathered his own daughter's child, render his tale of incest to the wealthy, white industrialist, Norton, near the beginning of the novel, the Invisible Man is torn between "fascination and humiliation" and confesses a "sense of shame" (68). Likewise, after Dr. Bledsoe, the black headmaster at the Tuskegee Institute–like college, angrily confronts the Invisible Man for exposing Norton to Trueblood, the narrator is shocked to see how the older African American "compose[s] his angry face like a sculptor, making it a bland mask" before returning to Norton's presence (102). Later, the Invisible Man is consumed by fury, "a numb violent outrage," when Bledsoe admits that he has always performed for whites to better his own position, that he has had to "act the nigger" to attain the status he now enjoys (143). Perhaps the ultimate marker of the narrator's uneasy relationship to black masking occurs toward the novel's finale, when he witnesses his contemporary Tod Clifton, an erstwhile African American member of the pseudo–Communist Brotherhood to which the Invisible Man belongs, selling the "Sambo Boo-gie Woogie" doll—a stereotypical toy that dances wildly when manipulated and bears a "black mask–like face" (431). The sight of Clifton bartering the abomination for money leaves the narrator enraged, feeling "betrayed" (433).

Driven by this uneasiness, Ellison's Invisible Man is consistently intent on distinguishing himself from this tradition of performance of which he is hyper–aware. The narrator wishes to avoid the peril of the mask and allow for the unrestrained presentation of an assertive self, a project he contrives to undertake through his "non–masked" oratorical performance. As Phillip Brian Harper argues, Ellison's narrator attempts to use his talent for speechmaking to redress his anxiety about "the problem of forging individual identity [within] the black community," a problem consistently exacerbated by the propensity of white subjects to view African Americans as an undifferentiated black mob (*Framing* 127–28). This is particularly recognizable after the battle royal of the novel's first chapter. Having been forced to assume the "performer's" role with a group of other young black men in a degrading and sexualized spectacle before a white male audience, the narrator struggles to assert his own identity—speaking ever louder, with increasing determination—as he presents a speech to that same audience afterwards. When the speech is apparently well–received by his white listeners, the Invisible Man admits that he "felt safe from grandfather, whose deathbed curse usually spoiled [his] triumphs" (32–33). Ironically, though, it is precisely *for* his performance that the narrator is rewarded, a fact of which, at this point, he seems naively unaware. Eventually, frustrated by the disappointments of his education, his working life, and his tenure in the Brotherhood, the Invisible Man even concedes, momentarily, at least, to the inevitability of his grandfather's decree and decides that he will "overcome them with yeses, [and] undermine them with grins" (508). Ultimately, though, he reverses this compromise in the narrative's closing pages, vowing to end his hibernation, "[shake] off [his] old skin," and commit himself—perhaps despite his invisibility—to a "socially responsible role" (581). Ellison's narrator thus continually recognizes his place alongside the voices of the past even as he attempts to mark his distance from them through the assertion of his own special voice. In this way, the Invisible Man wrestles with cross–generational ambivalence in a manner that recalls the beboppers, artists who were constantly aware of the jazz tradition they were in the process of reconstructing through their "politics of style." Fittingly, the novel marks the protagonist's contest with tradition, so dominant throughout the narrative, with a jazz–informed stylistic riff—simultaneously a quotation and a revision—that closes the prologue: "But what did *I* do to be so blue? Bear with me" (14).

The Invisible Man's turn on Armstrong's lyric at the end of the novel's prologue cues the Signifyin(g) discourse that ensues. Much like the bebop musicians who used Siginifyin(g) to mediate both affinity for and discomfort with their various musical and cultural influences, Ellison adopts the rhetorical mode to articulate his protagonist's ambivalent relationship to a larger black community and its expressive traditions. The Invisible Man continually defines his character against the cultural performance of other African Americans, revising notions of his own expressive self in accordance or conflict with the way other black subjects perform. As John Callahan argues in his essay, "Frequencies of Eloquence," the narrator's quest for self–identity in the novel is a pursuit of oratorical eloquence, an attempt to define himself as an individual voice. With his identity so irrevocably invested in his oratorical style, the narrator must create himself in conflict or congress with other African American speakers. Thus, speakers like Jim Trueblood and Homer Barbee influence the Invisible Man's oratorical development—despite his ambivalence toward them—through their improvisatory genius, specifically the ability to fashion speeches, stories, and songs according to the tastes and expectations of individual audiences (Callahan, "Frequencies" 65). Improvisation becomes paramount in the narrator's quest for identity; he must create himself through his ability to play to audiences. In this way, Callahan sees the trajectory of the narrator's story as commensurate with jazz performance, as the jazz soloist adapts each musical utterance according to the accompaniment of his bandmates and to the specific demands or emotional texture of his audience.

Ellison dramatizes this jazz–influenced productive tension by having his Invisible Man constantly adapting and revising his performed self to suit specific situations and interactions with others. While Callahan's interpretation is important to my reading of *Invisible Man* for its emphasis on orality and African American performative traditions, including jazz, it also suggests meaningful connections in the novel between oral texts and the written word. The narrative of the novel, Callahan argues, is about a failed orator, and its composition is an ostensible abandonment of the oral tradition for the literary that, in reality, wavers constantly between the spoken and written word. The book is, as Callahan writes, "an improvisatory, vernacular narrative of utterance," a bridge between its protagonist's past oral performances and the story's text, which constitutes the Invisible Man's current intervention into the conventionally literary (55).

In dramatizing this tension between orality and the written word, Ellison's novel is thus an important contribution in fiction to the "literary–jazz" tradition Hughes initiated through his poetry, a tradition that represents Bernard Bell's notion of "residual orality" through jazz expressivity. And through its various dramatic negotiations, Ellison's text enacts one of the key characteristics that Henry Louis Gates identifies in the Signifyin(g) black American literary tradition. As Gates opines, African American writers "read and critique the texts of other black writers as an act of rhetorical self–definition" (*Signifying* 122). In *Invisible Man*, Ellison expands on what Gates identifies here as literary Signifyin(g) and asserts the rhetorical mode's prevalence *across* expressive forms by exploring the relationship between his narrator and Louis Armstrong. As the Invisible Man repeats and revises Armstrong's lyric, he marks his own individual subjectivity against Armstrong's specific character, itself a metonymic example of a larger black cultural tradition based on "mastery of form." Thus, Invisible Man's self–definition occurs through a Signifyin(g) declaration of his difference from Armstrong and, by extension, from older modes of cultural performance. This move is a key starting point to Ellison's extended "improvisation" because it anticipates many of the key themes and stylistic traits that follow: the assertion of black subjectivity through sound via musico–textual quotation; the dramatization of political tension between the Double V generation and their antecedents; and a jazz–inspired dialogism in which these two strands meet. Using jazz to structure *Invisible Man*, Ellison orders the material fissures of collective African American subjectivity into an aesthetic statement that thrives on discursive competition.

Indeed, in his non–fiction writings on jazz, Ellison himself suggests the music thrives on paradoxical tensions between community and individualism, and between tradition and change. For example, in "The Charlie Christian Story," he writes:

> There is [. . .] a cruel contradiction implicit in the art form itself, for true jazz is an art of individual assertion within and against the group. Each true jazz moment [. . .] springs from a contest in which each artist challenges all the rest; each solo flight, or improvisation, represents (like the successive canvases of a painter) a definition of his identity as individual, as member of the collectivity and as a link in the chain of tradition. Thus, because jazz finds its very life in an endless improvisation upon traditional materials, the jazzman must lose his identity even as he finds it. (267)

Similarly, in the essay, "Living with Music," Ellison, while reminiscing about time spent with the great jazz musicians of his native Oklahoma City (many of whom later achieved fame on a national level), observes how

> [t]he delicate balance struck between strong individual personality and the group during those early jam sessions was a marvel of social organization. I had learned too that the end of all this discipline and technical mastery was the desire to express an affirmative way of life through its musical tradition, and that this tradition insisted that each artist achieve his creativity within its frame. He must learn the best of the past, and add to it his personal vision. Life could be harsh, loud and wrong if it wished, but they lived it fully, and when they expressed their attitude toward the world it was with a fluid style that reduced the chaos of living to form. (229)

Considering Ellison's comments in these two essays, one sees the importance of jazz as that which makes up the novel's structural core. For *Invisible Man* is a narrative that attempts to mediate between conflicting influences in the formulation of an individual African American subjectivity, while adhering to the modernist project of unifying the disorder of human experience through artistic expression.

Specifically, it is bebop's style of disjunctive exposition that Ellison uses to mediate his conflicting discourses. Just as Hughes employed the music's dialogical qualities in his musico–textual montage, Ellison fuses oppositional influences in an extended intertextual utterance. The novel frames various musical and verbal assertions by diverse voices within the Invisible Man's governing individual statement. Thus, the first–person narrator, much like bebop's Signifyin(g) soloists, is constantly mindful of the discursive legacies of those traditions that he simultaneously commands and subsumes within his own expository act. Ultimately—perhaps paradoxically—it is thus the narrator's acknowledgment of diverse voices in his narrative that allows for the full realization of his own individualism. This occurs because, in referring to the voices of others within his own expressive act, the Invisible Man creates a space for himself by accepting a place in tradition. It is a productive association with his communal roots rather than a radical break from the past. As Phillip Brian Harper suggests, as the narrator ceases to speak *to* the black community but rather *for* it—as evidenced by the novel's closing line, "Who knows, but that on the lower frequencies, I speak for you?"—"he becomes [. . .] the means through which the collective expresses its own subjectivity [. . . and he] finds his individual subjectivity in that of the community of which he is a part" (*Framing* 139). The effect is to manifest that uncertain relationship Ellison himself describes in his writings on jazz, in which the jazz musician perpetually "loses his identity as he finds it."

Like Hughes in *Montage of a Dream Deferred,* Ellison also effects bebop's disjunctive exposition through fragmented representation of various expressive styles, both verbal and musical. As Robert O'Meally notes, "*Invisible Man* is a capacious novel [. . . . ,] a rhetorical [tour] de force containing letters, sermons, fights, songs, political speeches, [and] dreams" ("Introduction" 2). Ellison nods to jazz music's comprehensive range of reference by cutting both verbal and musical expression together in his fragmentary mix. Musically, the novel features echoes of various approaches and traditions: the spirituals sung by the choir at the narrator's college campus; the folk blues he hears sung by Jim Trueblood in the South and by Petie Wheatstraw in Harlem; the urban, classic blues of Bessie Smith as rendered by his New York landlady, Mary; the strains of "Many a Thousand Gone" that accompany Tod Clifton's funeral march; the recording of "Jelly, Jelly" that plays on the jukebox for the hipsters at Barrelhouse's Jolly Dollar. Even beyond these overt musical references, the novel suggests African American musical traditions through a myriad of coy allusions: the narrator's self–chosen nickname Jack-the-Bear recalls both an African American folk song and a composition by Duke Ellington; Barrelhouse, the proprietor of the Jolly Dollar, shares his name with an early jazz style; the mysterious hipster B.P. Rinehart bears the moniker of a character from a Jimmy Rushing–Count Basie tune of the 1930s; the name of the gun–toting Dupre, who appears in the novel's climactic riot, suggests a folk blues and a Count Basie big–band number; the folk–rhyme, "They Picked Poor Robin Clean," which appears in the novel's hospital scene, was also a verse picked up in a Signifyin(g) riff–tune by Kansas City jazz musicians; the prophetic sign,

"The Time Is Now," that the narrator sees hints at Charlie Parker's "Now's the Time."[18] The effects of these varied allusions are twofold: for one, the blending of references brings a recognizably "black" influence to modernist expression, realizing Ellison's own early wish to make art "*Negro American*—to appropriate it, possess it, re–create it in our own group and individual images" ("Introduction: *Shadow*" 54, original emphasis); secondly, the range of allusions collapses time and tradition in an individualistic expressive act, such that Ellison, like the jazz musician, may offer a simultaneous critique of and an homage to past traditions in the "present" of his performance. Using bebop's fragmentary aesthetic and sounding a series of musical *obbligatos* from the African American collective past, Ellison signifies the tension between individual and community, represented by the "heterogeneous sound ideal" of diverse voices, while he negotiates the preservation of older forms and the need for their revision.

This literary process recalls the bebop musicians' revision of "traditional" styles, most notably the blues. As DeVeaux writes, jazz musicians like Gillespie and Parker maintained an ambivalent relationship with the blues, largely because of the way media and record labels cast the form as an untutored product of the rural black folk. As Gillespie later recalled, this representation was unsettling for the politically minded jazz musicians of his generation, all of whom were intent—like Ellison's narrator—on distancing themselves from the blanketing effects of stereotype and exaggeration: "[T]he bebop musicians didn't like to play the blues. They were ashamed. The media had made it shameful" (Gillespie 371).[19] And yet the influence of the blues in the jazz tradition was too significant to overlook, even for bebop's self–conscious iconoclasts. Thus, bebop musicians paid "tribute" to their cultural legacy through excessive revision and transformation. As Gillespie commented, "[The bebop musicians] busied themselves *making changes* [on the blues], a thousand changes in one bar" (371, my emphasis).[20] While the changes to which he refers here are of course the harmonic kind—chord changes—the statement effects a double–meaning. Bop musicians made a stylistic habit of altering their recreations of the past through individualistic revision by superimposing their own harmonic frameworks over the residue of cultural memory.

In using "cultural memory" here, I echo Samuel Floyd's concept from *The Power of Black Music*. Cultural memory, Floyd writes, is "a repository of meanings that comprise the subjective knowledge of a people, its immanent thoughts, its structures, and its practices; these thoughts, structures and practices are transferred and understood unconsciously but become conscious and culturally objective in practice and perception" (8). Furthermore, cultural memory, as Floyd points out, is connected with "cultural *forms,"* such as "music, where the 'memory' drives the music and the music drives memory" (8). That is, African American music evokes a distinctly black consciousness in its ongoing appeal to the materiality of the collective experience that shaped—and shapes—that consciousness. Bop musicians were ever cognizant of this African American history as they celebrated "black expressive traditions" while forging interventions into a larger field of modernist art. As Floyd observes, "their dialogical melodic, harmonic, and rhythmic juxtapositions of blues elements and European–derived extended chord structures [. . . .] reflected [. . .] not only the pleasure and excitement of musical discovery and achievement, but also the joy and exuberance of [black communal] myth and ritual" (143).

In *Invisible Man*, Ellison adopts the dizzying juxtapositions Floyd identifies in bebop, and uses them to facilitate his engagement with the past. As Thomas Marvin suggests, Ellison uses the narrator's contact with various musical personages in *Invisible Man* to dramatize both the cultural crossroads that Floyd locates in bebop, and a more general tension between the individual and the community. Reading figures like Trueblood, Petie Wheatstraw, and the Sambo doll as liminal and jazz–influenced—standing forever "at the crossroads where cultures meet"—Marvin argues that these figures all force the narrator to confront the paradoxical position of African Americans in American society (587). In addition, Marvin suggests that these black–musical characters consistently appear at times when the narrator is in danger of completely acquiescing to white power and control: Trueblood, when the narrator is in the presence of the dominating Mr. Norton; Wheatstraw, as the Invisible Man struggles to find work from white employers in New York; the Sambo doll, just before he is lost to the political maneuverings of the Brotherhood. Thus, in detailing the narrator's ambivalent search for identity in the midst of white influences, Ellison inserts personifications of black music that connect the Invisible Man to the African American past. The appearance of each of these various characters represents a recognizable assertion of the narrator's association to a black communal history—a history with a "slightly different sense of time" (as the narrator describes Louis Armstrong's music), than that provided by dominant discourses.

Indeed, Ellison is constantly engaged with American and African American history—and the inextricability of the two—throughout *Invisible Man*, a discursive interest he stylizes through bop–inspired dialogics and quotation. The novel continually employs bebop's palimpsestic negotiation with tradition to express both a complex ambivalence with African American experience and the relationship of the black subject to American history in general. Elliott Butler-Evans highlights the latter, arguing that throughout *Invisible Man*,

Ellison explores the recognition of the black subject "within the context of Western Culture" (119). Turning to Ellison's echoes of "canonical" writers like Dostoevsky, Joyce, Dante, and Melville, Butler-Evans writes that "Ellison's text engages in a radical appropriation and rearticulation of the sources rather than merely quoting or citing them" (119).[21] Butler-Evans's reading of this process is directed by Bakhtin's explanation of intertextuality: "The author can only use the discourse of the other toward his own ends, in such a way that he imprints on this discourse [. . .] a new semantic orientation. [. . .] A single discourse winds up having two semantic orientations, two voices" (qtd in Butler-Evans 120). Thus, as Butler-Evans argues, Ellison's referencing of canonical texts in "the act of writing [the novel] involves the reformulation of the dominant discourse" (121). And while Butler-Evans is interested in Ellison's relationship to the dominant discourse of a Western literary tradition, I would argue that the process he defines is integral to Ellison's reformulation of history, since the Western literary tradition represents the fixed repository of a dominant historical subjectivity. In reformulating the textuality of Western subjectivity, Ellison subverts the dominance of that record, loosening its fixed authority and subjecting it to the indeterminacy of improvisational play. The move is indebted to bebop's process of criticism and engagement through musical quoting. Bebop musicians frequently quoted phrases from "classical" music in their improvisations in a disruptive move that, according to Krin Gabbard, "undermine[d] distinctions between high and low art and [. . .] question[ed] the 'aura' that in the minds of most listeners surrounds [classical] composers" ("Quoter" 93).[22] However, the art of quotation in bebop, as Gabbard suggests, transcends aesthetics and is inextricably linked to the social, the historical; it "provides the jazz artist with modes of expression that are otherwise blocked by forces based in race, class, and popular taste" ("Quoter" 93).

Ingrid Monson articulates a similar point in her discussion of intermusicality in jazz, positing a kind of musical intertextuality based on the referencing of other musical "texts":

> Form [in jazz] never exists without its social component, its dialogic relationship to the other forms of discourse in its social world, both in the present and over time. The improvisational process in jazz underscores this point in a particularly vivid manner: the shape of a musical performance is the product of human beings interacting through music both in time and over time. (*Saying* 129)[23]

As Monson explains, the act of quoting in jazz disrupts social hierarchies in the way that Gabbard suggests, but also collapses time and allows the jazz improviser to engage with history and tradition by symbolically eliminating the distance between the individual in the present and the stacked experience of a collective past. Monson thus describes intermusical quotation in jazz performance as "an aural passage conveys to those with the sociocultural knowledge to recognize and interpret it a relation between a past performance and a present one" (*Saying* 127). Accordingly, Ellison's use of quotation collapses a temporal remove, placing two moments of cultural performance—his novel, each text he references—on the same temporal plane. The gesture allows an engagement with the past that reformulates dominant historical narratives in a shifting way, by appealing to readers across a range of "sociocultural knowledge." For example, Ellison appeals to the knowledge of readers well–versed in the literary canon he cites as he locates black subjectivity alongside that dominant discourse, both socially and temporally. On the other hand, those readers familiar with the various African American vernacular texts to which he refers—Armstrong's record, the blues, folk songs, sermons—are called upon to understand the inextricability of the novel's apparent black and mainstream intertexts. Thus, in his jazz–based allusiveness, Ellison proclaims the hybridity of American culture as he opens up formerly fixed canons and reformulates the place of the "invisible" black subject by collapsing the distance between his narrative and the dominant historical record.

Furthermore, Ellison's frequent quotation of black music in the novel is significant to the narrative's engagement with history because it both marks the status of those forms of music as repositories of African American cultural memory, *and* admits those vernacular repositories into its reformulated historical record. The Invisible Man's suggestion that history moves not like an arrow but a boomerang emphasizes, to borrow from Robert O'Meally's words, the novel's critique of a "deterministic or schematic tracing of history"; by association, the book's frequent appeals to African American culture "tell aspects of the American experience that do not get told in any other way" ("On Burke" 244–45). The novel's frequent turns to a black vernacular culture—which is often an unfixed text in its emphasis on orality and musicality—foreground improvisatory structures in order to acknowledge the *process* of history, and hence, history's inability to be expressed adequately in the fixed linearity of "finished cultural products" ("On Burke" 248–49).

Central to this project is Ellison's technique of referring to actual historical events and people while avoiding the establishment of one-to-one relationships between his narrative and "real" history. As John Callahan suggests, Ellison creates a "continuous present" in his novel by deliberately not particularizing his various historical referents. For example, Ras the Exhorter is *like* Marcus Garvey but not definitely so, since Garvey himself is mentioned in the novel; the book's black college resembles the Tuskegee Institute, but Ellison distinguishes at one point between the college's fictional Founder and Tuskegee's real founder, Booker T. Washington; and the race riot at the narrative's climax "bears some relation to the Harlem riot of August 1943, as well as to the Harlem riot of 1935" (Callahan, "Chaos" 134–35). I would augment Callahan's reading of the novel's temporal landscape as a "continuous present," by asserting the book's indebtedness to a jazz aesthetic. Recall, for instance, Ingrid Monson's explanation of quoting in jazz. Monson's suggestion that intermusicality places a jazz performer "in time" with voices of the past is, I would argue, essential to an understanding of Ellison's metaphor of history as boomerang, ever swooping back onto the historical subject rather than moving further and further away. History is necessarily vital, according to Ellison's novel; it is always open to suggestion and contribution from new voices, new subjects in its ongoing construction; it is always resistant to the unavoidable exclusions that result from attempts to create an authoritative record. As George Kent comments, Louis Armstrong and jazz are important to the novel's disruption of authoritative records on one level due to the music's "mode of breaking through the ordinary categories of Western clock time" (97). Moreover, as O'Meally notes, the subversive relationship between African American vernacular culture and mainstream history is particularly evident in the Invisible Man's imperative to an authoritative colleague in the Brotherhood, a white man married to an African American woman: "Ask your wife to take you around to the gin mills and the barber shops and the juke joints and the churches, Brother. Yes, and the beauty parlors on Saturdays when they're frying hair. A whole unrecorded history is spoken then, Brother. You wouldn't believe it but it's true" (*Invisible Man* 460).

Having realized this, Invisible Man disrupts the authority of the dominant discourse on a symbolic level at the novel's conclusion, by burning the various written texts in his briefcase: his high school diploma, the letter that began his initiation into the Brotherhood, an insulting anonymous note. Perhaps testifying to African American vernacular performance's enduring ambivalent relationship to these dominant discourses, though, Tod Clifton's Sambo doll refuses to burn.

The novel also represents the contestatory relationship between the dominant history and African American vernacular performance on a dramatic level, when Ellison's narrator describes the zoot–suited young men of Harlem and muses about their relationship to history:

What did [historians] ever think of us transitory ones? Ones such as I
had been before I found Brotherhood—birds of passage who were too

obscure for learned classification, too silent for the most sensitive
recorders of sound; of natures too ambiguous for the most ambiguous
words, and too distant from the centers of historical design to sign or
even to applaud the signers of historical documents? We who write no
novels, histories or other books. . . . What about those three boys, coming now along the platform, tall and slender, walking stiffly with swinging shoulders in their well–pressed, too-hot-for-summer suits, their
collars high and tight about their necks, their identical hats of black
cheap felt set upon the crowns of their heads with a severe formality
above their hard conked hair? It was as though I'd never seen their like
before: Walking slowly, their shoulders swaying, their legs swinging
from their hips in trousers that ballooned upward from cuffs fitting
snug about their ankles; their coats long and hip–tight with shoulders
far too broad to be those of natural western men. (439–40)[24]

The boys in their zoot suits and conk–styled hair impress heavily on Invisible Man's imagination and make him long to see the admission of their
existence into the dominant historical record. "They were outside the
groove of history," he reflects as they pass, and unsurprisingly he becomes
immediately aware of a "record shop loudspeaker blaring a languid blues,"
an African American musical echo that leaves him asking, "Was this the
only true history of the times, a mood blared by trumpets, trombones, saxophones, and drums, a song with turgid, inadequate words" (433)? Thus,
the scene juxtaposes a sartorial style—a kind of cultural performance—
which is such an integral part of the iconography of bebop's young revolu-
tionaries with a musical marker (however ambivalent) of an African
American past. In doing so, Ellison further marks his aesthetic–political
sympathy with the likes of Parker and Gillespie, young modernists outside
the "groove" of traditional history who redressed their lack of representation in that history through a "politics of style."[25]

In *Welcome to the Jungle*, Kobena Mercer discusses the conk and the
zoot suit as elements of a hybrid, improvisatory practice of aesthetic stylization in the black diaspora: "The patterns and practices of aesthetic stylization developed by black cultures in the West may be seen as modalities of
cultural struggle *inscribed* in critical engagement with the dominant white
culture and at the same time *expressive* of a neo–African approach to the
pleasures of beauty at the level of everyday life" (114, original emphasis).
Mercer reads these two signature trends in black fashion as part of a larger
expressive matrix in the 1940s that saw African American subjects engaged
in dialogic contest with mainstream styles. This matrix—which Mercer
claims should include jazz (with its emerging self–protective strategies

among black musicians) and the verbal contests and double–voiced address of black English—"encoded a refusal of passivity by way of a creolizing accentuation and subtle inflection of given elements, codes and conventions" (119). The conk, for example, with its

> element of straightening suggested resemblance to white people's hair, but the nuances, inflections and accentuations introduced by artificial means of stylization emphasized *difference*. In this way the political economy of the conk rested on its ambiguity, the way it played with the given outline shapes of convention only to disturb the norm and hence invite a "double take," demanding that you look twice. (119, original emphasis).

Similarly, the ostentatious zoot suit critiqued "oppression by the artful manipulation of appearances" (120). Its adoption by subaltern minorities, such as African American and Latino men, in the 1940s emphasized difference from a white mainstream in order to project an independence from that dominant culture: "With its wide shoulders, tight waist and baggy pants—topped off with a wide–brimmed hat, and worn with slim Italian shoes and lots of gold jewels—the zoot suit projected stature, dignity and presence: it signified that the black man was 'important' in his own terrain and on his own terms" (120).[26]

In his presentation of Harlem hipsters outside the groove of history, Ellison thus exploits the cultural dynamics Mercer describes, representing this broad "politics of style" in symbolic terms. The representation of the zoot suiters, along with Invisible Man's accompanying commentary, bridge the novel's dramatic narrative and Ellison's ongoing reformulation of history and dominant literary discourses through bebop quoting and collage. Ultimately, his consideration of their "outsiderism" underscores one of the novel's chief philosophical concerns, and indeed, one of the key political notions of the black modernism I am charting here: that even in its ostensible difference, and its seeming stylistic remove, the African American vernacular is inseparable from dominant formulations of American culture and history.

Chapter Four

"Here Where Coltrane Is": Jazz, Cultural Memory, and Political Aesthetics in the Poetry of Michael S. Harper

While Langston Hughes and Ralph Ellison offer the foundation for a jazz–influenced stream of African American modernist literature, the poet Michael S. Harper stands as one of their most noteworthy inheritors. Harper's work extends the innovations of Hughes and Ellison and sustains their hybridized aesthetic into a later historical context: through to the end of the twentieth century, decades removed from the New Negro renaissance, amidst changing tides in the American social landscape after the most mature period of the Civil Rights Era.[1] Harper's poetry fuses his predecessors' signal developments—Ellison's dialogic narration of history, Hughes's stylistic play—and argues for jazz music's enduring essential place in American culture. Like his jazz–modernist antecedents, Harper recognizes jazz as a medium that records "other histories" while it makes discursive interventions into mainstream culture through the "deformative" means of its shifting radical sound.[2] As the poet's work emphasizes, jazz may maintain the tradition of political–aesthetic engagement that influenced Hughes and Ellison even as political climes radically change. Though African American jazz artists after the 1950s, for example, continued to push the music outside the mainstream—almost as quickly as the mainstream could consume it—and presented an aesthetic correlative to emerging revolutionary black politics, they remained mindful of black American cultural traditions and an African American expressive past.

After bebop had settled into becoming the sound of mainstream jazz, the next—and some would argue, the last—revolutionary shift to redirect the continuity of the "jazz tradition" was a style known simply as "free jazz."[3] Gaining notice and cachet as the 1950s turned into the sixties, free jazz was an insurrection against longstanding improvisational practices. The music was led in spirit by Ornette Coleman, a former rhythm and blues saxophonist from Texas who popularized the style's name with a 1960 album title. Coleman's major innovation in free jazz was to create more space for improvisation in performance. Throughout all earlier jazz styles, improvisation had been structured around the convention of the solo round, with improvisers taking turns extemporizing over set harmonic patterns, like the twelve–bar blues or the thirty-two-measure template of the Tin Pan Alley popular song. Even bebop's revolt from the diatonic foundations of earlier styles had been grounded on a fidelity to harmonic patterns, to "playing the changes." Parker and Gillespie may have altered jazz vocabulary in their insistence that "new notes" could be superimposed over "old chords," but their improvisations remained ever mindful of those accepted song patterns as harmonic blueprints in the creative design. Coleman's music, on the other hand, looked to remove even those restrictions and allow for any note at any time by doing away with arranged harmonic frameworks altogether. As the saxophonist himself said in the liner notes to his influential 1959 record, *The Shape of Jazz to Come*, "[I]f I am just going to use the changes themselves, I might as well write out what I am going to play" (qtd in Williams, liner notes).[4]

Moreover, Coleman's free jazz stressed both an emphasis on group improvisation that included "the partial nullification of traditional divisions between soloists and accompanists," and a heightened "importance [on] energy and intensity as communicative elements" (Jost, "Free" 386). In dismantling the tradition of individual voices soloing in turn, free jazz made way for a more liberated improvisational aesthetic among performers. The solo–group tension so central to jazz was reconfigured, exaggerated perhaps, by doing away with the convention of successive solos over accompaniment and introducing a more consistently collective standard of play. Meanwhile, the productive tension that had defined previous styles of jazz emerged in somewhat overstated forms in this reconfiguration due to Coleman's emphasis on dynamics as a crucial quality of musical communication.[5] To some, his working quartet seemed perilously chaotic in their avant–garde presentation of four voices speaking simultaneously, loudly. However, it was precisely these qualities that also marked free jazz as a music firmly rooted in earlier African American traditions.

For one, free jazz's emphasis on group improvisation celebrated musical community as thoroughly as earlier African American music had. The rejection of solo improvisation for collective interaction invoked one of

African American music's primary historical functions—to mediate group experience and consciousness. This is true of African American music's earliest forms: the work songs that used antiphony to maintain community, and the spirituals that allowed for collective worship and prayer. As Samuel Floyd summarizes, "[i]n black culture, works of music are truly transactions between human beings and organized sound" (151). Thus, free jazz, paradoxically, innovated jazz musical tradition by venturing deeper into it. As Gunther Schuller notes, Coleman's groups "abandon traditional chorus and phrase structure," but their emphasis on "ensemble music" appears clearly "founded on traditional roots [as] it makes consistent use of spontaneous collective interplay at the most intimate and intricate levels" (230). As well, many read Coleman's experimentation with dynamics as an inheritance from the blues performance tradition in which he had been trained during his early career in Texas. Ekkehard Jost suggests that Coleman ignored "norms of intonation" in a way that resembled "archaic blues singing" ("Free" 387). Similarly, Amiri Baraka sees Coleman's sound as relying "to a great extent on a closeness of vocal reference that ha[d] always been characteristic of Negro music," and notes that the saxophonist "scream[ed] and rant[ed] in imitation of the human voice, sounding many times like the unfettered primitive [blues] shouters" (*Blues* 227). Baraka also reads significant stylistic connections between Coleman's sound and its immediate jazz predecessors, like bebop:

> Coleman's "Ramblin'" possesses a melodic line the spatial tensions of which seem firmly rooted in 1940's [sic] Gillespie–Parker composition and extemporization. The very jaggedness and abruptness of the melodic fabric itself suggests the boppers' seemingly endless need for deliberate and agitated rhythmical contrast, most of the melodies being almost extensions of the dominating rhythmical patterns. Whistle "Ramblin'," then any early [music by bop pianist Thelonious] Monk, e.g., "Four in One" or "Humph" or Bird's "Cheryl" or "Confirmation," and the basic *physical* similarities of melodic lines should be immediately apparent. (*Black* 74, original emphasis)

Likewise, John Litweiler suggests that Coleman's soloing on the early free jazz effort, *Something Else!,* from 1958, "is shot through with the adrenaline of Charlie Parker" (34–35). Thus, Coleman's music was not so much an impudent rejection of African American blues and jazz traditions as a measured extension of them.

While Coleman himself did not mark free jazz as explicitly emblematic of any kind of race politics, its reception and development were both inextricably associated with contemporaneous activity in African American politics. As Ted Gioia summarizes, around the time that free jazz emerged the notion of "freedom" had become an organizing ideal among African American civil rights activists:

> "Freedom riders" defied segregation in buses and terminals in the Deep South, often at great personal risk. The "Freedom Vote" of 1963 attracted tens of thousands of participants to mock elections that demonstrated the absence of real representative democracy in the South. The "Freedom Summer" of the following year found activists organizing to register African-American voters in large numbers in anticipation of the fall presidential election. The "Freedom Singers" chorus toured the country, giving concerts and raising money for the civil rights movement. Black leaders sought to form "Freedom Schools" and establish a "Freedom Democratic Party." The word was imprinted on the public's consciousness, dramatized in speeches by Dr. Martin Luther King, sung in hymns, brandished at Little Rock, Albany, Birmingham, Selma, and other battlegrounds of the civil rights movement. (338)[6]

Stressing the importance of "freedom" as a philosophical touchstone for African Americans in the early 1960s, Gioia argues that it "is impossible to comprehend the free jazz movement of these same years without understanding how it fed on this powerful cultural shift in American society" (338). Charles Hersch adds that free jazz

> represented political freedom in two ways: negatively, by rejecting musical rules and conventions that restricted individual expression and discarding traditional hierarchical roles within the small group; and positively, by musically creating a group of equals that in, in accord with [Martin Luther] King's idea of the redemptive community, maximized individual expression while maintaining great cohesiveness (97–98).

Just as bebop had done nearly twenty years earlier, free jazz marked a "deformative" intervention into American expressive practice by announcing radical black difference and establishing the foundation for a new African American avant–garde in jazz. The change in the music was representative of major shifts in black politics, just as bebop had registered a new assertive consciousness among African Americans after the Second World War. As Gioia stresses, the social importance of the new black avant–garde in jazz cannot be underestimated. In the past, those jazz musicians who had experimented with "freedom" and "atonality" had been white—pianist Lennie Tristano with his recordings of the late 1940s, Bob Graettinger in his experimental arrangements for the Stan Kenton big band, Jimmy Guiffre on his famous 1953 recording, "Fugue"—and the music had been grounded in a notion of the avant–garde rooted in European classical music.[7] Much of this music constitutes the material Gunther Schuller had in mind when he coined the term "Third Stream" in 1957 to "describe a merging of the most promising and progressive currents in jazz and contemporary classical music," a musical connection that allowed any experimentation to occur, suggests Gioia, within "the established order of things" (339). Free jazz, on the other hand, originated in a state of marginalization, in the fact that many of its innovators as experimental African American artists faced a kind of *de facto* exclusion from the mainstream. Because the music was "difficult," thriving on a traditionally modernist standard of aesthetic experimentation and artistic risk–taking, its composers and performers found themselves struggling financially at times. Historically, successful black musicians in America had achieved their economic gains as performing commodities, rewarded for their ostensible entertainment value in the mainstream. Early innovators like Louis Armstrong and Duke Ellington had been savvy manipulators of expectations in American entertainment. Even the bebop renegades of the 1940s who presented themselves as "serious artists" had been conscious of establishing their market value by reinventing those expectations. Free jazz embodied the radical avant–gardism valued in "high" modernist arts, taking bebop's concert–hall aspirations even further away from jazz music's popular beginnings. However, its development out of black music placed it in seeming opposition to progressive classical music, and thus removed it from the institutional means that allowed so–called serious music to develop.[8] Consequently, even after the pianist and composer Cecil Taylor had established himself in recording and performance as a key innovator in the free jazz movement, by the early 1960s he was forced by monetary woes to take a job as a dishwasher in a restaurant where, ironically enough, "records by Ornette Coleman, John Coltrane, and himself were played daily" (Wilmer, *People* 28).[9]

Because free jazz negotiated enduring racial inequalities in American culture and was a black sound that aggressively called for new perspectives in its challenges to musical convention, the music became an aesthetic marker of the nationalist politics that developed in the 1960s under the aegis of Black Power. As a political movement, Black Power came to fruition in the mid-to-late 1960s, developing out of the rhetoric of Stokely

Carmichael who ascended as leader of the Student Nonviolent Coordinating Committee (SNCC) in 1966. For years, SNCC had been a younger complement to Martin Luther King's Southern Christian Leadership Conference (SCLC), working in tandem with the older group in voter–registration drives, freedom rides, and non–violent protests. But many SNCC members became disillusioned with SCLC's vision of civil rights after setbacks in the early 1960s: the rise in unemployment among African Americans, the Sixteenth Street Baptist Church Bombing in Birmingham in 1963, the 1965 assassination of Malcolm X, and the Watts riot that memorialized black frustrations writ large as it left thirty–four people dead and another 1032 injured (Franklin and Moss 514). Carmichael was outspoken in voicing the disappointment of his SNCC colleagues, and unabashed in his criticism of SCLC's older civil rights leadership. Frustrated that traditional alliances between whites and blacks in the pursuit of civil rights had slowed the movement toward freedom, Carmichael "insisted that blacks must think in terms of 'black power' and use it to combat the 'white power' that had held them down" (Franklin and Moss 515). As Carmichael and Charles Hamilton wrote in 1967: "The concept of Black Power rests on a fundamental premise: *Before a group can enter the open society, it must first close ranks.* By this we mean that group solidarity is necessary before a group can operate effectively from a bargaining position of strength in a pluralistic society" (44). This rhetoric marked a shift toward a more separatist politics among many young African Americans, the culmination of which was 1967's Black Power conference in Newark, a gathering that called for the division of the United States into two separate nations, one for whites and one for blacks (Franklin and Moss 518).

With these separatist currents in the air, free jazz's radical sound was especially important to members of the Black Arts movement, a group of young African American artists who constituted, in critic and spokesman Larry Neal's words, "the aesthetic and spiritual sister of the Black Power concept" ("Black Arts" 184). Much like the intellectuals who dominated the Harlem Renaissance, the artists and critics who constituted the Black Arts movement were committed to the use of art as a vehicle for social reform. But this younger generation of political artists differed from their antecedents in their critical assumptions and specific approach. While the Harlem Renaissance had tried to engineer social change by appealing to white Americans through artistic excellence, the Black Arts collective subscribed to Black Power's separatist rhetoric and sought reform predominantly by rallying African Americans themselves. As Neal asserted, African American culture needed to answer Black Power's imperative for "Black people to define the world in their own terms" ("Black Arts" 184).

On an aesthetic level, this meant that the "cultural values inherent in western history must be either radicalized or destroyed," and that what was "needed [was] a whole new system of ideas" (Neal, "Black Arts" 185). Iconoclastic, radical, deformative, free jazz seemed an ideal medium for precipitating this reconfiguration. What musicians like Ornette Coleman and Cecil Taylor "[had] done, basically," to quote Amiri Baraka, was "to restore jazz to its valid separation from, and anarchic disregard of, Western popular forms. They [had] used the music of the forties with its jagged, exciting rhythms as an initial reference and ha[d] restored the hegemony of the blues as the most important basic form in Afro-American music" (*Blues* 225).[10] Frank Kofsky offers an even more uncompromising assertion of free jazz's relationship to Black Power. Writing about the new music in a 1966 essay, "Revolution in Black Music" (later collected in *Black Nationalism and the Revolution in Music*), Kofsky argues that the "avant–garde movement in jazz [was] a musical representation of the ghetto's vote of 'no confidence' in Western civilization and the American dream—that Negro avant–garde intransigents, in other words [were] saying through their horns [. . .] 'Up your ass, feeble–minded ofays!'" (131). This rejection of white ideologies, and white aesthetics, in free jazz complemented contemporary ventures in Black Arts literature which foregrounded black vernacular expression and underscored collective anger. Perhaps the best example is Haki Madhubuti's elegy for John Coltrane, "Don't Cry, Scream" an excerpt of which reads:

SCREAMMMM/we-eeeee/screech/teee   improvise
aheeeeeeeee/screeeeeee/theeee/ee   with
ahHHHHHHHHH/WEEEEEEEEE/scrEEE   feeling
    EEEE
we-eeeee WE-EEEEEEEEEWE-EE-EEEEE

the ofays heard you &
were wiped out, spaced.
one clown asked me during
my favorite things, if
you were practicing.
I fired on the muthafucka & said,
"i'm practicing." (97–98, lines 102–13)

However, the relationship between free jazz and Black Power was not merely the rhetorical construction of Black Arts intellectuals and sympathetic commentators; rather, African American performers and composers themselves began to emphasize their relationship to the new politics as the 1960s wore on. Speaking to Valerie Wilmer late in the decade, saxophonist Archie Shepp—a free jazz composer of "explicitly" political tunes like "Malcolm, Malcolm—Semper Malcolm" and "Call Me By My Rightful Name"—maintained that "[i]t is precisely because of the emerging identity of the Negro that jazz is beginning to take on a unique character," and argued that "the new black expression [would] play a tremendous part in the shaping of the new ethic" (qtd in *People* 158). Pianist Cecil Taylor was similarly outspoken in asserting the necessary relationship between his music and black radical politics, proclaiming that "[s]hutting your mind to the happenings was the final bankruptcy that the academy left us with, the current life in America *now* is the material for artists" (qtd in Wilmer, *People* 30, original emphasis). In the late 1960s, Taylor could not have embodied Black Power's separatist ethos more when he called for a disassociation between black musicians and the predominantly white music business on which they had historically depended. Urging black artists to boycott jazz clubs, record companies, trade papers, and federated unions, Taylor insisted, "Let's take the music away from the people who control it" (qtd in Kofsky 144).

Furthermore, this political sense was evident not only in offstage comments by black free jazz musicians in the 1960s and seventies, but also in their onstage performance. "As black nationalism developed," Wilmer summarizes, "becoming visible in the adoption of African and Islamic customs, names and dress, so the music broadened to contain obvious references to the strands that had been woven into the fabric of contemporary jazz" (*Serious* 27–28). References to Africa abounded in the new music: from Sonny Murray's 1969 *Homage to Africa* suite, to brass player Clifford Thornton's "free interpretations of melodies derived from rituals connected with two Yoruba deities" (Wilmer, *Serious* 28), to the striking performances of the Art Ensemble of Chicago, a collective that performed under the motto "Great Black Music—Ancient to Modern." Emphasizing connections between the new music and "non–Western" influences, the AEC used rhythmic instruments from other cultures (such as bells and rattles) and frequently incorporated a performative "Africanness" onstage by painting their faces in ceremonial designs or wearing African robes.[11]

Yet free jazz also enjoyed currency and meaning beyond its black nationalist context. As with earlier jazz styles, free jazz in some instances arrived at an intersection between radical cultural politics and mainstream acceptance. That is, while artists like Archie Shepp and the AEC used the music to facilitate a deformative cultural performance, other black musicians already firmly established in a jazz mainstream began to adopt elements of the avant–garde sound in a move that brought the style closer to the cultural center. The most notable artists from this group were the trumpeter Miles Davis and the saxophonist John Coltrane.[12]

By the early 1960s, Davis was the best–paid and arguably the most famous black musician to have come of age amidst the bebop movement after World War II. A bona fide commercial success with strong–selling LPs like *Porgy and Bess* (1958), *Kind of Blue* (1959), and *Someday My Prince Will Come* (1961) under his belt, Davis was a figure of considerable wealth and certifiable celebrity—a millionaire, as well as a cultural icon recognized by *Life* and *Playboy*.[13] Throughout the 1950s, the trumpeter moved between straight–ahead bebop and moody, bluesy ballads played with his trademark mute. Davis had staked his career on a cultivated cool and a reserved stage demeanor, approaching solos with economy and emotion. As free jazz began to garner notice around the turn of the decade, he was initially dismissive, assessing Coleman's music with his characteristic asperity: "Hell, just listen to what he writes and how he plays it. If you're talking psychologically, the man is all screwed up inside" (qtd in Chambers II: 19).[14] By the mid–1960s, though, Davis did an aesthetic about–face, "forgetting" earlier criticisms and integrating aspects of free jazz into the sound of his quintet. On records like *ESP* (1965), *Miles Smiles* (1966), and *Nefertiti* (1967), Davis turned his music toward a more Colemanesque collective interaction, maximizing collaboration with a younger group of sidemen that included drummer Tony Williams and pianist Herbie Hancock.[15] The move brought free jazz—or at least a facsimile of it—away from the fringes and closer to mainstream audiences through wide–release records for Columbia and big–ticket performances at jazz festivals and Carnegie Hall.

Yet despite this turn to free jazz stylistics, Davis appeared removed in his politics from the new black nationalism. While he was by no means apolitical, the trumpeter's social sense was, nevertheless, never easy to sketch, never as explicit as that of younger contemporaries like Cecil Taylor and Archie Shepp, or even of other bebop–rooted musicians like Charles Mingus who had integrated civil rights protest into his music with compositions like "Haitian Fight Song" and "Fables of Faubus," an ironic tribute to Arkansas's notoriously segregationist governor.[16] At best, Davis's move toward free jazz might be read as a moderate's acknowledgment of the music's aesthetic significance and a distant nod to the new black politics; at worst, the trumpeter might be accused of pandering to vogue and using elements of free jazz to maintain credibility among hip listeners attuned to the new thing. In any case, his enigmatic isolationism hardly lent itself to celebration by a generation of outspoken young artists and activists who advertised their agenda through strident calls for reform and a collective politics.

Davis never gave any indication that his experiments with free jazz were governed by much more than aesthetic interest. In contrast, his contemporary and former bandmate, John Coltrane, seemed to bridge Black Arts social expression, conventional civil rights activism, and a more traditional art-for-art's-sake aestheticism throughout the 1960s—in all, an amalgamating tendency that impressed radical black poets like Haki Madhubuti and Amiri Baraka, and that made him a central figure in and model of inspiration for the hybrid modernism of Michael S. Harper.[17]

In Harper's poetry, Coltrane emerges time and again as an iconic marker of the maelstrom of ambivalence, innovation, and acknowledgment central to African American expressivity in the wake of Black Power. Harper's poetic project recognizes the Black Arts movement's social interests and radical aesthetics without espousing its nationalistic rejection of more conventionally "Western" artistic traditions and the "white influence" of an accepted canon. The poet's turn to Coltrane in formulating a later hybrid literary aesthetic is perhaps unsurprising given the saxophonist's dizzying combination of iconoclasm and homage throughout the politically charged 1960s. Of all the jazz soloists that constitute the music's conventionally accepted pantheon, perhaps none stands so firmly at the crossroads of diverse styles, aesthetics, and cultural politics as Coltrane. An apprentice as a horn player in the rhythm and blues groups of Philadelphia in the 1940s, a sideman within Miles Davis's late–bop quintet of the mid–1950s, and leader of his own revolutionary group amidst the free jazz milieu of the 1960s, Coltrane was a musician who embodied jazz music's comprehensive impulse, its ability to encompass myriad African American musics within its own composite tradition.

It is the last phase in the saxophonist's career—Coltrane's gradual turn from bebop to a more free style in the 1960s—that made the musician an important galvanizing force in the 1960s formation of black nationalism and its political community, a figure whom Frank Kofsky argues needs necessarily to be discussed in the same social contexts as Malcolm X.[18] On a number of levels, Coltrane's work of the 1960s notably positions the saxophonist next to his black nationalist contemporaries in free jazz. For one, his turn to a group–oriented collective expression seemed to acknowledge the importance of communal politics. As Kofsky writes, the "collective improvisation" of the music, including that of Coltrane's quartet, "symbolize[d] the recognition among musicians that their art [was] not an affair of individual 'geniuses,' but the musical expression of an entire people—the black people in America" (140). Moreover, Coltrane's turns to the non–white cultures of Africa and India for inspiration appeared to signify his sympathy with, again in Kofsky's words, "the larger decision of the Negro ghetto to turn its back on an exploitative and inhumane white American society" (140). In efforts that included his stepped–up emphasis on rhythm (which by the late 1960s featured the use of two drummers), and compositions like *Africa/Brass* (1961), "Dahomey Dance" (1961), and "India" (1961), Coltrane appeared to support Black Power's rejection of traditionally white, Western values and aesthetics. Indeed, in Coltrane's relentless push for new sounds, for new approaches to improvisation, he seemed undeniably a product of the new radicalism—discontented with the old expressive modes and politics, hungry for reform, and restless for change.[19]

However, though many commentators stress Coltrane's ceaseless exploration and drive for innovation, the saxophonist was undoubtedly mindful of jazz tradition. As Bill Cole notes, even in the late 1950s, when the restlessness that spurred the musician's stylistic development was kicking into high gear, Coltrane was busy "study[ing] the history of jazz—not only his own music [that is, the late–period bebop of which he was an accepted master], but any music that he could possibly find theoretical works on" (82–83). As the musician himself said in a 1960 interview for *Down Beat,* "I'm very interested in the past, and even though there's a lot I don't know about it, I intend to go back and find out. I'm back to [early New Orleans reed player] Sidney Bechet already" (qtd in Cole 83). Accordingly, this academic interest in jazz history found its way into Coltrane's music, as with the 1960 tribute, "Blues to Bechet," played on Bechet's signature horn, the soprano saxophone, and included on an album of blues themes for Atlantic Records, *Coltrane Plays the Blues.*[20] As well, even after Coltrane had established his famous quartet, the group with which he performed and recorded much of his most radical experimentations in the early 1960s, the saxophonist still signed to do more "traditional" sessions for Impulse Records, including a 1963 session that joined his group with the crooner Johnny Hartman for a set of ballads and standards, and a famous meeting with Duke Ellington the year before.[21]

Moreover, as a political subject, Coltrane built on established modes of social expression in jazz. His music was certainly emblematic of bebop's "politics of style," the African American militancy through musical virtuosity that Parker and Gillespie had intensified in their work. Coltrane's political aesthetics could be ostensibly overt, as with the 1963 anthem "Alabama," composed in response to the Sixteenth Street Baptist Church bombing earlier that year in Birmingham, but at other times thrived on savvy rhetorical play, as in his 1961 variations on Rodgers and Hammerstein's "My Favorite Things," a wholesale deconstruction of one of the cultural products of mainstream whiteness. Ultimately, as a political voice, Coltrane seemed more interested in stimulating dialogue than in registering complaint or marking withdrawal. "My Favorite Things" is dialogical, as the best of bebop had been, subverting the dominance of the mainstream artifact by engaging with the piece rather than rejecting it outright, as Black Arts ideology might have called for. Furthermore, even in the saxophonist's "explicitly" political material, he aligned himself more with Martin Luther King (and, by extension, the SCLC's vision of civil rights through exchange) than with any separatist impulse. "Alabama," for example is modeled on the rhythms of King's elegiac sermon for the victims of the Sixteenth Street Baptist Church bombing. As Bill Cole argues, the saxophonist's appeals to King's expressive genius seemed part of Coltrane's sympathetic attempt "to articulate the plight of African-American people and all oppressed people throughout the world" (151). Coltrane was certainly vocal in his support of King's life and politics, as evidenced in his famous musical tribute, "Reverend King" (1966).

In all, Coltrane embodied a version of the phenomenon Craig Werner calls "gospel politics," namely, an expressive push for civil rights governed by dialogue within and across racial borders, through aesthetic connection and ideological exchange. As Werner argues, African American music of the 1950s and sixties was essential to the mobilization of civil rights energies in its simultaneous capacity to promote black community and stimulate political coalitions across racial lines. The predominance of antiphony in black expressivity is central to this social process, as Werner explains:

> The core of gospel politics lies in the "call and response" principle of African-American culture. The basic structure of call and response is straightforward. An individual voice, frequently a preacher or singer, calls out in a way that asks for a response. [. . .] The response can affirm, argue, redirect the dialogue, raise a new question. Any response that gains attention and elicits a response of its own becomes a new call. (11)

In the 1950s and sixties, Werner suggests, African American music carried the ethos of call and response into a larger social arena, generating "political and spiritual implications" out of mass–media exposure and movement between white and black cultural space (11). At times this antiphony could be directed at strengthening black community (Mahalia Jackson singing "I've Been 'Buked and I've Been Scorned," for example, at the 1963 March on Washington, or James Brown leading a chorus of young African American voices in the anthem, "Say It Loud (I'm Black and I'm Proud)"), or at negotiating revolution with a non–black listenership (Otis Redding performing "I've Been Loving You Too Long" to a mostly white audience at 1967's Monterey Pop Festival, or Sam Cooke on mainstream AM radio singing "A Change Is Gonna Come").[22]

John Coltrane's most famous recording, the 1964 Impulse Records release *A Love Supreme,* is one of the key musical texts in the articulation of gospel politics. *A Love Supreme* embodies the gospel impulse in African American music in its expressive emphasis on dialogue and community, and as the embodiment of democratic ideals. "At its best," Werner writes, "the gospel impulse helps people experience themselves *in relation to* rather than *on their own*" (28, original emphasis). Accordingly, "Coltrane opens [the record] with a blues cry but [Jimmy] Garrison's bass immediately establishes the heartbeat riff that keeps Coltrane's spiritual quest in touch with the beloved community" (Werner 131). Thus, the record dramatizes the gospel impulse's advancement of kinship and cooperation. Moreover, in the record's unwavering assertion of spiritual community, presented through its recurring vocal refrain, "A love supreme" (sung by Coltrane and his quartet members), the album affirms the necessity of communion central to gospel politics:

> Whatever its specific incarnation, gospel redemption breaks down the difference between personal salvation and communal liberation. No one makes it alone. If we're going to bear up under the weight of the cross, find the strength to renounce the Devil, if we're going to survive to bear witness and move on up, we're going to have to connect. (Werner 31)

Coltrane articulates a vision of this community himself in the prayer featured in the album's liner notes. Calling for a commitment to peace among his audience, the saxophonist emphasizes antiphonal dialogue in his insistence that "[o]ne thought can produce millions of vibrations" (liner notes). The sentiment corresponds with the less metaphorical vision of dialogue and community Coltrane offers in a 1966 interview with Frank Kofsky, in which the musician comments on the relationship of his work to racial difference. Whether an audience is white or black, Coltrane remarks, "doesn't matter. I only hope that whoever is out there listening, they enjoy it," that they "show what they feel" and "respond" (qtd in Kofsky 226).

Coltrane's self–declared emphasis on dialogue and exchange—the embodiment of Werner's gospel politics—parallels Michael Harper's explanation of his own social concerns. Influenced by the primacy of connection in jazz and an Ellisonian collaborative ideal, Harper's also work attempts to engage in dialogue with various American expressivities, including specifically black creative modes and broader historical and literary discourses. One of the guiding concerns of Harper's early creative development as a student in the University of Iowa's famous writing workshop was the question: "How would it be to solo with that great tradition of the big bands honking you on? Could one do it in a poem?" ("Poetic" 29). Moreover, informed by Ellison's vision of democracy in American expression, Harper admits to the necessity of tension in this exchange:

> Now all you have to do is get the albums and listen to the Blue Devils band and you'll know what I'm talking about. That became the nucleus of Count Basie's band. I tell you that because it seems to me that we have this ongoing dialogue—I think that Ellison said it best in an essay where he corrected Irving Howe for approaching his particular novel (that is, *Invisible Man*) in the wrong way. He said that he was in "a continuous antagonistic cooperation" with Mr. Howe and others. I think that that is a good expression for our use here—"antagonistic cooperation," which is the willingness to disagree about the way in which we see what we call reality. (Young et al 140)

Articulating a version of this sentiment in an earlier interview with James Randall, Harper expresses the necessary implications of dialogue in literature, explaining how a fidelity to black political concerns and a commitment to the expansion of received literary traditions intersect in his work:

> The icons of much of the heroism and resistance to oppression by Black Americans are implicit in all of my work—which is to say, I have a certain perspective on events, on America, on the language, on culture, and on cross–fertilization. I have Irish ancestry, but I don't have to be an Irishman to see the value of Yeats, or Synge, or Joyce. I had the luck to know that one has to place oneself in a continuum of consciousness. I did not see many voices from my own ancestors ably represented in our literature, and I wanted to do my part, to testify to their efforts and achievements, and the values implicit in the making of this country and its character. (17)

While the celebration of a recognizably African American identity is central to this project, Harper self–consciously does not position himself within the Black Arts movement with which his early career is roughly contemporary. Speaking of the development of black poetry in the late 1960s, Harper admits that "we lost our sense of what had gone before, and made accusations of people who had worked conscientiously and relatively quietly for change" (qtd in Rowell 796). The poet continues: "I remember when people wouldn't read Ellison and Hayden, not to mention Tolson. Beneath much of the rhetoric was misinformation and inexperience" (796). Ultimately, he concedes, he is unable to dismiss those earlier "cultural bearers" whom Black Power rejected. "Greater access to wider horizons was what I appreciated most," Harper declares. "I wanted to write well; I also wanted to be a responsible citizen" (796).

In Harper's poetry, the figure of Coltrane marks the intersection of these various ideological and aesthetic streams, embodying a dialogue in which history converges with the present, and black social consciousness addresses the paradoxes of American democracy. Harper uses Coltrane's life and music in his metaphorical exploration of thematic concerns like the importance of history, especially the use of black expressivity as an alternate history that counters dominant historical discourses; the inextricability of the black experience from the American cultural landscape at large; and the dialogic relationship that black culture bears with the mainstream which it simultaneously influences and opposes. Throughout Harper's Coltrane poems, the great saxophonist's music is the sonic marker of African American cultural memory, an echo that recurringly evokes the past and asserts black identity by voicing a call that anticipates and demands response.

In its celebration of black identity, Harper's work is not unlike that of the poets of the Black Arts movement, whom Sascha Feinstein notes "adopted Coltrane's sound as a musical embodiment of black nationalism in the United States" (116). However, Harper does not use the music as a marker of a transcendent, essential blackness, or as a rhetorical model for black separateness, but rather as the symbol of a collective African American memory informed by material influence and historical specificity. Harper uses Coltrane's music to mark African American cultural memory, as defined by Samuel Floyd, as "a repository of meanings that comprise the subjective knowledge of a people, its immanent thoughts, its structures, and its practices" (8).

Harper perhaps best represents the power of Coltrane's music to invoke black cultural memory in his most famous poem, "Dear John, Dear Coltrane." The poem begins with an allusion to Coltrane's music as its epigraph, the repetition of the vocal refrain "*a love supreme, a love supreme*" from Coltrane's famous album. The quotation is both musical (in its reference to the composition's famous four–note theme, to which the lyrics are sung on the album) and textual (in its appeal to the lyrics themselves)—a sign that recalls Coltrane's music in both its tonality and its iconicity. The intertextual–intermusical gesture evokes African American cultural memory in its allusiveness. The move compacts time, placing two moments of creative performance—Harper's poem and Coltrane's music—on the same temporal plane, and thus establishing African American community through its superimposition of seemingly removed historical points. It functions in the same manner that Ingrid Monson observes in intermusical quotation in jazz performance, as quoted in Chapter Three, "an aural passage conveys to those with the sociocultural knowledge to recognize and interpret it a relation between a past performance and a present one" (*Saying* 127). In addition, the poem's introductory appeal to Coltrane's work through musico–textual quotation—a quotation that Harper often sings or chants in public readings of the poem—summons the complex historical juxtaposition that begins the first stanza:

> Sex fingers toes
> in the marketplace
> near your father's church
> in Hamlet, North Carolina— (*Songlines* 25, lines 1–4)[23]

The scene Harper describes is a slave auction, a moment from historical experience which the music remembers, juxtaposed against a biographical referent from Coltrane's own life—the geographical space of his father's church in Hamlet. This temporal juxtaposition and telescoping of time is a technique that Harper employs throughout. Appealing to Coltrane through the pronoun "you," Harper conflates this address with other moments from a collective black history, like the movement of escaped slaves:

> you tuck the roots in the earth,
> turn back, and move
> by river through the swamps,
> singing: *a love supreme, a love supreme.* (*Songlines* 25, lines 11–14)

Or Harper narrates Coltrane's biography alongside the emergence of jazz amidst twentieth–century urban migration:

> You plod up into the electric city—
> your song now crystal and
> the blues. You pick up the horn
> with some will and blow
> into the freezing night:
> *a love supreme, a love supreme*— (*Songlines* 25, lines 19–24)

As Harper himself says in a 1972 interview with John O'Brien, the aim of the poem "is redemptive both in terms of black experience and in terms of the painful private life of black musicians. The suffering is both personal and historical and when it's internalized in the music of Coltrane, for example, it becomes a kind of cultural process" (97). And this process seems a specific manifestation of Floyd's argument that African American music stimulates black cultural memory by juxtaposing diverse historical moments. Harper's juxtaposition restores African American community across temporal planes, redressing the fact that, as he says above, black Americans, in formulating new strategies to resist white supremacy, had occasionally "lost [a] sense of what had gone before." In bringing together these various historical moments, Harper bridges the gaps that he perceives in the collective cultural memory.

Harper's representation of Coltrane's music as a significant marker of that cultural memory is also important because it presents the music as a key record of African American history, as an alternate account that counters the ideological biases of the mainstream's record. For Harper, black history is best collected not within the dominant discourse of white documentation, but rather through the African American oral vernacular, through the music and voices of African Americans themselves. As the poet says of African American history: "There are terrific losses in America that are taking place. And many people don't even know they're there, because nobody took the time to write them down. [. . .] And out of that memory and out of that loss comes a kind of ritual content, which is to say the framing of the experience and the presentation of the experience" (Young et al 144). The historical juxtapositions of "Dear John, Dear Coltrane" dramatize this ritual, placing diverse moments in a black collective experience together and locating them within a layered history expressed by Coltrane's sound. As Gayl Jones observes, Harper uses jazz to restore "landscape and history" and to bring a "sense of continuity of tradition"—a continuity that is perhaps elsewhere disrupted by the power and imposition of mainstream historical record, or more significantly, by the profound historical rupture caused by the forced diaspora of the Middle Passage (54).

In "A Narrative of the Life and Times of John Coltrane: Played by Himself," Harper again represents music's attempt to repair the ruptures in African American historical record. As the title of this poem suggests, Harper uses Coltrane's music to mark African American historical tradition, by referencing the title of Frederick Douglass's famous narrative of 1845. The gesture is ironic, though—a Signifyin(g) move. Harper asserts Coltrane's place as a unique voice in the black historical record, not unlike Douglass, but in revising the title of Douglass's narrative (most significantly with the substitution of the word "played" for "written"), Harper registers ambivalence about the ability of that written historical record to speak for the African American collective. In doing so, Harper recalls the tension between written, textual literacy and vernacular literacy that Douglass himself dramatizes. That is, though Douglass, in describing his experience of learning to read (despite the wishes of a master who wished to keep him illiterate) proclaims that literacy could counter "the white man's power to enslave the black man," he argues that it was vernacular literacy, as embodied by the special root he was advised to carry by his fellow slave, Sandy Jenkins, that was ultimately crucial to his drive for freedom (58). Carrying the root with him, Douglass was inspired to resist the violence of the overseer Covey. "This battle with Mr. Covey," Douglass recalls, "was the turning–point in my career as a slave. It rekindled the few expiring embers of freedom, and revived within me a sense of my own manhood" (79).

Harper's play with the uncertainty about "written" literacy also considers the position Douglass's text inhabits in relation to the documents with which it was published. Douglass's narrative is dialogical, characterized by tension between the writer's account of his own life and the extraneous authenticating texts that precede it, namely, letters from white abolitionists William Lloyd Garrison and Wendell Phillips. Though Robert Stepto has argued persuasively for the rhetorical dominance of Douglass's text over these introductory letters, there is nonetheless a recognizable tension in the aggregate design of the narrative as a whole. As Stepto himself concedes, a reading of the introductory letters reveals how "Garrison is [. . .] interested in writing history [. . .] and recording his own place in it" (29). A close reading of the texts from Garrison and Phillips reveals their claims to authority as they endorse the "authenticity" of Douglass's textual record. For example, Garrison writes:

> Mr. Douglass has very properly chosen to write his own Narrative, in his own style, and according to the best of his ability, rather than to employ some one else. It is, therefore, entirely his own production; and considering how long and dark was the career he had to run as a slave,—how few have been his opportunities to improve his mind since he broke his iron fetters,—it is, in my judgment, highly creditable to his hand and heart. (32)

Similarly, Phillips, in addressing Douglass, adds, "Again, we have known you long, and can put the most entire confidence in your truth, candor, and sincerity. Every one who has heard you speak has felt, and, I am confident, every one who reads your book will feel, persuaded that you give them a fair specimen of the whole truth" (36–37). Considering these tensions, Harper himself says of Douglass's narrative in an interview, "Frederick Douglass, a great orator, *and writer,* had to prove his literate insights; in many ways [African Americans are] still proving we can read and write" (qtd in Randall

17, original emphasis). Ultimately, the poet's appeals to Douglass's narrative signify on the textual conflicts therein and critique the white texts' unfounded claims to authority.

Harper's "Narrative of the Life and Times of John Coltrane" dramatizes these conflicts over textual histories in two key moments, both of which represent the tendency of dominant historical records to subsume, distort, or expunge the cultural experience of African Americans. In the poem's third stanza, Harper, speaking as Coltrane in a first–person voice, notes the tenuous relationship his music (shaped by experience) bears to the literature that comments on it: "into *sheets of sound* labeling me / into dissonance" (*Songlines* 187, lines 19–20, original emphasis). Here Harper acknowledges the suggestion of dissonance in the term "sheets of sound"— white jazz critic Ira Gitler's coinage for Coltrane's playing—and notes the process by which textual records may exclude or misrepresent African American cultural products. Moreover, in the poem's fourth stanza, Harper, still speaking as Coltrane, turns to jazz photography, and expresses dissatisfaction with the way his person is represented in lasting record:

> I never liked the photo taken with
> Bird, Miles without sunglasses,
> me in profile almost out of exposure:
> these were my images of movement;
> when I hear the sacred songs,
> auras of my mother at the stove,
> I play the blues: (*Songlines* 187, lines 21–27)

The final three lines of the stanza counter the distortion represented in the first four. The photograph of Coltrane with Charlie Parker and Miles Davis cannot capture what the music he plays can—the specificity of memory, the details of his character.

As these two examples from "A Narrative of the Life" reveal, Harper sometimes voices his broader commentary about the failings of historical discourse metaphorically, through the specificity of jazz history itself. In the poem "Bandstand," for example, from the sequence, "My Book on Trane," Harper writes of Coltrane's brief tenure in the Thelonious Monk Quartet, a tragically under–recorded period in the saxophonist's career:

> Monk's dissonant hat
> willing every change of direction;
> all those influences in your head
> touching the wrong target—

none of this recorded (*Songlines* 168, lines 1–5)

After describing the mentor role that Monk played in the emergence of Coltrane's virtuoso technique, Harper notes how their musical interaction went largely unrecorded, undocumented. However, as the poem's first stanza comes to a close, the poet attests to the historical significance of the moment: these musicians are dressed in their "common clothes" (presumably dressed down as they play for themselves, away from the expectations of paying audiences), appealing here to "the ancestors," those silenced members of the tradition for whom they speak in the present. In "Polls," another piece from "My Book on Trane," Harper again uses jazz to represent the tension between official history and black music's alternate discourse. That poem begins in a conversational voice, with an African American jazz fan lamenting the victory of white saxophonist Paul Desmond over John Coltrane in a magazine's best–of poll:

—I'm not saying Desmond can't play—
but *Playboy* was embarrassed,
sounding like swing all over again:
whuhfolks creating jazz— (*Songlines* 170, lines 4–7)

That is, the official record proposed by jazz journalism and the music market belies the alternate history of the music that the speaker himself recognizes outside that discourse. As Harper offers this suggestion, he also returns to one of the thematic strands that defines "Dear John, Dear Coltrane": Coltrane's music bears the expression of suffering and the unrestricted declaration of black lived experience. As the speaker says of Coltrane's music:

Some knew such playing
is possible
only when you're ready to die. (*Songlines* 170, lines 18–20)

Furthermore, as the poem concludes, Harper dramatizes the strain of Coltrane's alternate history against the strength of the dominant record:

Most whites always keeping score,
making it too easy to find the way,
guaranteeing you'll never find loss,
black and white on paper,
in the ground. (*Songlines* 170, lines 21–25)

Thus, the discourse of the mainstream ultimately tries to subsume the sound of Coltrane's music and suppress his body. The intensity of his voice, the playing that is possible as he nears death, is threatened by the termination of his life. The losses articulated by Coltrane are threatened by the limits of his own existence, by the fact that the musician as a living historical record is doomed to end up "in the ground." For Harper, this is especially perilous given Coltrane's ability to speak for the African American community and give voice to the ruptures of history, as with the slave auction sequence that follows the "love supreme" refrain in "Dear John, Dear Coltrane."

However, in documenting these potential losses and dramatizing the tension between written record and vernacular expressivity, Harper seeks to confront this threat and complement the history that Coltrane himself articulates through music. The poet's attempt to locate the history of slavery and its violence through the black body in jazz performance reflects what Saidiya Hartman identifies as a crucial part of African American strategies for redressing the ruptures and atrocities of the past: namely, recording those atrocities through the daily physical performance of black Americans, reiterating them through the black body's vernacular practice. Observing how vernacular practices like the performance of juba (a slave dance in which hands, knees, and thighs are clapped in rhythmic pattern) incorporates presentation of the black body's pain, Hartman suggests how black performativity articulates the memory of that violence against the threat of its erasure:

> In this instance, memory is not in the service of continuity but incessantly reiterates and enacts the contradictions and antagonisms of enslavement, the ruptures of history, and the disassociated and dispersed networks of affiliation. It is by way of this reiteration or differential invocation of the past and by way of this memory of difference that everyday practices are redolent with the history of captivity and enslavement. This working through of the past is a significant aspect of redress. (74)

In locating African American history within Coltrane's music and marking the saxophonist's body as a living record of that past, Harper presents jazz as another medium for vernacular resistance, a performance that mediates the tensions of history and, in Hartman's words, "exploit[s . . .] the constraints of domination" (54).

Harper's consideration of the body in "Dear John, Dear Coltrane," and in the sequence "My Book on Trane," voices the material history of

African Americans and examines the legacy of containment and violence continually enacted on the black body. As the above poems illustrate, Harper often represents African American history as expressed by black sound and black bodies, specifically through jazz—the vernacular sound that resists the containment of fixed record and thrives on the immediacy of physical performance. A quick glance at the titles of other poems shows how this idea recurs in Harper's work: "History is Your Own Heartbeat," "Blue Ruth: America," "Sack 'a Woe: Gallstones as History," "History as Bandages: Polka Dots and Moonbeams," and "Dead Day: Malcolm, Feb. 21." This theme is especially clear in another of his Coltrane poems, "Here Where Coltrane Is." In this poem, the speaker remembers fallen civil rights leaders Martin Luther King, Jr. and Malcolm X as he listens to a recording of "Alabama," Coltrane's memorial to the victims of the Sixteenth Street Baptist Church bombing. Again, the saxophonist's music beckons and shapes the specifics of African American cultural memory. As the speaker concludes, while immersed "in the six notes which [became] an anthem," Coltrane's lament and life are inextricable from the social concerns that inspire the song:

> For this reason Martin is dead;
> for this reason Malcolm is dead;
> for this reason Coltrane is dead. (*Songlines* 37, lines 28–30)

Because Coltrane is a galvanizing force in his ability to stimulate cultural dialogue and celebrate racial pride, the poem laments the musician's passing as the loss of another catalyst for social change. The speaker then recognizes that the pain of this history endures, is transformed perhaps, in the sound of the music, and in the bodies and sounds of the music's African American cultural inheritors: "in the eyes of my first son are the browns/of these men and their music" (*Songlines* 37, lines 31–32). That is, amidst these losses, the living historical records of black music and black bodies remember the pain of the past and offer its redress in the possibilities for change each inheritor possesses.

However, though Harper's turn to the African American body, through Coltrane's music and its effects, invokes African American cultural memory and expresses the historical details of that collective consciousness, the move also complements the poet's broader dialogue with American history and culture. As John Callahan notes, Harper is "interested [. . . in] ties formed by the shared experience of American life" ("Testifying" 90). In "Here Where Coltrane Is," Harper asserts the inextricability of African American material experience from other American physical and cultural spaces. The poem's setting marks a confluence of shared black and white histories; the speaker listens to Coltrane's music in his "Victorian house," a house situated in a neighborhood populated by "clear white/children who love [his] children" (*Songlines* 37, lines 7, 14–15). Thus, the sufferings of the past, such as the murders of the Baptist church children, Martin Luther King, and Malcolm X are remembered within a racially integrated, and ostensibly non–confrontational physical space. As Harper himself says of the poem, "it's about the necessity of creating a continuum for children, a dynamic, personal, and aesthetic process which presupposes human inter-action and contact" (qtd in O'Brien 101). Coltrane's music, and the speaker who listens to it, remembers specific moments of struggle from the black past but looks to a redemptive moment in a shared American future. This is perhaps most evident in that, even in the recording of "Alabama," with its haunting tribute to the specificity of black experience, the speaker is inspired to remark in the poem's opening lines that ultimately "[s]oul and race/are private dominions," individual aspects of character that stimulate the larger dialogue without (Harper *Songlines* 37, lines 1–2).

This broad dialogue thrives on Harper's specific ability to invoke the cultural memory of slavery—arguably the most horrific moment in a collec-tive American experience—in order to work against a silencing of the pecu-liar institution's atrocious legacies in the mainstream record. The poet's jazz–influenced invocation of that material past engages with slavery's spe-cific acts of violence in order to redress them. Most notably, Harper responds to slavery's depersonalization of the African American subject as non–speaking chattel, a body perpetually severed in representation from the consciousness contained therein. As Hortense Spillers argues, discus-sions of the enslaved African American body need to recognize a distinction "between 'body' and 'flesh' and impose that distinction as the central one between captive and liberated subject–positions. In that sense, before the 'body' there is the 'flesh,' that zero degree of social conceptualization that does not escape concealment under the brush of discourse, or the reflexes of iconography" (457). That is, slavery's material history constitutes a series of crimes—capture, containment, violence—against the black body as "flesh," which re-emerge on a discursive level as a forcible construction of the African American body as dehumanized object, a sign of Otherness and emotional negation. As Spillers writes, "the captive body reduces to a thing" and "embodies sheer physical powerlessness that slides into a more general 'powerlessness,' resonating through various centers of human and social meaning" (457).

Beryl Wright and Lindon Barrett have each articulated versions of how these "centers of human and social meaning" operate in slavery's discourses and their continued legacy. Wright discusses the complicity of white specularity in the exertion of "social control" over the African American subject (397). Building on the influential work of feminist film critic Laura Mulvey, Wright argues that one of slavery's discursive legacies is the emergence of two specific categories of white voyeurism: a "gaze of obliteration that erases physical presence and denies interiority," and a "gaze of [public] surveillance that assumes—despite its contradictions—the privilege of interior penetration and interpretation" (400). The latter, Wright suggests, is "a gaze that assumes the right to look for purposes of identification and control; a gaze that collects data for a public archive of the body" (400). These two forms of the dominant gaze function toward the same end: reducing the observed African American body entirely to its exterior physiological characteristics, thereby disallowing a potential subject status for African Americans, based on the assumption that black humanity never transcends its well–catalogued physical qualities. Similarly, Barrett shows how the discursive power of slavery turns on a series of dichotomies that equate blackness with illiteracy and the body, and whiteness with literacy and the mind. In slavery's ideological framework, Barrett maintains that "[r]ace as a symbolic boundary is conflated with literacy as a symbolic boundary, a conflation both overdetermined by and reifying the antithesis of body and mind" (420). The fusion of these various symbolic categories occurs at the level of the body in different ways: for instance, access or restriction to literacy, or the occupation of the status of subject or object in antebellum America, hinged on which side of the mind–body split one was assigned.

Harper foregrounds America's discomforting and enduring fixation on black corporeality to ironize it and throw it into disarray. The poet subverts the depersonalization of the black subject by juxtaposing representations of the black body as object of the obliterating gaze with bodily representations of jazz and jazz musicians as human subjects. For example, in "Dear John, Dear Coltrane," the objectified black bodies of the opening lines blend seamlessly into the second–person account of the musician's biography—more specifically, into the narrative of Coltrane's own body and its decline due to liver cancer:

> Sex fingers toes
> in the marketplace
> near your father's church
> in Hamlet, North Carolina—
> witness to this love
> in this calm fallow of these minds,
> there is no substitute for pain:

genitals gone or going,
seed burned out. (*Songlines* 25, lines 1–10)

The effect of this association is a granting of voice and self to the previously silenced black subject. That is, Harper's conflation of John Coltrane's physicality with the discursive corporeality of unnamed slaves bestows voice and interiority upon the latter by virtue of the former's unquestioned expressiveness. By the poem's end, the silenced bodies of the past speak through the "expressive corporeality" of Coltrane's music, represented by the recurring echoes from *A Love Supreme* that appear with each reference to the musician's body and its pain:

Dawn comes and you cook
up the thick sin 'tween
impotence and death, fuel
the tenor sax cannibal
heart, genitals, and sweat
that makes you clean—
a love supreme, a love supreme—

* * * * *

So sick
you couldn't play *Naima*,
so flat we ached
for song you'd concealed
with your own blood,
your diseased liver gave
out its purity,
the inflated heart
pumps out, the tenor kiss,
tenor love:
a love supreme, a love supreme—
a love supreme, a love supreme— (*Songlines* 26, lines 43–54)

Furthermore, Harper's phallic accent in the poem—Coltrane's decline marked as "impotence," the recognition of "genitals" among the "heart" and "sweat" of the musician's performance—signifies on another unsettling trope: white anxiety over the black male body and the ensuing attempts to contain it. As Harper himself notes, the poem "begins with a catalogue of sexual trophies of whites, a lesson to blacks not to assert their manhood.

Black men are suspect because they are potent, and potency is obviously a great part of Coltrane's playing and of the music of contemporary black musicians" (qtd in O'Brien 97). By underscoring the phallic in "Dear John, Dear Coltrane," Harper addresses and condemns the practice of lynching as a vehicle through which whites historically sought to police the black male subject, particularly in the late nineteenth and early twentieth centuries. The poet calls attention to Coltrane's body to underscore how lynching constituted, as Robyn Wiegman writes,

> the imposition of an extreme corporeality that defined [the African American male subject's] distance from the privileged ranks of citizenry. With the advent of Emancipation and its attendant loss of the slave system's marking of the African-American body as property, lynching emerged to reclaim and reassert the centrality of black male corporeality, deterring the now theoretically possible move toward citizenry and disembodied abstraction. (94)

Harper's evocation of lynching's violence amidst the poem's historical juxtaposition marks the act's ongoing relevance, its ongoing significance as a symbolic gesture of white domination.

Repeatedly, Harper uses an exaggerated emphasis on the jazz musician as supermasculine entity to subvert two enduring misrepresentations created by the distorting power of a dominant white gaze: the first is of the African American jazz virtuosi, and the second, by extension, is of the black male subject. In Harper's poetry, the black jazz musician constitutes an iconic representation of black masculinity as a whole. Thus, Harper's casting of Charlie Parker as "the hardest, longest penis / in the Mississippi urinal" in "'Bird Lives': Charles Parker in St. Louis," parodies the tendency of the white spectator to imagine its black male Other as a figure of exaggerated sexual potency (*Songlines* 50, lines 28–29). Recall, as Frantz Fanon argues, this racialized hyperbole stems from a psychological need among whites to depersonalize the black subject by overstating male difference. Thus, "[t]he white man is convinced that the Negro is a beast; if it is not the length of the penis, then it is the sexual potency that impresses him. Face to face with this man who is 'different from himself,' he needs to defend himself. In other words, to personify The Other" (170).[24]

This discourse of black corporeality frequently finds it way into writing on jazz because the music seems unavoidably governed by a genius of the body. That is, because jazz improvisation, by its very nature, eschews the studied recreation of fixed texts and pre-composed repertory, the aesthetic character of the music appears to emerge simply from each performer's physical self. Jazz emphasizes the performer before the composer; thus, the brilliance of Charlie Parker's or John Coltrane's music is absent when either Bird or Trane leaves the building. As Bruce Johnson suggests, the centrality of improvisation in jazz is frequently misunderstood when observed through the mind–body hierarchy that dominates European cultural discourses. European "high culture," Johnson suggests, venerates art that comes from the mind, which it reads as the "site of the highest civilization" (3). As such, discourses informed by this ideology tend to denigrate jazz and regard it as a lower form, crudely visceral because it is a music in which "the body is the primary site of the music" (3). This is a trope that begins in early assessments like Anne Shaw Faulkner's "Does Jazz Put the Sin in Syncopation?" but endures throughout later periods, even after the music had made a supposed entry into the mainstream. Even seemingly sympathetic discourses ascribe an inexorable physicality to jazz music. The music's mythology frequently turns on a celebration of physical bravado in its estimation of jazz genius. While occasional legends in jazz, such as Miles Davis or Lester Young, may be appreciated for a softness of approach, the music's standard for admiration is generally superhuman physicality, a hyperbolic propensity for bandstand feats of derring–do. Consider, for example, Louis Armstrong's assertion that the famed New Orleans trumpet player Buddy Bolden "used to blow so loud and strong that, on a still day, they say, you could hear him a mile away" (*Swing* 12). Or observe the explicit suggestion of physical violence in the way Nat Hentoff describes Coleman Hawkins's famous cutting contests on tenor saxophone in the 1930s: "Like a fabled gunslinger for whom everyone would make more than ample room when he came into a bar, Hawkins would stride into a town and wait to be challenged. He never showed much outward emotion, but his eyes gleamed in anticipation of the next slaughter of the innocents" (*Listen* 43). This jazzman-as-physical-hero theme dominates the music's own oral history and is central to naturalizing the otherwise–produced suggestion that jazz is an inherently masculine enterprise. One of the most notable (and most humorous) examples of this discourse occurs in the title to Charles Mingus's musical memorial to Charlie Parker, "If Charlie Parker Was a Gunslinger, There'd Be a Lot of Dead Copycats."

Harper signifies on this discourse by describing the corporeality of African American musicians in overstated terms. The poet frequently ascribes an overt sexuality to the musician's black body while he foregrounds its materiality. A representative example is "Elvin's Blues," a dramatic monologue in which Harper constructs Coltrane's longtime drummer, Elvin Jones, as a figure of phallic intensity and grotesquely masculine viscerality. I quote it in its entirety:

Sniffed, dilating my nostrils,
the cocaine creeps up my
leg, smacks into my groin;
naked with a bone for luck,
I linger in stickiness,
tickled in the joints;
I will always be high—

Tired of fresh air,
the stone ground bread,
the humid chant of music
which has led me here,
I reed my song:

"They called me the black
narcissus as I devoured
'the white hopes'
crippled in their inarticulate
madness,
Crippled myself,
Drums, each like porcelain
chamber pots, upside down,
I hear a faggot insult my
white wife with a sexless grin,
maggots under his eyelids,
a candle of my fistprint
breaks the membrane of his nose.
Now he stutters."

Last Thursday, I lay with you
tincturing your womb
with aimless strokes I could not feel.
Swollen and hard the weekend,
penitent, inane
I sank into your folds,
or salved your pastel tits,
but could not come.

Sexless as a pimp,
dying in performance
like a flare gone down,
the tooth of your pier

hones near the wharf.
The ocean is breathing,
its cautious insomnia—
driven here and there—
with only itself to love.

(Songlines 7–8)

Harper's choice of Jones as subject is apt here, considering a perpetual tendency in jazz commentary to cast the drummer's genius in primitive, physical terms—a depiction that too often seems to turn on racial essentialism. For example, in the liner notes to an upbeat 1964 recording between saxophonist Stan Getz and pianist Bill Evans—two white players generally lauded for the delicacy of their playing—James Isaacs calls attention to the anomalous nature of the session's hardness. "The brighter musical hues" of the record, Isaacs notes, "contrast boldly with the cooler or more melancholy colors that were primary in both principals' palettes" (liner notes). Isaacs explains the break from Getz's "melodic mastery" and Evans's "singularly introspective artistry" by acknowledging the influence, on drums, of a dark presence from without— "a force of nature named Elvin Jones" (liner notes). Picking up on this representational trend in his dramatic monologue, Harper casts Jones as unceasingly violent, a phallic threat. However, the poet's move subverts the primitivist bent of the discourse it adopts by tending toward repulsive language. While the primitivism of Isaacs's writing comes from celebratory intentions, Harper problematizes that celebration of the jazz musician as physical dynamo by throwing the trope into grotesque hyperbole. Thus, Jones's viscerality is vicious and infertile, his ostensible potency presented in a sterile but relentless sexual encounter. Likewise, the drummer's musical genius—evidenced by his momentous acts of physical performance—is denigrated through metaphor. The drums on which he excels, besting his white contemporaries, are cast in scatological terms, as upturned chamber pots, redolent, presumably, with the excess of physicality—that is to say, shit. Like Charlie Parker with "the hardest longest penis in the Mississippi urinal" in "*'Bird Lives!,'*" the jazz musician is reduced to exaggerated body as a site of corporeal excess.

Harper's juxtaposition of hyperbolic sexuality and corporeal excess is transgressive, aimed at unsettling the high–low, self–Other binaries that thrive amidst white supremacy and inform representations of the black body. Harper's representations provoke a white ambivalence about the black body that moves between affected disgust and unchecked desire, and troubles the easy binary that white discourses attempt to assert between the "purity" of the white body and the "grotesqueness" of its black Other. As Peter Stallybrass and Allon White suggest, the primary site of contradiction [in the formulation of social hierarchies], the site of conflicting desires and mutually incompatible representation, is undoubtedly the "low." Again and again we find a striking ambivalence to the representations of the lower strata (of the body, of literature, of society, of place) in which they are both reviled and desired. Repugnance and fascination are the twin poles of the process in which a *political* imperative to reject and eliminate the debasing "low" conflicts powerfully and unpredictably with a desire for this Other. (4–5, original emphasis)

Stallybrass and White argue that the symbolic assertion of the low—of, for instance, the "grotesque body"—disrupts the perpetuation of these social hierarchies by upsetting that desire and constantly reminding the dominant class of that which it seeks to disown. Explaining the process of this transgressive resistance in detail, they write:

A recurrent pattern emerges: the "top" attempts to reject and eliminate the "bottom" for reasons of prestige and status, only to discover, not only that it is in some way frequently dependent upon that low–Other [. . .] but also that the top *includes* the low symbolically, as a primary eroticized constituent of its own fantasy life. The result is a mobile, conflictual fusion of power, fear and desire in the construction of subjectivity: a psychological dependence upon precisely those Others which are being rigorously opposed and excluded at the social level. (5, original emphasis)

Harper's use of jazz musicians here is particularly important because, as Ingrid Monson argues, jazz musicians after bebop, with their avant–garde, "outsider" style, have too often been received by whites in stereotypical terms that associate nonconformity with "sensual intensity" and "social transgression" ("Problem" 405, 413).

Accordingly, Harper repeatedly juxtaposes the celebration of the jazzman's visceral supermasculinity with grotesque corporeality in his Coltrane poems. Recall, in "Dear John, Dear Coltrane," for instance, the tenor saxophonist is reduced to a twofold failure of the body: the sickness of the liver that eventually claimed his life and the impotence that Harper imagines as a result of that malady:

Loss, so great each black
woman expects your failure
in mute change, the seed gone.

*****

So sick
you couldn't play *Naima,*
so flat we ached
for song you'd concealed
with your own blood (*Songlines* 25–6, lines 16–18, 43–47)

While less overtly phallic, "Solo" also emphasizes the grotesqueness of
Coltrane's physical decline:

Infections of the middle ear
gave you the inflection
you couldn't hear,
patterns given in pleurisy,
each breath killing your timing
until you drowned (*Songlines* 171, lines 15–20)

In "Pulp Notes," Harper casts Coltrane's physical degeneration in canni-
balistic terms:

Smack took my wrists
but the blood wouldn't give up
until I developed cancer,
no musician's disease,
a string man raised on pigmeat
eating himself. (*Songlines* 179, lines 31–36)

Thus, Harper uses Coltrane's collapse to represent the ultimate futility of
celebrating the jazzman's exaggerated physicality, challenging that myth of
the body by underscoring its artificiality. If jazz is merely a genius of the
body then its expressive power is ultimately doomed because Coltrane's
body will inevitably decay. Rather than reconfigure the primitivist bent of
jazz discourse into a "strategic essentialism" by celebrating the jazzman as
physical hero, Harper deconstructs the discourse with an exaggeration of
its central precepts. The bodily aspects of the jazzman's physicality are
emphasized to the point of disgust.

But Harper's dialogue with the discourse of African American corporeality is not always centered on the black male subject. Rather, the poet
resists the dominant, male–centered view of black community that Philip
Brian Harper has outlined: namely, that "healthy" African American identity is "fundamentally weakened wherever [black] masculinity appears to
be compromised" (*Men* ix). The poet's reparative dialogue with America's

dominant discourses does not subsume African American female subjectivity within an exclusively masculinist venture. Instead, he vocalizes the way that black women have also been wronged by a discursive matrix that simultaneously negates and controls blackness. Music is metaphorically central to this strand in his work as well, as in his memorial to Bessie Smith, "Last Affair: Bessie's Blues Song." The poem laments the accidental death of the great blues singer and emphasizes the loss of her expressivity as a violation of the singer's body:

> Disarticulated
> arm torn out,
> large veins cross
> her shoulder intact,
> her tourniquet
> her blood in all–white big bands:
>
> *Can't you see*
> *what love and heartache's done to me*
> *I'm not the same as I used to be*
> *this is my last affair*
>
> Mail truck or parked car
> in the fast lane,
> afloat at forty–three
> on a Mississippi road,
> Two–hundred pound muscle on her ham bone,
> 'nother nigger dead 'fore noon.
>
> *Can't you see*
> *what love and heartache's done to me*
> *I'm not the same as I used to be*
> *this is my last affair*
>
> Fifty–dollar record
> cut the vein in her neck,
> fool about her money
> toll her black train wreck,
> white press missed her fun'ral
> in the same stacked deck:

Can't you see
what love and heartache's done to me
I'm not the same as I used to be
This is my last affair

Loved a little blackbird
heard she could sing,
Martha in her vineyard
pestle in her spring,
Bessie had a bad mouth
made my chimes ring:

Can't you see
what love and heartache's done to me
I'm not the same as I used to be
this is my last affair
                        (*Songlines* 63–64)

As with the poems that observe male musicians, Harper's speaker interrogates the discourse that, in attributing an exaggerated physicality to Smith, negates her interiority, her expressiveness. This is especially clear in the pun of the first line. "Disarticulated," the medical term that describes one of the injuries suffered by Smith in her fatal car crash (the separation of her arm from her body), also summarizes the voicelessness caused by the lack of white recognition that the speaker reports. Her significance as a notable black artist is undermined by a white spectatorship unwilling to see beyond the "negative" signifying power of her black body. Thus, in dying, even the Empress of the Blues is merely a "'nother nigger dead 'fore noon." Harper looks to redress that offense in the poem by installing the italicized echo of Smith's voice into this malevolent discourse. The poem's acknowledgment of Smith's lyricism—manifest in the recurring italicized verse—protects against its erasure in a discursive matrix that tries to diminish the loss of her voice as an incidental consequence of her body's demise.

Harper also vocalizes the importance of black female subjectivity to his dialogue with the discourse of black corporeality in "Blue Ruth: America." Written for a dying female relative, the poem is less overtly "musical" than the Bessie Smith memorial, but the nod to the blues in the title does mark its continuity with Harper's ongoing vernacular concerns. Moreover, the poem is the first in a sequence of poems entitled "Ruth's Blues," which recalls the blues' expressive power, even if it does not always mark explicit stylistic innovation on the form. "Blue Ruth: America" emphasizes the importance of its subject's existence to the preservation of an African American historical record, just as the Bessie Smith poem marks the blues singer's death as a threat to that record's security:

> I am telling you this:
>
> the tubes in your nose,
> in the esophagus,
> in the stomach;
> the small balloon
> attached to its end
> is your bleeding gullet;
> yellow in the canned
> sunshine of gauze,
> stitching, bedsores,
> each tactoe cut
> sewn back
> is America:
> I am telling you this:
> *history is your own heartbeat.* (*History* 3)

Though the poem makes an apparent concession to the discourse of black corporeality in its seemingly unironic appraisal of the black female subject as bodily object, Harper offsets that potential slip with the framing statement, "I am telling you this." On a literal level, the declaration emphasizes the importance of the black body's interiority to the subject it addresses— that is, the statement delineates Ruth's subjectivity by appealing to her not as corporeal flesh but as repository, a vital being in whom American history rests. Secondly, the second–person appeal of the poem's framing statement invokes Harper's ongoing American dialogue by extending the symbolic importance of Ruth's interiority to the reader. The poem asserts the crucial subjectivity of the supposedly dormant black body by superimposing it on the reader's own consciousness through the statement's direct appeal. Thus, Ruth's heartbeat is as central to American history as any other American reader would hope his or her own is. This rhetorical move is solidified with the savvy of the poem's title, "Blue Ruth: America," which juxtaposes the acknowledgment of Ruth's subjectivity (voiced by the invocation of her name) through African American expressivity (marked by the descriptor, "blue") and the country to which her being makes invaluable historical and discursive interventions. The continuity I suggest Harper marks through this gesture—between Ruth, as call, and reader, as response, in a communal formulation of historical record—seems compounded by the fact that this poem frames the "Ruth's Blues" sequence with "Here Where Coltrane Is," one of Harper's most telling testaments to both the strength of black genealogies, and the potential for cross–racial connection in America.

Naming is central to Harper's broad dialogue with America and constitutes another rhetorical gesture for which he is indebted to his post–war jazz influences. Jazz has always emphasized the performative importance of naming, for example, through its accent on nicknames (King Oliver, Duke Ellington, Armstrong as "Satchmo" or "Pops"), or, more importantly, in the music's fondness for self–commemorative song titles (Lester Young's "Lester Leaps In," Lionel Hampton's "Hamp's Boogie Woogie"). Bebop amplified the importance of naming, perhaps as another exaggerated rhetorical gesture within its ongoing Signifyin(g) bravado. Countless bebop compositions underscore the expressive identity of their creator through explicit naming in the title: Parker's "Ornithology," "Bird's Nest," "Carvin' the Bird," "Bird of Paradise," "Yardbird Suite," and "Bird Gets the Worm"; Gillespie's "Dizzy Atmosphere," "Birks' Works" (after the trumpeter's middle name), "Dizzier and Dizzier," and "Dizzy's Business"; Monk's "Thelonious," "Blue Monk," and "Monk's Mood."[25] And while these pioneering bebop musicians certainly made the act of naming a crucial part of their performance, the trend carried on beyond them, remaining central to the expressive projects of their descendants. Harper's muse, John Coltrane, for example, was especially inclined toward the act, with compositions like "Blue Train," "Traneing In," and "Chasin' the Trane." For these musicians, the act of naming seems inextricable from their political intentions, from their will to redress social inequities through expressive style.

Kimberly Benston analyzes the importance of this rhetorical move within identity formation in African American culture. Beginning with a discussion of Malcolm X's famous renunciation of "Little," his family's surname, Benston argues that "[f]or the Afro-American [. . .] self–creation and reformation of a fragmented familial past are endlessly interwoven: naming is inevitably genealogical revisionism" ("I yam" 152). The move, Benston maintains, turns on the discursive power of the name in slavery, and redresses the slave master's attempts to restrict black subjectivity through naming: "Language—that fundamental act of organizing the mind's encounter with an experienced world—is propelled by a rhythm of naming: it is the means by which the mind takes possession of the named, at once fixing the named as irreversibly Other and representing it in crystallized isolation from all conditions of externality" (Benston, "I yam" 152).

To redress this offense, then, the African American subject renames himself or herself in an effort to erase that legacy of subjection and formulate a new identity that thrives on its own self–marked history and communal ties.

Harper employs this strategy in his poetry, announcing his own identity through naming. At times, this naming is self–referential, an announcement of presence through the invocation of his own name, as with the title of his collected poems, *Songlines in Michaeltree*. More often, though, Harper uses naming to assert his identity within a larger community by invoking the names of others. As Benston notes, Harper is a key developer of "the Afro-American praise poem, a vehicle for pre-serving and extending the spiritual legacy of his forebears (literary, cul-tural and familial) by repeating and interpreting their 'good names'" ("I yam" 165). One famous example of this form, which Benston notes, is "Alice," in which Harper uses "the titular heroine" (Alice Walker) to "[weave] a lineage of strong black women (encompassing Zora Neale Hurston and Harper's grandmother) and [bind himself] to it by 'writing / your name in theirs and in mine'" (165). The poet engages with jazz tra-dition in a similar way, through a constant celebratory naming of the jazz musicians by whom he is influenced: John Coltrane, most obviously, but also Charlie Parker, Elvin Jones, Bessie Smith, Bud Powell ("For Bud"), Paul Chambers ("Mr P.C."), Wes Montgomery ("Movin' Wes"), and Wayne Shorter ("On First Listening to *Native Dancer* by Wayne Shorter"). This act of naming establishes Harper's place in a jazz–based "continuum of consciousness" (to use the poet's own phrase). It also mimics jazz's own tendency toward invoking the name, which can include motivated homage through the naming of other musicians: for instance, Charles Mingus's "Duke Ellington's Sound of Love," or Thelo-nious Monk's "In Walked Bud."

In the poet's early poem, "Brother John," naming constitutes a central expressive mode. It is not, however, merely an acknowledgment within the title, but is the aesthetic means through which Harper develops his the-matic interests. I quote the poem at length:

Black man:
I'm a black man;
I'm black; I am—
A black man; black—
I'm a black man;
I'm a black man;
I'm a man; black—
I am—

Bird, buttermilk, bird—
smack, booze and bitches
I am Bird
baddest nightdreamer
on sax in the ornithology-world
I can fly—higher, high, higher—
I'm a black man;
I am; I'm a black man—

Miles, blue haze,
Miles high, another bird,
more Miles, mute,
Mute Miles, clean,
bug-eyed, unspeakable,
Miles, sweet Mute,
sweat Miles, black Miles;
I'm a black man;
I'm black; I am;
I'm a black man—

Trane, Coltrane; John Coltrane;
it's tranetime; chase the Trane;
it's a slow dance,
it's the Trane
in Alabama, acknowledgment,
a love supreme,
it's black Trane; black;
I'm a black man; I'm black;
I am; I'm a black man—

Brother John, Brother John
plays no instrument;
he's a black man; black;
he's a black man; he is
Brother John; Brother John—

I'm a black man; I am;
black; I am; I'm a black
man; I am; I am;
I'm a black man;
I'm a black man;

I am; I'm a black man;
I am:

(*Songlines* 3–4)

Dedicated to the fiction writer, John O. Stewart, "Brother John" reveals Harper's inclination for naming at its most involved. Using a stylized repetition and an almost ritualistic invocation of names, the poem formulates an antiphonal engagement with Harper's contemporary, Stewart, and his musical forbears, Charlie Parker, Miles Davis, and John Coltrane. Throughout, Harper's speaker imagines a new genealogy for himself, denoted by the title's naming of Stewart as "Brother John," and in the continual placement of the speaker's "I" voice within named appeals to the various musicians. Ultimately, this "genealogical revisionism" (to use Benston's phrase) acknowledges the expressive importance of the various figures it references, but also stimulates a dialogical tension between the identity of Harper's speaker and those of his antecedents. The named references to the musicians, for example, are continually displaced by the assertion of the speaker's "I." Eventually, the poem's first–person voice emerges alone, in the final stanza, which notes the enduring existence of Harper's personal voice with the open–ended statement "I am:" that closes the poem. In this way, "Brother John" is emblematic of Harper's ongoing dialogue with the world at large. It is one of the most representative statements of his continual negotiation of tradition, of community, and of America: an antiphonal engagement in which Harper's work answers previous calls while it anticipates other responses from without.

Chapter Five:

Albert Murray Brings It On Home: Revisioning Black Modernism in *Train Whistle Guitar*

In a sense, the fiction of Albert Murray carries the jazz–modernist tradition I have charted throughout this book full circle, maintaining the combined social and aesthetic interventions of Hughes, Ellison, and Harper by working against the myth of jazz music's constant stylistic progress and directing its gaze at the past. Whereas the other work I have examined used jazz to innovate American modernism through stylistic novelty and contemporaneous appeals to radical politics, Murray's work articulates its polemic and its aesthetic advance through "the shock of the old." His fiction, first published in the 1970s, looks back on the myths and expressivity that collect African American experience, primarily through its attention to past jazz styles. Indeed, I contend that it is Murray's use of jazz that enables him to assert the enduring importance of the black vernacular, and, at the same time, to re-envision history, repositioning African American traditions more centrally in the American imagination.

However, despite Murray's emphasis on revisiting and preserving America's cultural past, it would be myopic to describe his work merely as a kind of twentieth–century conservatism.[1] Rather, his retrospective narration heeds one of jazz's most integral, inherent aesthetic properties: experimental play with tradition, in which the individual soloist sorts out those qualities congruous with his personal style and rejects those that do not conform to it. For Murray, experimentation in the arts should not signify a departure from tradition but rather its preservation. As he writes in *The Hero and the Blues*, experimentation is "an action taken to insure that nothing endures which is not workable; as such, far from being anti–traditional, as is often assumed, it actually serves the best interests of tradition, which, after all, is that which continues in the first place" (71). Murray sees this elective interaction with the past as central to modernism in both music and literature; both the jazz musician and the writer must improvise against the past in a jam session with all that has gone before. In this way, Murray offers a vernacular complement to T.S. Eliot's famous argument from "Tradition and the Individual Talent": "No poet, no artist of any art, has his complete meaning alone. His significance, his appreciation is the appreciation of his relation to the dead poets and artists. [. . . W]hat happens when a new work of art is created is something that happens simultaneously to all the works of art which preceded it" (49–50). Accordingly, in practice, Murray marks his affiliation with his fellow jazz–modernists by stylizing individual experience.

In his seminal novel, *Train Whistle Guitar,* Murray recuperates earlier jazz styles and retrieves past moments from a collective African American memory within the narrative of an autobiographical *bildungsroman.*[2] Murray does so, I argue, to present his own variation on a modernist project of artistic self–creation while simultaneously enabling the preservation of a collective black history and culture against the threat of negation and erasure. In all, Murray's retrospective riffs on American culture, in narrating Scooter's coming-of-age, impart cultural history through a multilayered analogy: Scooter's life mirrors the development of jazz, which itself is a kind of shorthand for American "mongrel modernism" overall. For Murray, American culture is necessarily hybrid. As he writes:

> Identity is best defined in terms of culture, and the culture of the nation over which the white Anglo–Saxon power elite exercises such exclusive political, economic, and social control is not all–white by any measurement ever devised. *American culture, even in its most rigidly segregated precincts, is patently and irrevocably composite. It is, regardless of all the hysterical protestations of those who would have it otherwise, incontestably mulatto.* Indeed, for all their traditional antagonisms and obvious differences, the so–called black and so–called white people of the United States resemble nobody else in the world so much as they resemble each other. (*Omni* 22, original emphasis)

The specific implications of this cultural hybridity inform Murray's entire creative project. Speaking of himself and Ralph Ellison in the preface to their published letters, Murray recalls:

> Ellison and I regarded ourselves as being the heirs and continuators of the most indigenous mythic prefiguration of the most fundamental

existential assumption underlying the human proposition as stated in the Declaration of Independence, which led to the social contract known as the Constitution and as specified by the Emancipation Proclamation and encapsulated in the Gettysburg Address and further particularized in the Thirteenth, Fourteenth, and Fifteenth amendments. (xxiii)

Indeed, Murray's cultural criticism offers a blueprint for his narrative project: to integrate the specificity of his own distinctly Southern African American experience into America's own grand historical narrative. As John Gennari astutely notes: "Read alongside his critical and polemical essays and interviews, Murray's fiction would seem to have as its subject not simply the coming-of-age of an Alabama schoolboy, but the history and destiny of America itself" ("Slumming" 60). Murray's narrative is the dramatized end–product of what he calls the "vernacular imperative": "*to process (which is to say to stylize) the raw native materials, experiences, and the idiomatic particulars of everyday life into aesthetic (which is to say elegant) statements of universal relevance and appeal*" (*Nada* 77, original emphasis). Thus, his goal as a writer is to process his own local particulars into accessible dramatizations of universal human experience—or at least Murray's own idea of it.

In Murray's eyes, jazz is the medium which best meets the vernacular imperative. For example, as he writes of Duke Ellington, whom he considers the greatest of jazz composers, "no American artist working in any medium whatsoever in any generation has ever fulfilled the vernacular imperatives more completely and consistently. Not even Walt Whitman, Mark Twain, among the most illustrious of his literary ancestors" (*Nada* 78–79). Furthermore, Murray contends that "the 'jam session' [is] the representative anecdote for life in the United States" ("Improvisation" 192).[3] And if the jam session best captures the "antagonistic co-operation" of American life (a term Murray borrows from Ellison), then the jazz musician with his special talent for improvisation is the "representative man, [the] *hombre de epoca*, [the] all–purpose protagonist, whose personal best is exemplary" (*Nada* 16). For Murray, Americans are the representative people of the twentieth century, and jazz musicians are the quintessential Americans. As the character Jewel Templeton, a film actress and self–styled philosopher says in Murray's late novel, *The Seven League Boots, el hombre de epoca* "should be the natural product of the American experience, that [American] schools should be geared to turning out, given the ready accessibility to modern innovations in ever more precise and efficient communication and transportation facilities we enjoy" (206). Later in that same novel, Jewel's mentor, a knowledgeable French aristocrat, expands on this, proclaiming that jazz is the constitutive embodiment of modern American mobility and cultural hybridity, and thus best evokes twentieth–century life in total: "I insist that your wonderful American music is anything but the folk art of a subculture. It is the music that I find to be the very embodiment of the rhythms and disjunctures along with the sonorities and cacophonies of our epoch" (*Boots* 310). Read alongside Murray's cultural criticism, his fiction does seem, as Gennari argues, to offer an extended jazz–centered history of American culture. The views expressed here seem drawn directly from Murray's essays, in which he foregrounds the music's importance in statements like, "*it was through Louis Armstrong's definitive influence on jazz that the United States has registered its strongest impact on contemporary aesthetic procedure*" (*Nada* 54, original emphasis). And the rhetorical focus on jazz in Murray's cultural criticism and fiction is key to the writer's political project: to stress the valuable particulars of African American experience in discussions of universalism, and to redress past misrepresentations of the black American subject.

Yet Murray's relationship to jazz goes beyond commentary and rhetorical exercise. As John F. Callahan notes, the writer has an "almost proprietary" interest in the music ("Introduction," *Trading* ix). Murray's standards for jazz are high; in his mind, it is a medium designed for "heroic self–expression," to use his words, for the exaltation of the self within and against historical contexts (qtd in Wood 18). For example, ever trenchant when faced with a soloist who fails to meet Murray's standards for individualistic innovation and historical reverence, Murray comments on the stagnancy of second–generation bebop players in a 1959 letter to Ralph Ellison:

> The Curse of Charlie Parker is right. A bunch of birdshit scratchers. Most guys these days are not even passable creative musicians any more. A bunch of studio hacks. These guys are even more dependent on somebody else's clichés than our avante garde [sic] literary bores. These guys are concerned with fashion, not music. Old Duke is still reaching back, man; and when he hits, the continuity is always there, the newness, individuality, and the relevance. [. . .] (*Trading* 212)

Keeping his investment in tradition in mind, one is unsurprised perhaps to note that Murray has been active since the 1970s in shaping the direction that mainstream jazz has taken. As mentor to the influential jazz trumpeter, Wynton Marsalis, and as one of the creative directors of New York's Jazz at Lincoln Center program (along with Marsalis and Stanley

Crouch), Murray has tried to direct a younger generation's point of view back toward the past, emphasizing the importance of traditional jazz, of earlier modes of antiphonal performance, and of musical celebration as saving graces against the existential crises of contemporary American life. An elder statesman among American intellectuals, Murray suggests throughout his work that a turn to the past can constitute experiment, that engagement with expressive traditions need not always focus on novelty and disjunction. All of these notions figure into his novel, *Train Whistle Guitar,* and into his larger intellectual goal—to assert the vitality of African American culture and highlight its redemptive possibilities for America as a whole. As Murray himself says: "Today, America's only possible hope is that the *Negroes* might save us, which is what we're all trying to do. We've got Louis [Armstrong], Duke [Ellington], Count [Basie], and Ralph [Ellison], and now we're trying to do it with Wynton and Stanley. That's all we are—just a bunch of Negroes *trying* to save America" (qtd in Boynton 101, original emphasis).

By the 1970s, jazz, as one popular narrative of its history goes, was dead, or all but. Traditional jazz, that is, that music played by mainly acoustic combos with an emphasis on improvisation and swing, appeared less often in clubs or on record. Gone were young lions in big suits and berets, signifying on the changes to "How High the Moon." Jazz fusion, an electric amalgamation of rock, funk, and jazz, had become the sound of choice among younger musicians. More often than not, the albums likely to appear in record bins filed under jazz were of this pop–sounding, plugged–in style: Herbie Hancock and the Headhunters, with their Sly Stone–derived funk–soul grooves; Weather Report, with Joe Zawinul on synthesizer, and an electro–jazz fantasia; the Latin–tinged fusion of Return to Forever with Chick Corea on electric piano.[4] Beyond its tendency toward the electric and the electronic, jazz fusion broke with jazz tradition in its aesthetics. For one, the music was rhythmically centered around rock's steady 4/4 time, rather than the "uneven" syncopation of swing. As well, the music was more produced, defying the "haphazard" group improvisation of earlier jazz styles, and emphasizing instead an orchestrated studio polish with occasional solo breaks. Fusion was practiced, sounding more like contemporary pop music without the vocals, rather than the unrehearsed, potentially perilous music of earlier jazz styles. Its slickness was a far cry from, say, the first–take tightrope–walking of Miles Davis's *Kind of Blue,* a recognized landmark of group improvisation that nonetheless reveals the imperfection of the human touch, as with alto saxophonist Cannonball Adderley's uncertainty on the track "Flamenco Sketches."

Some versions of this "death of jazz" narrative appeal to aesthetics, arguing that the music collapsed under its own propensity for change. Having gone through so many stylistic shifts in the first three–quarters of a century—dixieland, swing, bop, free jazz—the music ran out of momentum, as it were. After all, what direction could experimentation take after Ornette Coleman and company had dismantled so many of the structures central to the music's performance? As Scott DeVeaux notes, free jazz precipitated an "inevitable" crisis in jazz, since it exaggerated a "narrative of jazz history" based on a "chain of continuous innovation" ("Constructing" 549). Thus, in this version of the music's history, the turn to fusion marks less a complete abandonment of jazz history than a necessary move toward novelty, answering the music's insistent call to make it new, to say what had not been said before.[5] Aside from an ostensibly "inherent" call for novelty in the jazz aesthetic, the other reason for fusion's proliferation in the 1970s was surely commercial. The music's rock–tinged sound appealed to listeners raised on the Top 40 in ways that previous jazz styles had not needed to. In the past, before the popularity of rock and roll, jazz improvisers had maintained an active engagement with popular music, recording current tunes from Tin Pan Alley, or from Broadway musicals. Rock music, perhaps because of its reliance on relatively simple chord progressions and rigid rhythmic feels, produced less "standard" material for improvisation. To preserve a viable economic place in a music industry flooded by non–jazz, jazz, it seems, compromised by moving closer to the hit parade.

As the 1970s moved toward the 1980s, the disappearance of traditional jazz did appear imminent; commercialism and innovation were flourishing at the expense, it seemed, of the music's history, of ties between what musicians were doing in the present and what had gone before. Certainly a number of musicians were still playing acoustic jazz, emphasizing swing and traditional improvisation, but that form had ceased to be the dominant mode. And for those who perceived jazz as an expressive repository of African American history and culture, in particular, the change was alarming. As Tom Piazza writes:

> [T]he sense of why jazz was important—of what jazz *was* in the first place—had become diluted; the music needed a revivifying, organizing metaphor. Certainly there was a sense that few young musicians, especially young black musicians, were bothering to learn how to play jazz anymore; few even seemed to ask what was involved in learning to play jazz. Most young musicians who thought they were learning to play jazz were learning from fusion and funk records, along with a handful of Coltrane records. The sense that in order to learn how to play jazz,

whatever that meant, you might have to go back and study, really dig
into some roots that extended back before the 1960s, was all but
unheard of, except among a handful of young white players who tried
to sound and dress like 1930s swing musicians. These archivist types
[. . .] could play very convincingly in the styles of earlier players, but
they were anachronisms, members of a consciously retro movement
rather than players bent on reimagining the idiom for themselves. (6)

Amidst these currents, Albert Murray began publishing the books that would
define him as a novelist, a cultural critic, and a jazz scholar. Murray's work, in
all its varied forms, pointed to an African American reclamation of the jazz
tradition, and insisted on the importance of that musical heritage in defining
American culture on the whole. The calls that he made in books like the novel,
Train Whistle Guitar, the essay collection, *The Omni-Americans,* and the
music history, *Stomping the Blues,* were responded to in kind by a group of
younger musicians who came of age in the 1980s and nineties. As Ted Gioia
writes of *Stomping the Blues,* in particular:

The publication of [. . .] Murray's book [. . .] served as an influential
attempt to recall jazz back to its origins as African-American music.
Murray emphasized the critical role of the blues [. . .] and celebrated
the sense of swing, so important to the jazz tradition, yet increasingly
obscured in contemporary currents of improvisation. Although Murray
could hardly have seen it at the time, his words would prove prophetic.
A new generation of jazz players, who came to prominence during the
next decade, would champion this same cause, initiating a host of new
efforts that attempted to promote the inherently African-American elements of the jazz tradition. (381)

This reclamation of the jazz tradition by young African American players
was led musically by the New Orleans trumpeter, Wynton Marsalis, a tech-
nically prodigious musician who came of age during the 1970s playing
bebop in a late incarnation of Art Blakey's Jazz Messengers.[6]

From the beginning of his career, Marsalis was audacious and outspoken, a young man brave enough to denounce the fusion work of Miles
Davis and lament the passing of jazz's acoustic age. But while Marsalis was
initially grounded creatively in the post–bop sound of the 1960s, under the
tutelage of Murray and Murray's disciple, Stanley Crouch, the young trumpeter's style became more musically comprehensive, looking past Coltrane
and Davis back to Armstrong and Ellington.[7] And off the bandstand,
Marsalis's expressed philosophy about art began to bear Murray's distinct

influence as the 1980s progressed—specifically, in Marsalis's arguments about the importance of jazz not just as black music but also as an emotional and intellectual cornerstone in American culture as a whole. Under Murray's influence, notes Tony Scherman, "Marsalis came to accept the idea that lies at the heart of his thinking on jazz—namely, that jazz is the most American of art forms, the distillation of the American spirit" (67). Indeed, Marsalis's comments about the music in a 1989 interview with Tom Piazza are unmistakably Murray–esque. Expounding on its relationship to American culture and politics, the young trumpeter opines: "Jazz music [. . .] addresses all the complexities of the mythology of America. You have the negotiation between individual rights and group responsibility, all of it. Just like Martin Luther King was trying to make Americans be more American, that's what jazz music tries to do. It gives us a spiritual architecture" (qtd in Piazza 81). Considering the indebtedness of Marsalis's thinking to Murray's, and the trumpeter's own considerable influence on the generation of young tradition–minded jazz musicians that came of age in the 1980s and nineties, one cannot deny that Murray's place in the jazz–modernist literary tradition is profound.

Whereas Hughes, Ellison, and Harper were largely influenced by what was going on around them musically, absorbing aesthetic influences and political possibilities from contemporaneous jazz styles, Murray has been active in shaping the jazz milieu around him through his publications. In directing the movement of mainstream jazz back through the music's tradition, Murray has not only imagined social and artistic potential in the music as his jazz–literary predecessors did, but has helped younger musicians envision and realize those possibilities in their own conceptualization of the music. Murray's relationship to the jazz world enacts a return to the past that makes good on the writer's own longstanding intellectual and creative projects, as best expressed in his cultural criticism and in the novel, *Train Whistle Guitar.*

Murray's first published book, *The Omni-Americans* (1970), is a work of social criticism that responds to white and black perceptions of African Americans following the height of the Civil Rights Era. In Murray's view, by the late 1960s, Americans subscribed too easily to an artificial cultural separation of blacks and whites, buying into this division either through the insidious legacy of white supremacy or through Black Power's forceful counter–offensive. On either side, African Americans were continually victimized: depicted by whites as an enfeebled social responsibility, or perceived by black nationalists as a battered ethnic faction in the white man's world, a group under siege and perpetually in search of empowerment. Both views, Murray argues, were short–sighted. Countering the "folklore of white supremacy" and the "fakelore of black pathology," he suggests that the African American experience is one of vitality, power, and self–respect. Moreover, it is an essential component of America's national character.

To make this argument, Murray emphasizes black American culture's improvisatory style and resilience of imagination, qualities which make African Americans central to a more general American rhetoric of self–determination. As he expresses in the introduction to *The Omni-Americans,* his political project

> is based in large measure on the assumption that since the negative aspects of black experience are constantly being overpublicized (and to little purpose except to obscure the positive), justice to U.S. Negroes, not only as American citizens but also as the fascinating human beings that they so obviously are, is best served by suggesting some of the affirmative implications of their history and culture. (6)

The "national" implications of this reparatory move follow; in delineating the vitality and originality of African American expression, Murray argues for its influence on America at large and maintains that "[e]thnic differences are the very essence of cultural diversity and national creativity" (3).

Accordingly, diversity and hybridity are essential to Murray's conceptualization of American identity. An antithetical voice in the face of Black Power rhetoric, Murray resists separatist impulses in *The Omni-Americans* and proclaims the inseparability of African American experience from American culture. His thinking, by his own acknowledgment, is influenced by Constance Rourke's *American Humor: A Study of the National Character* (1931) and *The Roots of American Culture* (1942).[8] As Rourke maintains, American character is a composite of three archetypes: the Yankee, the Native backwoodsman, and the Negro. Each of these types marks America's "mood of disseverance," a willingness to break from tradition and exhibit resilience amidst struggle: the Yankee in his rebellion against European control, the backwoodsman in his mastery of the wilderness, the Negro in his resistance to slavery (qtd in Murray, *Omni* 16). Murray extends Rourke's vision of American hybridity by asserting that African Americans perhaps exemplify American ideals better than any of the cultural types she defines as key to the American national character. Though this formulation of hybridity is problematic—turning on the unchecked reiteration of Rourke's discrete symbolic "types" rather than proposing a critical assessment of cultural cross–influence and exploring the blurred boundaries of Bakhtin's "organic hybridization"—the benefits of Rourke's celebration of the American Negro for Murray's political–aesthetic project are obvious. In Murray's eyes, the black American's embodiment of American cultural standards begins with the history of fugitive slaves before Emancipation. "The slaves who absconded to fight for the British during the Revolutionary War," Murray writes

> were no less inspired by *American* ideas than those who fought for the colonies: the liberation that the white people wanted from the British the black people wanted from white people. As for the tactics of the fugitive slaves, the Underground Railroad was not only an innovation, it was also an *extension* of the American quest for democracy brought to its highest level of epic heroism (*Omni* 18, original emphasis).

Noting the ongoing paradoxes between American idealism and the exaggerated mythology of white America, Murray succinctly remarks, "Nobody tried to sabotage the Mayflower" (18). Through all of this, Murray extends Rourke's reading of American culture with a rhetoric decidedly indebted to W.E.B. Du Bois's in *The Souls of Black Folk:*

> [A] concrete test of the underlying principles of the great republic is the Negro Problem, and the spiritual striving of the freedmen's sons is the travail of souls whose burden is almost beyond the measure of their strength, but who bear it in the name of a historic race, in the name of this the land of their fathers' fathers, and in the name of human opportunity. (Du Bois, *Souls* 16)

Thus, Murray argues forcefully for a reconsideration of African Americans as quintessential representatives of the national character—they *are* "the omni-Americans" of his title—and he reasons, in turn, that black expressive culture is necessarily central to America's self–definition. Again, Murray emphasizes the historical importance of slavery in charting how African Americans have embodied the freedom and resourcefulness at the heart of American national idealism: "In spite of the restrictions and atrocities of the plantation system, the personal and social intercourse among slaves was so fabulous in the richness of its human fellowship, humor, esthetic inventiveness, and high spirits that the masters [. . .] could only pretend to shrug it off as childishness" (62). Citing the legacy of that historical versatility in contemporary African American life, Murray insists that jazz musical expression is a representative example of the black American's ability to improvise within the paradoxes of democracy:

[W]hen the Negro musician or dancer swings the blues, he is fulfilling the same fundamental existential requirement that determines the mission of the poet, the priest, and the medicine man. He is making an affirmative and hence exemplary and heroic response to that which André Malraux describes as *la condition humaine.* Extemporizing in response to the exigencies of the situation in which he finds himself, he is confronting, acknowledging, and contending with the infernal absurdities and ever–impending frustrations inherent in the nature of all existence *by playing with the possibilities that are also there.* Thus does man the player become man the stylizer and by the same token the humanizer of chaos; and thus does play become ritual, ceremony, and art; and thus also does the dance–beat improvisation of experience in the blues idiom become survival technique, esthetic equipment for living, and a central element in the dynamics of U.S. Negro life style. (58, original emphas is)

The redemptive possibilities Murray reads in African American culture seem a far cry from the social science conclusions he declaims; black America is not mired in victimhood, he argues, but always affirming itself in the face of struggle.[9]

If *The Omni-Americans* constitutes Murray's intervention into African American cultural politics based on reclaiming black expressive traditions, then 1976's *Stomping the Blues* is his most detailed explication of black music's specific importance to the myths and rituals in which he finds vitality and social consequence. In *Stomping the Blues,* Murray expands on his cultural riffs from *The Omni-Americans* and proposes jazz and blues music as its own unique philosophical tradition: a socially binding force that oscillates between stark existentialism and a humanistic faith in redemption. Here Murray continues his attacks on both the problematic misconceptions of sociology and the limitations of black nationalism. A polemical work and a historical narrative, *Stomping the Blues* celebrates past blues and jazz masters to accentuate the resilience and vigor of African American cultural life and to counter further damaging narratives of black victimhood.

Perhaps Murray's most significant rhetorical move in *Stomping the Blues* is the distinction he proposes between the blues and the "blues as such." The blues, as a musical form or expressive mode, is the core, he asserts, of African American vernacular expression. The "blues as such" is the existential crisis, or attack of the blue devils that the music attempts to redress. The crisis of the "blues as such" stimulates, in Murray's words, *"the most fundamental of existential imperatives: affirmation [. . .] and continuity in the face of adversity"* (6, original emphasis). Thus, blues expression is never an admission of self–defeat, but a stylized *acknowledgment* of adversity through which the performer takes control:

> The blues as such are synonymous with low spirits. Blues music is not. With all its so–called blue notes and overtones of sadness, blues music of its very nature and function is nothing if not a form of diversion. With all its preoccupation with the most disturbing aspects of life, it is something contrived specifically to be performed as entertainment. Not only is its express purpose to make people feel good, which is to say in high spirits, but in the process of doing so it is actually expected to generate a disposition that is both elegantly playful and heroic in its nonchalance. (45)

Thus, when Jimmy Rushing sings, "Good morning blues, blues how do you do?" with Count Basie's Orchestra, he is not yielding to the power of visiting demons, but stylizing his own resistance to them, standing up to adversity by acknowledging it and vocalizing his authority through humor.

Ostensibly, this delineation of difference between "blues as such" and blues music seems grounded only in aesthetic debate, but the distinction is crucial to Murray's post–civil rights call to reconsider attitudes about African Americans. The assumption of melancholy and defeat in blues expression that Murray counters with his explanation of its workings complements his broader engagement with the delusions of "social science fiction." The confusion he seeks to eradicate about black music is similar to the misunderstanding he critiques throughout *The Omni-Americans*, namely, that African Americans are victims without the capacity to handle the inequities America has thrust upon them. In explaining the philosophical foundations of blues and jazz, Murray argues how African American expressivity constitutes "equipment for living" and acts as a socially meaningful force. Central to this is the communal ritual of black musical performance, an event that Murray calls the "Saturday Night Function," in which African American musicians and their audiences enact an empowering rite through antiphony and exchange. Murray explains:

> [O]f all the age–old ways of dispelling the ominous atmosphere that comes along with the blues [as such], the one most people seem to have found to be the most consistently effective all told also turns out to be essentially compatible with a great majority of the positive impulses, urges, drives, cravings, needs, desires, and hence the definitive purposes, goals, and ideals of their existence. [. . .] The blues counteragent that is

so much a part of many people's equipment for living that they hardly ever think about it as such anymore is that artful and sometimes seemingly magical combination of idiomatic incantation and percussion that creates the dance–oriented good–time music also known as the blues.

Hence the dance hall as temple. Hence all the ceremonially deliberate drag steps and shaking and grinding movements during, say, the old downhome Saturday Night Function, and all the sacramental strutting and swinging along with all the elegant stomping every night at such long-since-consecrated ballrooms as, say, the old Savoy, once the glory of upper Manhattan. And hence in consequence the fundamental function of the blues musician (also known as the jazz musician), the most obvious as well as the most pragmatic mission of whose performance is not only to drive the blues away and hold them at bay at least for the time being, but also to evoke an ambiance of Dionysian revelry in the process. (16–17)

Murray thus concurs with the black nationalists who argued that art and social concerns are inextricable, but he differs from Black Arts figures in the African American art he champions.[10] The swinging rites of the dance hall reveal the complexity and verve of African American experience, he insists, and in that vital assertion of community lies the real emotional and political hope for blacks in the United States.

Furthermore, Murray's attention to jazz and blues aesthetics in *Stomping the Blues* asserts the music's place within American culture. In a chapter entitled, "Folk Art and Fine Art," Murray counters assessments of the blues idiom that mark that black musical expression as an untutored art form due to its folk beginnings. Opposing the primitivist misconceptions that plague readings of black vernacular expressivity, Murray contends:

[T]he assumption that folk expression is the unalloyed product of a direct stimulus/response interaction with natural environmental forces is fallacious. Folk expression is nothing if not conventional in the most fundamental sense of the word. Far from being spontaneous, as is so often supposed, it is formal. It is of its very nature traditional. The exact opposite of unadulterated invention growing out of the creative ingenuity of individuals uninhibited by regulations and unencumbered by the whims of fashion, it conforms to rigorously restrictive, local, regional, which is to say provincial, ground rules that have been so completely established and accepted as to require little if any enforcement as such beyond initiation and apprenticeship instruction. (203–04)

The blues idiom—the folk blues, the jazz that emerges from it—is undeniably a mode marked by a unique grammar and formal expectations. And while Murray argues that even at the folk level there is a sophistication to blues expression that is too often overlooked, he also argues that in the formal innovation of jazz, the blues idiom achieves a level of folk–inspired stylization that rivals the best of American so–called fine art. For Murray, no creative figure embodies this passage more than Duke Ellington, whose blues–tinged compositions are the quintessence of American expression. "Not unlike Emerson, Melville, Whitman, Twain, Hemingway, and Faulkner in literature," Murray writes, Ellington

> converted more of the actual texture and vitality of American life into first–rate universally appealing music than anybody else. Moreover, he [did] so in terms of such vernacular devices of blues musicianship as vamps, riffs, breaks, fills, call-and-response sequences, idiomatic syncopation, downhome folk timbres, drum–oriented horns, strings, and so on. (224)

In all, Murray is relentless in stressing the music's Americanness. For instance, his celebration of Ellington here extends the ongoing political project begun in *The Omni-Americans*. He asserts Ellington's place among the canonical figures of American literary expression and thus marks the connectedness of jazz to icons who defined the fixed repository of American ideas. Moreover, in assessing the specifics of Ellington's technique as composer, Murray validates various blues and jazz musical techniques, a gesture that breaks down ostensible division between black expressivity and American fine art. It asserts the inextricability of the blues idiom (and the African American vernacular) from the aesthetics and stylization that presumably define American artistic greatness. Jazz and blues are hybrid forms, he maintains, "native to the United States," a "synthesis of European and African musical elements, the product of an Afro-American sensibility in an American mainland situation" (63).

An attention to the aesthetics of the distinctly American blues idiom is always key to Murray's exaltation of black expressive life. Throughout *Stomping the Blues*, Murray is insistent about the control and discipline that inform African American vernacular performance. Redressing the ubiquitous misconception that the black vernacular's emphasis on improvisation thrives merely on unbound spontaneity, Murray is quick to argue that blues and jazz performance turn always on communal standards and cultivated traditions. "[B]lues–idiom merriment," he suggests, "is not marked either by the sensual abandon of the voodoo orgy or by the ecstatic trance of religious possession," but rather, by a "unique combination of spontaneity, improvisation, and control" (50). Community is also integral to the artistic discipline of the blues idiom; it is an expressive tradition shaped significantly by the shared standards of performer and audience. The context of each improvised statement yields essential aesthetic imperatives. As Murray writes, "no matter how deeply moved a musician may be, whether by personal, social, or even aesthetic circumstances, he must always play notes that fulfill the requirements of the context, a feat which presupposes far more skill and taste than raw emotion" (98). Thus, blues expressivity constitutes its own formal, "classical" tradition, a heritage defined by training, standards, and discipline.

Published in 1974, *Train Whistle Guitar* dramatizes the various polemical threads from these key works of cultural criticism, asking for a reconsideration of black culture within the United States. A seemingly simple coming-of-age narrative that traces the maturation of Scooter, a young African American, growing up in the deep South of the 1920s, the novel in fact enacts a reconsideration of history. Like the cultural criticism, *Train Whistle Guitar* revises long–accepted cultural divisions between blacks and whites. Like Ellison, his contemporary and close friend, Murray addresses the need to revise historical divisions between black and white in American cultural space. Throughout *Train Whistle Guitar*, Murray's adolescent hero, growing up in Gasoline Point, Alabama, recognizes conflicts between "book history" and the vernacular histories to which he is privy: the fireside reminiscences of his parents and their friends; the barber–shop signifying of the town's older men; the blues and jazz performances of Luzana Cholly, a guitar–playing drifter, and Stagolee Dupas, the town's resident jookhouse piano player. Murray fashions his novel from a jazz aesthetic on both representational and structural levels. The book looks to the music in its vivid descriptions of musical performance, and stylizes its narrative around attempts to evoke jazz sound through call-and-response figures, unorthodox semantics, and intertextual riffs.

Throughout, the novel illustrates the vitality and complexity of African American life through its vivid representations of black expressive rituals. As Warren Carson astutely writes, "Absent are the pathological and degrading implications so common to the historical and sociological interpretations offered by other scholars. Instead, Murray's theory of the black Southern experience pivots on the wholesomeness of the black community, especially in terms of how well the community prepares its young to cope with the larger society" (287). Furthermore, the narrative of Murray's novel dramatizes his own faith in "omni-Americanism," in the hybrid character of cultural life in the United States. His young protagonist, Scooter, revels in a kind of cultural versatility, equally at home in the indefinite "briar patch" of the African American vernacular and in the fixed canons of the local schoolhouse. Murray uses his hero's cultural dexterity to critique the ostensible division between the two cultures. Scooter's self–definition, throughout the novel, depends on a constant engagement with diverse expressive modes. Like a jazz performer negotiating the various complementary and antagonistic turns of history and tradition, Scooter determines his own character through a playful interaction with cultural influences. In this way, he mimics Murray's own assessment of the jazz and blues performer's musical self–definition in *Stomping the Blues:* "It is not so much what blues musicians bring out of themselves on the spur of the moment as what they do with existing conventions. Sometimes they follow them by extending that which they like or accept, and sometimes by counterstating that which they reject" (126).

Importantly then, Murray's novel foregrounds jazz's conventions of antiphony and dialogue, stylistically emphasizing statement and counterstatement throughout. Antiphonal figures—so central to black music, from gospel to blues to jazz—function throughout the book as affirmations of black community: a signal call is made by one speaker, demanding a response from another that performs their shared experience. In its opening second–person narration, for example, the book syntactically engages the reader in a call-and-response structure based on Scooter's reminiscences. The passage offers a stylistic enactment of community between text and reader:

> There was a chinaberry tree in the front yard of that house in those days, and in early spring the showers outside that window always used to become pale green again. Then before long there would be chinaberry blossoms. Then it would be maytime and then junebugtime and no more school bell mornings until next September, and when you came out onto the front porch and it was fair there were chinaberry shadows on the swing and the rocking chair, and chinaberry shade all the way from the steps to the gate. (1)

On one level, the style reflects the workings of memory; the "you" of the narration is the Scooter of the past consciously called into being by his narrating in the present. As Wolfgang Karrer argues, the narrator's "split of self address (I–you) [. . .] create[s] nostalgia, because [it] serve[s] to enhance the cathectic value of the memory traces and of the act of recalling them" (132). But the narration also extends its participatory reminiscences to the reader, creating at once community and historical consciousness. The antiphonal relationship of this extension is emphasized by the novel's italicized first–person "breaks," solo moments in which Scooter asserts himself as caller, emphasizing his sense of self outright and articulating his identity through voice and character. Consider, for instance, the passage that follows the novel's opening:

> *I used to say My name is also Jack the Rabbit because my home is in the briarpatch, and Little Buddy (than whom there was never a better riddle buddy) used to say Me my name is Jack the Rabbit also because my home is also in the also and also of the briarpatch because that is also where I was also bred and also born. (4)*

The turns to first–person assert Scooter's individual voice against the expressive collective he evokes into consciousness through the second–person narration. While the narrator invites participation and response from those he addresses throughout the novel, he also asserts his own expressive authority by emphasizing the centrality of his own "I."

As well, this early first–person section is especially important in its reflexive play with Scooter's concern about identity formation, and its insistence on musical expressivity as central to that self–definition. The passage continues:

> *And when I also used to say My name is also Jack the Bear he always used to say My home is also nowhere and also anywhere and also everywhere.*
>
> > *Because the also and also of all of that was also the also plus also of so many of the twelve–bar twelve–string guitar riddles you got whether in idiomatic iambics or otherwise mostly from Luzana Cholly who was the one who used to walk his trochaic–sporty stomping–ground limp–walk picking and plucking and knuckle knocking and strumming (like an anapestic locomotive) while singsongsaying Anywhere I hang my hat anywhere I prop my feet. Who could drink muddy water who could sleep in a hollow log. (4–5)*

Foregrounding the improvisational nature of Scooter's self–actualization, Murray shows his young hero here as unfixed in name: he is Scooter, yes, but "also Jack the Bear." Later, Scooter confirms his indeterminacy all the more, announcing that he "also used to call [himself] Jack the Nimble and Jack the Quick" (31). Murray's hero is willfully open to change and combinations; Scooter's (and Murray's) oft–used verbal lick, *"also and also,"* is itself a shorthand signifier for the hero's figurative place at the crossroads.

Fittingly, one of Scooter's signature gestures in moments of personal, emotional importance is the crossing of his fingers.

As the above passages register, Scooter's indeterminate qualities are informed by jazz expressivity. Indeed, Scooter's "also"s and crossed fingers connect him to Luzana Cholly, the novel's train–hopping bluesman, who defies fixity on both metaphorical and real levels in his tendencies toward self–mythologizing and travel. As Scooter recalls:

> I still cannot remember ever having heard anybody saying anything about Luzana Cholly's mother and father. [. . .] Nor did he seem to need a wife or a steady woman either. But that was because he was not yet ready to quit the trail and settle down. [. . .]
>
> The more I think about all of that the more I realize that you never could tell which part of what you heard about something he had done had actually happened and which part somebody else had probably made up. Nor did it ever really matter which was which. Not to anybody I ever knew in Gasoline Point, Alabama, in any case, to most of whom all you had to do was mention his name and they were ready to believe any claim you made for him, the more outrageously improbable the better. (14–15)

Cholly's fluidity inspires Scooter, who is quickly developing his own Signifyin(g) prowess. Both characters become, in the novel, part of the blues expressive matrix, which Houston Baker calls "a nonlinear, freely associative, nonsequential meditation" (*Blues* 5). Central to this matrix is the idea of the crossroads, offering an iconographic representation of the blues as "a point of ceaseless input and output, a web of intersecting, crisscrossing impulses always in productive transit" (3). In the novel, crisscrossing impulses in the formation of expressivity and performance are key to the community Scooter and Cholly enjoy. For Scooter, Cholly represents one set of performative possibilities in the quest for identity. His blues expression and wandering lifestyle signify vernacular histories and mobility, evident in the way "he was forever turning guitar strings into train whistles which were not only the once-upon-a-time-voices of storytellers but of all the voices saying what was being said in the stories as well" (15). Cholly embodies Baker's assertion that "blues and its sundry performers offer interpretations of the experiencing of experience" (7). Fittingly, then, Scooter performs various tributes to Cholly amidst his own inchoate self–creation—fashioning, for example, his own version of Cholly's "sporty–limp walk," or hopping a freight train with Little Buddy (9).[11]

While Scooter looks to Cholly as a mentor figure, the boy's antiphonal relationship with his contemporary Little Buddy is just as significant to his expressive self–creation. We find in the boys' relationship a jazz–based formation of identity that thrives on exchange. The complementary, antiphonal nature of their interaction is evident from the above "I" passage. Scooter's assertion of indeterminacy (in naming himself both Jack the Rabbit and Jack the Bear) is answered and extended by Buddy's paradoxical assertion of placelessness and omnipresence (his home being "nowhere," "anywhere," and "everywhere"). This mutual self–definition occurs throughout the novel, in the boys' various moments of Signifyin(g) and oral play. Much like Ellison's Buster and Riley, Murray's Scooter and Buddy continually form their own identities through performative interaction, as when they plan their freight–hopping adventure:

> Stand up, Little Buddy said, with his cap square too, Step down.
> And give me your hand for Chickasaw Bend, Alabama, I said and held my arms out palms up and then let them fall.
> Chickasaw Bend, Mobile County, Aladambama United Tits of a Milk Cow, one time, Little Buddy said.
> Been long hearing tell of it.
> And ain't but the one.
> Oh but will there be one?
> Oh stand up step up step down.
> Oh whosoever will.
> Let him come and give me your hand.
> And give God your heart, brother.
> One for Chickasaw.
> I thank you, praise be, I thank you.
> Two for Chickasaw Bend.
> Amen Amen Amen Amen.
> Hey, that's all right about your goddamn school, Little Buddy said.
> Hey, call us the goddamn school this time.
> We got your goddamn school, I said. I got your goddamn school right here. (39)

The boys' Signifyin(g) in this "leapfrog" exchange allows for the collaborative formation of identity based on rebellion from the conventional institutions of church and school. Their mock preacher–congregation exhortations parody the religion with which they have been raised, while their defiance about the "goddamn school" from which they are skipping to pursue their freight–train adventure girds them as renegade partners in crime. In resisting the conventions of society, while engaging *with* those very conventions, the boys enact a jazz–like communal performance. They signify on form (the sermon) and on custom (the expectation that they attend school). The cross–references of the performance recall the formal revision in jazz that Murray reads elsewhere in his cultural criticism. Noting, for example, that the "equipment for living" proffered by black music is comprehensive in its range of influences and unflinchingly playful in its reworking of other sources, Murray writes in *Stomping the Blues* that "[w]hatever were the ultimate origins of the solo–call/ensemble–riff-response pattern" in blues–based music, "the chances are that blues musicians adapted it from [. . .] church renditions" of popular spirituals (27), and that "the spirit of caricature" is essential to jazz borrowings from the church, as when Louis Armstrong "legitimized the iconoclasm of his secular use of sacred music with an unmistakable element of parody" (36).

Yet Scooter and Buddy's Signifyin(g) exchanges do not always function as motivated "parody" or "formal critique" (Gates, *Signifying* xvii). At times, their performance constitutes homage, as when they riff on Luzana Cholly's name and character. When the bluesman walks by, the boys erupt into a celebratory naming ritual:

> *Say hey now Mister Luzana Cholly.*
> *Mister Luzana Cholly one time.*
>
> * * * * *
>
> *Mister Luzana Cholly all night long.*
> *Yeah me, ain't nobody else but.*
> *The one and only Mister Luzana Cholly from Bogalusa bolly.* (11)

Alongside their fastidious efforts to copy his "sporty–limp walk," Scooter and Buddy's Signifyin(g) tributes solidify community through vernacular expression and enable an emerging self–definition through association. However, their efforts to produce individual performative characters are influenced by other local heroes as well. Planning their freight train episode, for instance, Scooter and Buddy wish they were joined by Gander Gallagher, a black man who once managed to steal wheels for a go–cart from "under a nightwatchman's nose" (20). Speaking in their usual hyberbolic acclaim, the boys express their desire to be like Gallagher by toasting that he could "steal lightning if he [had] to" (20). Furthermore, their performative appreciation of African American heroes extends beyond the local, as when Murray's narrator recalls a boyhood worship of Jack Johnson, the black heavyweight champ also lauded by Ellison's Buster and Riley. Scooter muses on

> *the also and also of Jack Johnson who was by all accounts and all odds*
> *the nimblest footed quickest witted Jack of them all; who could spring*
> *six feet backwards and out of punching range from a standstill, who*
> *could salivate a Spanish fighting bull with a six–inch uppercut, whose*
> *eyes and hands were so sharp that he could reach out and snatch flies*
> *from mid–air without crushing them.* (31–32, original emphasis)

In considering Johnson, Murray's narrator also recognizes the danger of performance for blacks in America. Imagining himself in the boxer's persona, Scooter acknowledges threats against a confident African American identity:

> *Because when the ku klux klan got mad and put on its white robes and*
> *started burning crosses just because somebody said bring me my coffee*
> *as black and strong as Jack Johnson and my scrambled eggs all beat up*
> *like poor old Jim Jeffries, I was the one they wanted to come and lynch.*
> *I was not as black or as big as Jack Johnson and I was never going to*
> *have all my hair shaved off, but all the same as soon as I stepped into*
> *the prize ring I was the one who had set out from Galveston, Texas,*
> *not only to see the sights of the nation and seek my fortune wherever*
> *the chances were, but also to become the undisputed heavyweight*
> *champion of the world.* (31–32, original emphasis)

Scooter is unflinching in his desire to be like the famous heavyweight and thus assume a militant stance against white supremacy and control. Embodying Murray's vernacular "equipment for living," the boy hero finds empowerment in identification with the nimble, quick–witted black standard–bearer. A far cry from the pathological victim role Murray insists that "social science fiction" imagines for young African Americans, Scooter suggests that performing a version of Johnson's identity fortified his social resolve, that he imagines crossing "old John L. Sullivan's color line" (of segregation in nineteenth–century boxing) "every time [he] stepped into the workout circle around the punching bag" (33).

As the novel progresses, Scooter's self–definition turns on a personal, jazz–informed engagement with American racial conflicts. While Murray celebrates performative ritual and an unconventional musician's life, he also recognizes demands on African Americans to negotiate broader American expectations. That is, though figures like Luzana Cholly and Gander Gallagher are attractive as heroic figures in their maverick ways, Scooter is urged toward convention and "antagonistic cooperation" with the America that lies beyond the local vernacular of Gasoline Point. In this, Murray narrates Scooter's development in the 1920s in light of contemporaneous debates from the Harlem Renaissance. While the boy fantasizes about being unfettered by social convention (as he imagines Luze is) he is also unable to escape expectations engendered by Du Bois's so–called "Talented Tenth"—namely, the hope that the elite ten per cent of African American society will advance the entire race through its individual achievements. For instance, Scooter's bookish interest in history is monetarily rewarded by the family friend Sawmill Turner, a self–made black businessman. As Turner tells him, Scooter's enthusiasm about education may potentially profit African Americans as a community, and, as such, necessarily demands encouragement and nurturing:

> He came and stood in front of my chair then. This boy is worth more than one hundred shares of gilt–edged preferred, and the good part about it is we all going to be drawing down interest on him. Then he handed me a five–dollar bill [. . .] and told me to buy myself a fountain pen; and he told Mama he was going to be the one to stake me to all the ink and paper I needed as long as I stayed in school. All I had to do was show him my report card. (74)

Turner is not alone in recognizing Scooter's academic potential and attributing a kind of messianic hope to the boy. After Scooter recites a variety of historical American texts to family and friends (including the Declaration of Independence, the Gettysburg Address, and the Preamble to the Constitution), he moves other black adults to acclaim: "That boy can just about preach that thing right now," and "That boy can talk straight out of the dictionary when he want to" (68–69). The expectation that Scooter engenders is evocative of the middle–class hope in higher education that flourished throughout the New Negro movement of the 1920s. As David Levering Lewis writes: "Education for progress was the ideal that united the Talented Tenth, transcending divisions of personality, politics, and ideology. All else failing—exercise of ballot, protection under the law, inclusion in labor unions and professional bodies—it was the rare Afro-American bourgeois who faltered in his faith in higher education" (157).

Accordingly, Scooter's aunt, Miss Tee, is similarly impressed by his scholastic achievements, urging him on with: "*This is My Mister who can write his name all by himself. Show them My Mister. This is My Mister who can do addition and subtraction all by himself. Show them My Mister. And show them how My Mister can also recite from the Reader all by himself"* (55, original emphasis). However, though Miss Tee's praise appears to reaffirm the Talented Tenth faith in education, Scooter's stylized remembrance simultaneously offers a vernacular critique of that middle–class principle. That is, Scooter's recollections of Miss Tee's invitations to perform are antiphonal, a signal call that demands response. At the same time, her praise resembles blues verse in its tripartite structure: a repeated thought with subtle variation ("This is My Mister who can do X by himself. Show them My Mister"), followed by a more varied statement of resolution. In working this vernacular echo into his dramatization of Talented Tenth concerns about education, Murray dismantles the division between so–called high and low cultures engendered by those bourgeois sentiments. In remembering his scholastic achievement as a site of blues antiphony, Scooter explores the complex relationships and networks of cross–reference that inform his development.

In fact, what Murray does is offer a vision of hybridity, by juxtaposing the vernacular performance of the blues with the traditional academic performance at which Scooter excels. The boy's facility with the fixed texts of American history is as much a part of his subject formation as is his ability to respond to the classic blues. Murray, I would argue, intends the two to be interdependent, complementary. Neither constitutes a product of discrete blackness or whiteness: book learning is not the province of whiteness, nor is the blues a black form necessarily removed from the academy. Rather, both represent the organic processes of exchange always at work in American culture. Ultimately, African American potential lies not merely in pursuing conventional education, nor in exercising vernacular savvy, but in recognizing the inseparability of the two. The importance of this exchange is something Luzana Cholly realizes, and accordingly, Luze acknowledges and encourages Scooter's academic ability. Recognizing the productive connections between the black vernacular in which Scooter is well–schooled and the scholastic world in which he excels, Luze argues that "the young generation was supposed to take what they were already born with and learn how to put it with everything the civil engineers and inventors and doctors and lawyers and bookkeepers had found out about the world and be the one to bring about the day the old folks had always been prophesying and praying for" (30). Scooter's promise turns on his versatility: on his mastery of the expressive rituals with which he is surrounded and on the academic genius nurtured by Miss Metcalf's classroom.

Murray fuses these two instructive modes in the segment of the novel devoted to Scooter's consideration of history. Here, Scooter's various types of learning are amassed and set in juxtaposition. Thus, his schooling in the town's particulars, like the operation of trains and sawmills overlaps with his introduction to geography and literature at school, which encounters the historical narrative of his parents' and their friends' fireside reminiscences. Murray superimposes these ostensibly disparate strands in the chapter to mark their relevance to each other. Scooter's earliest, most local, considerations of time and history—"I already knew how to mark the parts of the day by the sawmill whistles long before I learned to read time as such from the face of a clock" (50)—are not unrelated to the knowledge he acquires at school, or the communal memory he inherits from his elders.

All three inspire the narrator to consider the world at large in relation to his own burgeoning sense of self. For example, his early ability to mark time by the whistles is conveyed in relation to the personal details of his own life: the whistle signals the times at which he awakes, has breakfast, and makes his way to school. Similarly, his schooldays contribute to the formation of his complex identity: Miss Tee renames him, calling him "My Mister"; moreover, the literature he encounters inspires him to re-envision himself as an inheritor of many other imaginative traditions.

In turn, this combination of empathy and imagination informs Scooter's reaction to his elders' narration of history around his parents' fireplace. Listening to a story about his Uncle Walt escaping a lynch mob, Scooter internalizes the narrative:

> [I] got up and saw Uncle Walt sitting by the fire in Papa's clothes talking about how he had made his way through Tombigbee Swamp. He slept in Uncle Jerome's bed and Uncle Jerome slept on a pallet in front of the fireplace. They put ointment on the bruises and rubbed his joints down in Sloan's Liniment, and he slept all day the next day and the day after that too, telling about it again the second night by the fire with his feet soaking in a tub of hot salt water, and I could see it all and I was in it too, and it was me running through the swamps, hearing them barking, coming, and it was me who swam across the creek and was running wet and freezing in the soggy shoes all the next day. (66)

Thus, as with his consideration of Jack Johnson's mythology, Scooter views the attempted–lynching narrative as a defining component in his own development. Like the jazz musician who internalizes tradition and figures himself within and against it in every moment of performance, Scooter envelops past histories into his own expressive formation.

This formation is most evident throughout the "History Lessons" chapter as he consumes the various oral narratives and alternative histories passed on by the elders, and saves them within his own storehouse of expressive material. The historical record that Scooter derives from the African American adults in his life is, by its very nature, unfixed, subjective, and Murray's hero is aware that the diverse products of his education are all also open to variation in vernacular performance. As Scooter recognizes at one point, while listening to fireside stories, "Everybody had his own way of telling about it" (59). Acknowledging the importance of that versatility, one is not surprised, then, that when Scooter remembers his Uncle Jerome's account of the Civil War, his imagination interrupts to reaffirm his own playfulness as expressive subject:

> [H]e used to say that the color of freedom was blue. The Union Army came dressed in blue. The big hand that signed the freedom papers signed them in blue ink which was also blood. The very sky itself was blue, limitless (*and gentleman, sir, before I'd be a slave, I'll be buried in my grave*). *And I said My name is Jack the Rabbit and my home is in the briarpatch.* (67)

While Scooter's development is certainly analogous to the jazz musician's creative growth, Murray emphasizes the connection dramatically by emphasizing changes in black music as the narrative progresses. Early in the novel, Luzana Cholly, the embodiment of folk anonymity, is Scooter's most dominant influence. But as Scooter begins to integrate the various American possibilities from his composite education, the boy is more attracted to the jazz music of Stagolee Dupas, Gasoline Point's refined champion of barrelhouse piano. In the self–reflexive correlation between the development of jazz, and Scooter's emergence as "the hero as improviser," to use Murray's words, Stagolee symbolizes a move in black expressivity toward hybrid stylization and aesthetic refinement ("Regional" 6). As Scooter recalls, the piano player was "to honed steel and patent leather what old Luzana Cholly was to blue steel and rawhide" (99). Stagolee embodies the stylized versatility to which Scooter himself aspires, equally at home "vamping the chords to 'Nearer My God to Thee,'" "adding some of his own verses" to the folk ballad "Stagger Lee," or "playing sheet music" of contemporary tunes like "Ain't She Sweet" and "My Blue Heaven" (99, 124). As well, Stagolee is a picture of technical virtuosity: "[W]hen you heard him vamping into his own very special stop–time version of 'I'll See You in My Dreams,'" Scooter recalls, "you knew he was about to ride out in up–tempo, riffing chorus after chorus while modulating from key to key so smoothly that you hardly noticed until you tried to whistle it like that" (124).

Stagolee's ubiquity in the novel's late sections corresponds with Scooter's own schoolboy maturation into the realization of New Negro promise. With this, Murray further rewrites the black vernacular and jazz more centrally into American modernism. That is, countering the historical undervaluing of jazz in the 1920s, Murray's revision figures the music as the quintessential, folk–based product of aesthetic, urban sophistication. Listening to Stagolee perform variations on old ragtime tunes, for instance, Scooter "think[s] about the good time places in such patent leather avenue towns as St. Louis, Missouri and Reno, Nevada and San Francisco, California, where he had played when he was on the road" (124). This same urbanity comes through in Stagolee's sartorial expression, as well, as when Scooter recalls him "wearing a sporty gray checked pinchback suit, a black silk shirt open at the collar, and a black and gray hound's tooth cap, with the visor unsnapped" (132). For Scooter as emerging improviser and potential New Negro hero, Stagolee represents a performative possibility that balances traditional refinement and downhome expressivity. As Scooter acknowledges near the novel's conclusion, it is Stagolee who ultimately influenced his education and improvisational approach more than Luze:

> [S]o much of what I was to learn about music comes more directly from Stagolee Dupas than from Luzana Cholly, (who was there first but whom I never saw or heard practicing and never heard even mention either a note or a key signature by name). Because he (Stagolee) was the one who was if anything more concerned with instrumentation than with lyrics (which as often as not he only scatted anyway—even when the words were his own) (124–25).

Finally, Murray's reconceptualization of American modernism through the optics of his own biography and the emergence of jazz has its dramatic correlative in the novel's last chapter, when Scooter learns the truth of his parentage: that he is the biological son of his parents' friend Miss Tee. This crisis of genealogy—the discovery that he is not who he thought he was—liberates Scooter from any fixed vision of his own identity, a liberation which is essential to Murray's reworking of American history and modernism. The revelation renders Scooter an orphan who may define himself by choice rather than lineage. As Buddy voices to Scooter, the discovery of the secret is as "good as giving you the inside claim on old Luzana and old Stagolee and old Gator Gus and them and all that. Because man you welcome to Old Lady Metcalf and all that old school stuff" (182). Thus, Scooter is a hero who possesses the freedom to embody American ideals as tinged by the organic exchange of the black vernacular and by academic learning; he is a protagonist well–trained in Signifyin(g)'s liberatory strategies. The improvisational potential inherent in Scooter's release from genealogy symbolizes Murray's own self–asserted independence from closed–minded cultural conceptions and fixed notions of identity. As the writer himself says in a 1974 interview, when discussing the novel: "I counterstate the sociology...I extend Mann's Joseph stories, Nick Adams in a story like "In Our Time", and *Portrait of the Artist as a Young Man*. Luzana Cholly, the guitarist, is Odysseus, Beowulf, Roland and all the heroes to Scooter. Auden talked about the 'true ancestor' whom you don't find by going back along a straight line" (Gelfland 10). Open to the aesthetic possibilities and freedom from history that he perceives to be his true American birthright, Murray offers a vision of the past—of America, of modernism, of jazz—that is malleable, unfixed, open to the artist's individual will.

Coda

In closing, I cannot help but return to Ken Burns's *Jazz,* the document with which I began this book. When the film aired in ten parts on PBS throughout January 2001, at the start of the new century, the occasion seemed a palpable marker of jazz music's ascendancy in the American popular imagination. It was a grand gesture of acclamation, maybe, that sought to reverse the rough–going to which the music had been first subjected in the century of its birth. After being denounced by Anne Shaw Faulkner as a primitive threat to national decency in the 1920s, celebrated by Norman Mailer as the "music of orgasm" in the late 1950s (4), and even pronounced prematurely dead in the 1970s, jazz was now being widely fêted. Burns himself said in a number of interviews that the jazz film completed an "American trilogy" for him, a three–part historical panorama that included his previously acclaimed documentaries on the Civil War and baseball.[1] After decades of being "outside" the mainstream, or worse, just plain forgotten, jazz had, through Burns's work, attained an incontrovertible place in a virtual American hall of fame: it was now placed alongside the war that had helped define the country's turbulent character and the pastime that had later tried to distract us from it.[2]

And though few people I know actually sat through all nineteen hours of Ken Burns's *Jazz,* the new century began, it seemed, with jazz music everywhere. Promotional tie–ins for the Burns film abounded. Record stores advertised the documentary with posters bearing the black-and-white likenesses of jazz giants ranging from Louis Armstrong to Ornette Coleman. There was a series of compact discs associated with the film on sale everywhere, a pile of "greatest–hits" type collections for nearly every major artist in the pantheon. Booksellers offered the "companion volume" to the film, a weighty coffee table book, authored by Burns and his creative partner Geoffrey C. Ward, which featured hundreds of stunning archival photos to complement its narration of the music's history. And this frenzy of *Jazz* cross–promotion was not limited to predictable goods. Never one to miss out on a marketing occasion, even Starbucks got into the game. In the winter of 2001, one could not order a latté without being pushed to buy the coffee–chain's "Light Note" blend or hearing "West End Blues," "Ornithology," or "Maiden Voyage" over the café sound system.[3]

Of course, jazz had been building in exposure. In the accumulation of interest since the 1980s, jazz experienced an unprecedented period of celebration that ran almost parallel to the career of its supposed savior, Wynton Marsalis. Indeed, as the career of the young trumpeter developed, straight–ahead acoustic jazz appeared to be in the midst of a mainstream reclamation that carried throughout the last two decades of the century. For instance, jazz was frequently showcased on television's top–rated sitcom, *The Cosby Show* in the mid–1980s: there were allusions to classic bebop records by the show's jazz–loving patriarch, Cliff; a poster of Marsalis that hung prominently in the bedroom of the family's teenaged son, Theo; and guest appearances by famous jazz musicians like Lena Horne and Dizzy Gillespie.[4] In 1987, Marsalis and his quintet, dressed in tailored suits and performing hard bop, appeared as musical guests on NBC's *Saturday Night Live*—generally a high–profile platform for rock acts riding the top of the hit parade.[5] Moreover, in 1990, Marsalis appeared on the cover of *Time* magazine for an article advertising the emergence of a jazz renaissance, while in the summer of that same year, Spike Lee released *Mo' Better Blues,* a glossy feature film about jazz musicians starring Denzel Washington and offering lush performance scenes with music dubbed by trumpeter Terence Blanchard and the Branford Marsalis Quartet.[6] Then in 1991, Marsalis, Murray, and Crouch founded the Jazz at Lincoln Center program, a high–budget repertory that presented concerts, film programs, and lectures, in the interest of celebrating and preserving "classical" jazz. The program eased jazz into one of the country's prominent artistic institutions, and six years later, Marsalis was awarded the 1997 Pulitzer Prize for his jazz oratorio, *Blood on the Fields,* a piece performed and recorded with the Lincoln Center Jazz Orchestra under the aegis of the JALC program. The Pulitzer honor marked an obvious highpoint in the trumpeter and composer's career, but also constituted a telling sign of the mass acceptance and institutionalization of "traditional" jazz. The music had come a long way since its early denigration, or even since 1965, when the Pulitzer committee had rejected Duke Ellington's nomination for a special award for composition.

However, in citing these various events I do not mean to suggest that they are merely fortuitous, an arbitrary and collective change of heart regarding jazz among the American public. Rather, I would argue that the move that jazz made in the last quarter of the twentieth century, away from the so–called margins and toward the center of institutionalized, "accepted" American cultural life, came in part as a result of the political–aesthetic strategies of the writers whose work I have charted throughout this book. That is, while jazz influenced the modernist literature of Hughes, Ellison, Harper, and Murray, these writers, with their aggressive social involvement and appeals to the African American vernacular, established the music as an inviolable part of the hybrid cultural landscape to which they all attest. All four writers break down racialized borders in American culture and underscore how black expressivity is inextricable from the mainstream. And all four look to that expressivity with the historian's eye in reclaiming the stories, myths, and songs imperiled by cultural hierarchies and the menace of racism. Unsurprisingly, three of the four figure into the text of Ken Burns's *Jazz,* the cultural document I read here as the culmination of this jazz renaissance. Burns's segment on Duke Ellington and the Cotton Club quotes from Langston Hughes, citing his criticism of the venue's Jim Crow practices; the film's reconstruction of bebop's origins draws on Ralph Ellison's reminiscences of Minton's Playhouse from his essay, "The Golden Age, Time Past"; and Albert Murray appears on–camera at various times in the documentary, offering commentary on the music's capacity for ritual and salvation.

Indeed, of the four writers in this book, Murray has likely influenced the repositioning of jazz most tangibly. For one, as discussed in Chapter Five, his mentorship of Wynton Marsalis, the most high–profile jazz musician to emerge since the 1960s, is a noticeable influence on Marsalis's career trajectory and on the rhetoric that guides his public persona. The trumpeter's early work appeared locked in a 1960s hard bop style, rich in its technical proficiency but at times rigid in its disregard of the rest of the jazz tradition. As his career progressed, though, and, presumably, as the influence of Murray and Murray's own protégé, Stanley Crouch, grew stronger, Marsalis's playing and composing grew more historically expansive in their approach: there was more blues in his tonality, more New Orleans second–line rhythms in his attack, and an almost Ellingtonian grandness in his writing, with a tendency toward longer pieces and extended ensemble work. And off the bandstand, Marsalis is decidedly Murray–esque in his speech. His innumerable attestations to the democratic idealism in jazz—that the music offers a vision of what America will be when the country truly becomes itself—is a little bit *Omni-Americans,* a little bit *Stomping the Blues.*

But Murray's influence on the reconsideration of jazz effects larger cultural currents, as well. As John Gennari argues, *Stomping the Blues* is important to a more widespread re-evaluation of African American culture rooted in the academy. *Stomping the Blues,* Gennari writes, with its efforts to

> develop an aesthetic theory of jazz indigenous to the music, a theory fully attuned to the cultural values, the aesthetic criteria, and the social practices of the milieu in which the music has been created [. . .] . , pointed jazz criticism in the direction that Henry Louis Gates, Jr., and Houston A. Baker, Jr., have been traveling in recent years in their search for an African-American vernacular literary theory. ("Criticism" 453)

While Gennari reads Murray's vernacular–centered approach to jazz as a methodological influence on the work of those signal African American literary theorists, Baker himself acknowledges the influence of *Stomping the Blues* on his formulation of blues expressivity in *Blues, Ideology, and Afro-American Literature* (12). Thus, Murray's work is important beyond the implications it wields for jazz itself. *Stomping the Blues*'s determined rendering of the jazz tradition as both a wellspring of aesthetic complexity on par with the best of modernist art, and an intricate practice that must be read necessarily by its own expressive standards, is significant for its influence on the pervasive reformulation of the American literary canon, and the critical approaches to it, that Gates and Baker have inaugurated in their work over the past two decades.

However, these connections between Murray's approach to jazz and Gates's and Baker's recent reconfiguration of American literary studies do not operate merely through broad influence and analogy. The increasing institutionalization of both African American literary studies and jazz music in the United States are ends toward which jazz modernism has been doggedly pressing since its birth. Rooted in the Harlem Renaissance, in a political project based on intellectual excellence and race pride, the tradition mapped in this book has always tried to empower black expressivity, by pushing it to a more recognizable place in the so–called center of American life, and by asserting a cultural relevance that really should have been clear all along. These jazz modernists have always maintained that the music and their writing were inseparable from both the aesthetic innovations of twentieth–century literature and art, and from the political interests of African Americans.

Of course, these four writers—Hughes, Ellison, Harper, and Murray—have affirmed these connections and influenced the parallel resituation of jazz and black literature in varying ways. The foundational pair of Hughes and Ellison do so largely on discursive grounds, through innovative stylistics which reveal associative possibilities between black music and modernist literature, and through the polemic of their essays. Perhaps no document articulates the inevitability of these aesthetic connections more forcefully than Hughes's "The Negro Artist and the Racial Mountain." Harper and Murray, on the other hand, build on these expressive foundations, but have also influenced the twofold institutionalization of jazz and black literature beyond the limits of the page. For example, Harper's anthology, *Chant of Saints: A Gathering of Afro-American Literature, Art, and Scholarship* (1979), edited with Robert B. Stepto, is a signal text in the re-evaluation of African American culture, a unique assemblage of poetry, fiction, "traditional" scholarship, and music commentary that anticipates the interdisciplinary critical perspectives that have dominated (African) American cultural studies since the 1980s. Meanwhile, Murray has been a particularly distinct force in the reassessment of African American vernacular culture and its place in the American grain.

In some ways, then, this complementary substantiation of black literature and music in American culture thrives on a network of cross–influence and productive association: jazz influences black literature in the formation of a unique modernist style, which in turn influences the aesthetic trajectory of the jazz tradition and its reception in the national imagination. At the heart of this dizzying relationship, though, is the incontestable and crucial fact that both jazz, and the African American modernist literature it influences, belong at the center of this collective imagination. As I have argued throughout this book, one cannot narrate America's becoming–modern without acknowledging the significance and influence of jazz and African American literature. Both offer, to paraphrase and reconfigure Wynton Marsalis's remarks from the Burns film, visions of American culture as it *has* become itself: hybrid, allusive, playful, and unmistakably alive to its own paradoxes and complicated history.

Notes

NOTES TO THE INTRODUCTION

1. Though I quote Burns's use of Fisher's article here, I cite from the original text (as collected in Nathan Irvin Huggins's *Voices from the Harlem Renaissance*) to maintain accuracy with its punctuation and presentation.

2. A notable scholar who does not subscribe to this conservative view is Alfred Appel, Jr. In *Jazz Modernism: From Ellington and Armstrong to Matisse and Joyce,* Appel argues for the place of jazz musicians like Louis Armstrong, Duke Ellington, and Fats Waller in any broad consideration of modernist art. As Appel suggests, the comprehensive aesthetic of these musicians—drawing from vernacular cultures and mass–produced commodities—is essentially similar to the transformative style characteristic of the artists traditionally seen as defining modernism, including James Joyce, Henri Matisse, and Pablo Picasso. Appel writes: "To call Armstrong, Waller, et al., 'modernists' is to appreciate their procedures as alchemists of the vernacular who have 'jazzed' the ordinary and given it new life" (13). While Appel limits his discussion primarily to jazz musicians of the first half of the twentieth century, his broad suggestion that jazz should be central to any definition of a modernist style is similar to arguments I propose throughout this book.

3. I return to this essay in Chapter Three, to discuss how Ellison's fiction appears so informed by his formulation of a jazz aesthetic, as articulated here.

4. Examples of Ellison's description of jazz as language, or product of voice, occur in the essays, "The Golden Age, Time Past," when he writes that the jazz musician's ultimate goal is to "[achieve] that subtle identification between his instrument and his deepest drives which will allow him to express his own unique ideas and his own unique voice" (245); and "What These Children Are Like," when he argues that "jazz musicians are invading the backwoods with modifications of language, verbal as well as musical" (544).

5. In this, I wish to build on Hazel Carby's productive argument that critics must never let "patriarchal sensibilities speak for themselves" (as she suggests

Cornel West does in critical work on W.E.B. Du Bois) but must instead subject those sensibilities to rigorous examination "so that we may follow and grasp their epistemological implications and consequences" (10–11).

6. As Carby writes: "Davis's concept of freedom remains limited to the misogynistic world of jazz, and it manifests itself principally in the musical relations among the male instrumentalists with whom he worked" (136). However, as Carby also points out, Davis does not leave women absent from his autobiography, but rather positions them in rhetorically convenient ways: "The various women described in *Miles* are carefully given their place in his material world: they may service his bodily sexual and physical needs, but are albatrosses around his neck when he wants to fly with other men in the musical realm of 'genius' and performance" (145). An interesting contrast to Davis's gendered depiction of jazz as a site of freedom is Julie Dawn Smith's criticism that despite African American free jazz's "critique of [. . .] racial oppression" and European free improvisation's "critique of class structures," "[n]either free improvisation nor free jazz [. . .] extended their critiques to include the aesthetic, economic, or political liberation of women" (229–30).

7. Improviser and composer Pauline Oliveros emphasizes this gender exclusion when she recalls: "By the end of the sixties, my experience with improvisation was almost exclusively solo or with groups of men. [. . .] Even though I was included in the groups that I worked with, I felt an invisible barrier. As I had noticed early in life, males bond strongly around music and technology and leave women out of their conversations and performance" (54). Moreover, Oliveros calls attention to the way these gendered exclusions are rendered natural through critical practice, as when male critics celebrate male improvisers for their technical prowess but describe female improvisation purely in affective terms. See Oliveros, 54.

NOTES TO CHAPTER ONE

1. Oliver, Armstrong and Morton were all from the same Southern city, New Orleans, and all initially moved to the same Northern city, Chicago, which in the early 1920s was momentarily the center of jazz activity. Oliver arrived in Chicago in 1918, Armstrong (at Oliver's invitation) in 1922, and Morton also in 1922. As Eric Porter argues, the development of jazz in the early decades of the twentieth century must necessarily be understood through the context of black migration:

> Jazz emerged when black musicians and other African Americans became immersed in modern life at the end of the nineteenth century and the beginning of the twentieth. A series of domestic migrations brought rural African Americans to urban areas and southerners to the North. In urban areas throughout the country, musicians of different social backgrounds encountered one another in formal

and informal educational networks, where they built upon existing vernacular forms and transformed them with the tools of Western music. (6)

2. Indeed, it was quite likely *because* of those unmistakably African American features that jazz was so hungrily consumed by white audiences and listeners. I explain this relationship in my detailed discussion of the 1920s cult of primitivism.

3. As Art Lange and Nathaniel Mackey write in the note that begins their volume, *Moment's Notice: Jazz in Poetry and Prose,* "That jazz music is the United States' best known indigenous art form all but goes without saying" (i). Robert O'Meally argues as much in his edited collection, *The Jazz Cadence of American Culture,* suggesting that jazz is so central to the "electric process of American artistic exchange" that it is no challenge for the student of American culture to read "[j]azz as metaphor, jazz as model, jazz as relentlessly powerful cultural influence, jazz as cross–disciplinary beat or *cadence*" ("Preface" xi, original emphasis). Burton Peretti adds in his *Jazz in American Culture* that the music "is an ingrained element of American styles and attitudes" (4).

4. Other examples that confirm this arrival in the past decade abound. Note the 1997 Pulitzer Prize awarded to Wynton Marsalis—the first ever awarded to a jazz musician—for his extended composition, *Blood on the Fields;* consider the panegyric reminiscences devoted to Duke Ellington in the American media over the spring of 1999 to commemorate the composer's centennial anniversary.

5. Curiously, among the artists Bell includes as members of the "jazz movement" are T.S. Eliot and Igor Stravinsky.

6. I speak of the Harlem intelligentsia as a somewhat unified group here because, with few exceptions or degrees of variation, most established African American intellectuals during the period did not esteem jazz as an inherently progressive cultural form. I do not mean to suggest, though, that Harlem's intellectuals acted homogeneously regarding all matters concerning art and racial politics during the period. Consider, for example, the different reactions to Carl Van Vechten's *Nigger Heaven,* which I discuss in n. 9.

7. The exclusion of jazz from *The Crisis* is perhaps less surprising given the periodical's conservatism. As George Hutchinson writes in *The Harlem Renaissance in Black and White:* "*The Crisis* fulfilled a longstanding dream of Du Bois to edit a 'high class journal' circulating among 'the intelligent Negroes' and binding them together in a pursuit of 'definite ideals'" (142). These "definite ideals" seemed inextricably linked to Du Bois's own comfortable middle–class background though, for as Hutchinson summarizes, the material that "*The Crisis* wanted to see [took] the black middle–class point of view as normative" (153). Du Bois's neglect of jazz, then, contrasts notably with the attention paid to the music by more class–inclusive movements in Harlem. As Eric Porter writes, for instance, "During the 1920s, the leftist African Blood

Brotherhood (ABB) and Marcus Garvey's United Negro Improvement Association (UNIA) sponsored jazz and blues performances as a means of galvanizing support for their causes" (7).

8. Locke himself was more vocally appreciative of jazz by late in the Harlem Renaissance, celebrating figures like Louis Armstrong and Duke Ellington in his 1936 book–length study, *The Negro and His Music*. However, as Eric Porter points out, "Locke's celebration of jazz went only so far. While he celebrated jazz artistry and the accomplishments of jazz musicians, he considered the form something of an artistic dead end" (45). Porter suggests that Locke's limited validation of jazz lies both in the intellectual's "continued investment in high culture and in a recognition of the restrictions facing black musicians working in the idiom" (46).

9. Though I cite Van Vechten's novel here as an obvious example of problematic representations of jazz—and by extension African American culture—by white writers, *Nigger Heaven* was not universally dismissed by black intellectuals at the time of its release. Instead, reactions to the book were somewhat divided. As Robert F. Worth notes, James Weldon Johnson praised the novel in an *Opportunity* review, while Charles Johnson wrote in a letter to Van Vechten just after the book's release that it was a novel "springing from emotions other than patronizing sympathy" (qtd in Worth 463). W.E.B. Du Bois, on the other hand, was infuriated by the novel and advised readers in his 1926 *Crisis* review "to drop the book gently in the grate" (518). Langston Hughes himself offered a defense of the novel, even "ventur[ing] to say that more Negroes bought it than ever purchased a book by a Negro author" (qtd in Worth 465). Hughes's defense of the novel is complicated by his own material involvement in its success, however, as he wrote many of the blues lyrics that Van Vechten quotes in the narrative. Nevertheless, even though some key black intellectuals defended Van Vechten's novel, it is hard to overlook the troubled specularity it brings to representations of African American cultural life. Consider, for instance, the ethnographic feel of the "glossary of . . . unusual Negro words and phrases" presented as an appendix to the novel. Such seems indicative of the discomforting voyeurism that Van Vechten brought to his dealings in Harlem—a quality lampooned by jazz lyricist Andy Razaf in the song, "Go Harlem," with the rhyme, "Go inspectin' like Van Vechten" (qtd in Worth 462).

10. Eric Porter argues that this exclusion might also be explained as a result of the Harlem intellectuals' anxiety that jazz was merely a commodity in a mass–produced culture, rather than an example of "fine art." See Porter, 11–12.

11. Du Bois was adamant about his belief that African American art should be a vehicle for social progress rather than a mere aesthetic exercise. This is most clear in the essay "Criteria of Negro Art" (1926), in which he exclaims, "I do not care a damn for any art that is not used for propaganda" (514).

12. W.E. Yeomans purports that Eliot's poetic rhythm seems distinctly jazz–influenced in a number of pieces, including the very brief "Shakespeherian Rag"

section of *The Waste Land, Sweeney Agonistes* and selected lyrics from *Old Possum's Book of Practical Cats.* Examples of Williams's jazz–influenced verses include "Shoot It Jimmy" (which I discuss in this chapter) and "Old Bunk's Band," written for famed New Orleans trumpeter Bunk Johnson. Loy turns to jazz in "The Widow's Jazz" and "Negro Dancer," a poem apparently written for Josephine Baker. For examples of Sandburg's and Lindsay's jazz–influenced verse, see "Jazz Fantasia" and "The Congo," respectively.

13. In a 1957 interview later excerpted in the poet's *Paterson,* Williams expanded on his earlier thoughts: "We poets have to talk in a language which is not English. It is the American idiom. Rhythmically, it's organized as a sample of the American idiom. It has as much originality as jazz" (*Paterson* 222).

14. It is worth noting here that in his essay, "Jazz at Home," from Locke's *New Negro* anthology, J.A. Rogers also recognizes jazz as a new product of the urban landscape, noting that the music "bears all the marks of a nerve–strung, strident, mechanized civilization" (218). However, though Rogers admits that the music is temporally modern, the emphasis of his essay identifies jazz as an art waiting to be transformed. Rogers announces that jazz certainly has a great future, citing that the evidence of this is its "sublimation" (his term) into the orchestrated endeavors of composers like George Gershwin and Will Marion Cook.

15. This tendency among the white moderns to view jazz as both emblematic of black Otherness and symbolic of ultra–modernity captures a disturbing paradox that Michael North summarizes in *The Dialect of Modernism.* As North argues, modernist writers were invariably attracted to African American expressivity and yet were unwilling to grant full acceptance to black culture. Thus, "the image of racial and cultural unity" ostensibly celebrated by the white modernist avant–garde "is always shadowed by its twin opposite, racial oppression" (North 138).

16. Consider, for example, the difference between the biographical notes for William Carlos Williams and Hughes in Prentice–Hall's *Anthology of American Literature,* a commonly used university textbook. Whereas Williams is lauded as a "prime literary innovator," and acknowledged as being "a significant force in the freeing of poetry from the restraints and predictive regularity of traditional rhythms and meters" (1258), Hughes is remembered merely as "one of the dominant voices speaking out for black culture in white America in the latter half of the twentieth century" (1382).

17. As Steven Tracy notes, Hughes's work also responds wholeheartedly to Pound's call for poetry to respond to the sequence of the musical phrase, not the metronome (*Blues* 141).

18. Douglas summarizes the "mongrel" development of American modernist culture as arising out of a fortuitous intersection of "black" and "white" projects: "[A]t the moment that America-at-large was separating itself culturally from England and Europe, black America, in an inevitable corollary movement, was recovering its own heritage from the dominant white culture. [

. . .] Although these movements can be and usually are studied separately, they are at bottom, as the terms 'Aframerica' and 'Aframericans' were meant to suggest, inextricable; whites and blacks participated and collaborated in both projects" (5). North writes in the preface to his study, "The white vogue for Harlem has long had an accepted place in histories of the 1920s, and the shallow Negrophilia of this period has often been acknowledged in accounts of the Harlem Renaissance. But it is less often acknowledged just how far this racial cross–identification went or how widespread it was. Writers as far from Harlem as T.S. Eliot and Gertrude Stein reimagined themselves as black, spoke in a black voice, and used that voice to transform the literature of their time. In fact, three of the accepted landmarks of literary modernism in English depend on racial ventriloquism of this kind: Conrad's *Nigger of the 'Narcissus,'* Stein's "Melanctha," and Eliot's *Waste Land*. If the racial status of these works is taken at all seriously, it seems that linguistic mimicry and racial masquerade were not just shallow fads but strategies without which modernism could not have arisen" (i).

19. Douglas concedes early on in her study that her "focus will be more on the whites than on the blacks," admitting that her "perspective is perhaps inevitably a white one" (6). North does attempt to bridge "black" and "white" expressivities more significantly in his study, but his point of departure is always the racial masquerade and linguistic imitation practiced by white modernist writers. His chapters on Claude McKay and Zora Neale Hurston center mainly on their responses to this practice of cultural appropriation.

20. I should be clear here that I do not mean to discredit the work of scholars who do analyze the influence of African American subjectivity and expressivity on so–called white American culture, especially since this change in perspective was so long in coming. As Toni Morrison writes:

> There seems to be a more or less tacit agreement among literary scholars that, because American literature has been clearly the preserve of white male views, genius, and power, those views, genius, and power are without relationship to and removed from the overwhelming presence of black people in the United States. This agreement is made about a population that preceded every American writer of renown and was, I have come to believe, one of the most furtively radical impinging forces on the country's literature. The contemplation of this black presence is central to any understanding of our national literature and should not be permitted to hover at the margins of the literary imagination. (5)

21. My complementary use of Bhabha and Bakhtin here is indebted to Robert J.C. Young's *Colonial Desire: Hybridity in Theory, Culture and Race*. In his discussion of various theories of hybridity, Young juxtaposes Bakhtin's notion of "the undoing of authority in language through hybridization" and Bhabha's relocation of that idea to "the dialogical situation of colonialism" (22).

22. In *Writing Between the Lines,* Aldon Nielson also reads the Williams and Hughes poems together, but Nielson finds the two poems to be "strikingly" alike in what he reads as a mutual celebration of "the pure productivity of human speech and the improvisational power of jazz rhythm" (190). Nielson does concede, though, that "it is true that black and white Americans sometimes speak the same language differently" and "that the same words mean differently depending on who speaks them and in what setting" (190).

23. As Spencer summarizes, the myth of the Old Negro turned on the white–created stereotype that African Americans were "immoral, criminal, and mentally inferior" (2). Alain Locke writes in *The New Negro* that the Old Negro was "more of a myth than a man" (3). He elaborates:

> The Old Negro, we must remember, was a creature of moral debate and historical controversy. His has been a stock figure perpetuated as an historical fiction partly in innocent sentimentalism, partly in deliberate reactionism. . . . So for generations in the mind of America, the Negro has been more of a formula than a human being—a something to be argued about, condemned or defended, to be "kept down," or "in his place," or "helped up," to be worried with or worried over, harassed or patronized, a social bogey or a social burden. (3)

Henry Louis Gates adds that the pointed self–creation of black Americans into "New Negroes" was intended to subvert "stereotyped figments" of white "racist minds" like "Zip Coon," "Sambo," and "Mammy" ("Trope" 140–1).

24. In defining mastery of form and deformation of mastery, Baker suggests that the ur-texts for these two modes of cultural performance are Booker T. Washington's famous "Atlanta Compromise" address of 1895, where he assumes the minstrel mask of ostensible "accommodation," and W.E.B. Du Bois's vernacular–influenced *The Souls of Black Folk.*

25. Spencer argues that African American music needs to occupy a more central place in any study of the New Negro renaissance in the arts. He insists that any study of pre-WWII Harlem that compartmentalizes the arts according to traditional disciplinary boundaries is short–sighted and doomed to overlook the innumerable cross–influences that defined black literature and the performing arts of that period. His contention reinforces my own desire to discuss the work of Hughes in close context with goings–on in early jazz.

26. Edward E. Waldron, for instance, is not content to assert that Hughes's blues poems capture "the mood, the feel and the spirit of the blues," but feels it necessary to proclaim that "the blues poems of Langston Hughes *are* blues as well as poetry" (140). Similarly, Richard K. Barksdale sees Hughes's music poems as examples of "folk poetry," the intent of which he believes is to "communicate the rich folk culture of Black people" (96). While I do not disagree with Barksdale's reading of the importance of that

vernacular culture to Hughes's work—an influence that I address in detail—I disagree with his implicit underestimation of Hughes's place in American literary practice when he oversimplifies the poet's work as "orature" (106). Even critics who wish to place Hughes in a broad American literary context fall into the peril of justifying the poet's position within an African American folk collective. David Chinitz, for instance, argues that Hughes's blues poems are successful because of the poet's "self–concealing art": the ability to replicate the spontaneity of the blues while maintaining a level of literary sophistication that is evident under critical scrutiny (182). Yet even though Chinitz exhibits faith in the stylistic complexity of Hughes's work as literature, he is moved to justify the poet's place in a folk context by explicating the techniques of orature that render Hughes an "authentic" blues voice. In all, this collective critical unwillingness to separate Hughes from the folk constitutes in my mind a needless resistance to acknowledging Hughes's place within a modernist literary sphere.

27.   Tracy defines the "classic" blues as the "highly arranged, dramatic, stage–influenced vaudeville style" that was recorded by singers like Mamie Smith and Bessie Smith in the 1920s ("Tune" 72). These blues were composed and refined for recording and publication, unlike the improvised folk blues that had long flourished within the African American vernacular.

28.   Throughout this chapter I provide line numbers for all references to Hughes's poetry in which I do not cite the complete poem.

29.   Examples of critics who make this division are Patricia E. Bonner in her article, "Cryin' the Jazzy Blues and Livin' Blue Jazz: Analyzing the Blues and Jazz Poetry of Langston Hughes," and Lynette Reine-Grandell in her article, "Langston Hughes's Invocation of the Blues and Jazz Tradition Under the Double–Edged Sword of Primitivism."

30.   As Tracy reports, "In the nineteenth century both of these terms ["blues" and "blue devils"] found their way into the writings of people like Thomas Jefferson, Washington Irving, and Lord Byron" (59). The *Oxford English Dictionary* lists its earliest usages of "blue" and "blue devils" to refer to states of despondency as occurring in 1550 and 1781, respectively. In his history of the blues, *Stomping the Blues,* Albert Murray, whom I discuss at length in Chapter Five, distinguishes between "blues" as universal human emotion and "blues" as a specifically African American musical tradition by calling the former "the blues as such" and the latter simply "the blues."

31.   On jazz's genealogical debt to blues, consider Eileen Southern's summary in *The Music of Black Americans:* "The most distinctive features of jazz derive directly from the blues. Jazz is a vocally oriented music; its players replace the voice with their instruments, but try to recreate the voice's singing style and blue notes by using scooping, sliding, whining, growling, falsetto, and the like" (367). On the symbiotic relationship between jazz and blues, consider Ted Gioia's assessment that despite the generic differences I outline in this chapter, "the two styles, blues and jazz, have remained intimate bedfellows over the years [. . .] an intimacy so close

that, at times, it is hard to determine where the one ends and the other begins" (20).

32. For example, Armstrong provided cornet accompaniment on "St. Louis Blues," "You've Been a Good Ole Wagon," "Cake Walkin' Babies from Home," "Careless Love Blues," and "I Ain't Goin' to Play Second Fiddle," all from 1925. Smith also employed the services of other noted jazz instrumentalists, like pianists Fletcher Henderson and James P. Johnson, trombonist Jack Teagarden, clarinetist Benny Goodman, and tenor saxophonist Coleman Hawkins on various recordings between 1924 and 1933.

33. Armstrong's most famous blues recordings of the period include "West End Blues," "Potato Head Blues," and "Basin Street Blues." Ellington's notable blues recordings from the 1920s include "Yellow Dog Blues," "Tishomingo Blues," "Rent Party Blues," and "Harlem Flat Blues." Morton's memorable blues takes include "Smoke House Blues," "Sidewalk Blues," "Dead Man Blues," "Original Jelly–Roll Blues," "Cannon Ball Blues," and "Wild Man Blues."

34. Expanding on this comment, Tracy writes, "The jazz musician has a tendency to be more sophisticated, to improvise in a more complex manner and at greater length and to de-emphasize the words of songs and subordinate them to instrumental expressiveness and variations, though the jazz player often imitates the human voice" (*Blues* 245).

35. "Jazz as Communication," revised for 1958's *The Langston Hughes Reader*, was originally published as "Jazz: Its Yesterday, Today and Its Potential Tomorrow" in the *Chicago Defender* in July 1956.

36. Chinitz champions Hughes's "authenticity" as a blues voice throughout the article. As I note above, Chinitz's notion of "authenticity" is one I find uneasy because I see it as rehearsing the primitivism that too often dominates criticism of Hughes's work.

37. As Richard K. Barksdale notes, "most of [Hughes's] folk poems have the distinctive marks of orature. They contain many instances of naming and enumerating, considerable hyperbole and understatement, and a strong infusion of street talk rhyming" (96).

38. For Gates's extended exploration of West African oral traditions as the foundation of African American Signifyin(g) practice, see *The Signifying Monkey*, 3–88. In *The Power of Black Music*, Samuel Floyd also argues at length for a reading of African American expressivity through West African syncretisms. See 14–86.

39. Sheppard argues that at the heart of much modernist writing is the grim belief that traditional modes of language use do not adequately convey the chaos of modern life. The modernist artist, then, seeks to reconfigure language through experimentation of form. Collage is key to this. As Sheppard notes, in modernist literature, "[t]ime becomes a series of fragmented instants, and a sense of continuity gives way to discontinuity" (327).

40. Similarly, Clyde Taylor compares the experimental aesthetic of modernist artists like Picasso, Stravinsky, and Pound to the oral–musical expression of African Americans. In both artistic strains Taylor argues that creativity

exhibits an "indifference to faithful representation of the world" and forms a new aesthetic out of expressive fragments as a response to chaotic and disorienting experience (3).

41. Given that this poem was written some time between 1924 and 1926—considering the release date of the popular song it quotes at length and its initial publication in *The Weary Blues*—it seems that Hughes consciously invokes established "white" modernist techniques here (particularly those of T.S. Eliot in *The Waste Land*) in his multivocal style.

42. Born in New Orleans in 1889, Williams was an African American songwriter and lyricist of merit and considerable success. Many of his compositions have become jazz standards, including "Basin Street Blues," "Royal Garden Stomp," "Careless Love," and "Tishomingo Blues." In the 1920s, Williams performed in Europe with a number of notable black performers, including Josephine Baker and Fats Waller, and in *Black Manhattan* (1930), James Weldon Johnson included him among the most outstanding "coloured writers of popular song" (115).

43. Hughes rehearses this opposition to the written text in other places in his work. For example, in his first autobiography, *The Big Sea*, he describes throwing all of his books overboard while en route to Africa as a young shiphand. Hughes exalts the moment as one of liberation—in part from "being black in a white world"—as he ventured closer to the more welcoming cultural space he expected from his destination.

NOTES TO CHAPTER TWO

1. Even during the 1920s, as Jervis Anderson notes, when jazz was first enjoying widespread popularity, Harlem's African American stride piano innovators like James P. Johnson and Willie "the Lion" Smith often "played to full houses but for small paychecks" (129). As Smith himself later recalled: "To the Harlem cabaret owners, to all night-club bosses, the money was on a one-way chute—everything coming in, nothing going out. [. . .] It was your job to draw in the customers. All the owner had to do was count the money" (qtd in Anderson 129). By the dawn of the 1940s, African American musicians were still frequently underpaid, as Dizzy Gillespie remembered:

> Realizing that I had something very imaginative and unique going for me, I stopped accepting jobs where the salary was too low and unreflective of my talents and contributions as a soloist. Jazz musicians were paid some pitifully low wages at that time, as sidemen, and since I had no group of my own established, people considered me a sideman. That status—and the little money that went along with it—I refused to accept. I ended up working at a furious pace for about a year with over *ten different bands*, trying to make each one give me what I wanted. I

refused to stay in any one place for too long, demanded
special treatment, and if I didn't get it, I'd leave and go
someplace else. (152, original emphasis)

Gillespie's restlessness in this passage and his dissatisfaction with the economy of jazz around the early 1940s anticipate the various factors that led
to the development of bebop.

2. Commenting on the Original Dixieland Jazz Band, Ted Gioia writes:

[T]he history of recorded jazz was initiated with an event
that remains to this day clouded in controversy. And, as
with so many of the loaded issues in the story of the music,
the question of race lies at the core of the dispute. In an
ironic and incongruous twist of fate, the Original Dixieland Jazz Band (ODJB), an ensemble consisting of white
musicians, was the first to make commercial recordings of
this distinctly African-American music. Raised in New
Orleans, these five instrumentalists—leader and cornetist
Nick LaRocca, clarinetist Larry Shields, trombonist Eddie
Edwards, drummer Tony Sbarbaro, and pianist Henry
Ragas—joined forces and performed in Chicago in 1916,
then opened in New York in January 1917. During an
engagement at Reisenweber's Restaurant, the group
attracted large audiences with its novel and spirited music,
and spurred the interest of East Coast recording companies. Columbia was the first to record the band, but hesi-
tated to release the sides because of the unconventional
and ostensibly vulgar nature of the music. Soon after, the
Victor label overcame such scruples, and a second session
produced a major commercial success in "Livery Stable
Blues." (37–38)

3. As Scott DeVeaux notes, "a report in *Billboard* at the end of 1940 noted
that employment for black entertainers had declined some 25 to 30 per-
cent from the peak levels of two to three years earlier" (*Birth* 147). Moreover, by the end of the 1930s, some venues (like the storied theaters and
ballrooms of Harlem) that had previously showcased black bands now
turned to white musicians for their entertainment.

4. White swing musicians, particularly Benny Goodman and Tommy Dorsey,
also appeared prominently in many American feature films in the late 1930s
and early forties. Conversely, as Krin Gabbard writes, "For many years black
artists were simply left out [of American movies] or confined to short performance scenes that could be excised by nervous exhibitors" (*Jammin'* 6).

5. This "coronation" of white musicians began much earlier when Paul
Whiteman, a white bandleader, pronounced himself "The King of Jazz" in
the 1920s. (That moniker served as the title for a 1930 Hollywood feature

film that starred Whiteman as well.) Another antecedent for this tradition of white musicians claiming ascendancy in jazz through naming is the aforementioned Original Dixieland Jazz Band.

6. During the Swing Era, Dizzy Gillespie recalled

> only one major white band [. . .] hired black musicians on a permanent basis to play with them, and that band was Benny Goodman's. Of course, the white bands got most of the jobs that paid best, and the black musicians, the major creators, as a rule were frozen out. They used all kinds of excuses to justify this evil, such as the trouble mixed bands might provoke among racist customers and employers, the problems of finding restaurants, hotels, water fountains, toilets, and other public accommodations for the black members of the troupe. (*To Be* 157)

7. As well, many jam sessions took place at Monroe's Uptown Place, also in Harlem. Monroe's was a small basement club that attracted musicians for after-hours meetings. Though the club was certainly an important site in the development of bebop, most recollections of the period mention it less than Minton's. Keeping this in mind, I use Minton's throughout this chapter as a metonymic marker of the Harlem sessions that gave birth to the new music. Furthermore, it is worth noting the significance of the fact that Minton's—a friendly site of midwifery for the new music—was owned by the first black delegate to the New York local of the American Federation of Musicians. As Dizzy Gillespie later noted, in the 1930s and forties, the AFM assigned

> big fines for playing jam sessions, and the union had "walking" delegates who would check on all the places that were frequented by jazz musicians. [. . .] One guy in California would follow you around to see if you were going to a session. He belonged to the "colored" local out there at first, and then they merged and put him in charge as "walking" delegate for places where the "colored" musicians would be playing. He'd follow you around just waiting to see you pick up your horn without a contract, and fine you a hundred to five hundred dollars. We were somewhat immune from this at Minton's because Henry Minton who owned the place, was the first "colored" union delegate in New York. Unfortunately, to the young jazz musician, the union has always been just a dues collector. On our level we never saw it as being of any real benefit, and sometimes it kept us from gaining experience. The union benefited the classical musicians and created things for them, but the jazz guys got nothing. (*To Be* 139–40)

While Gillespie speaks in this narrative of differing treatment of musicians according to the style of music they played, the fact that so many of the working jazz musicians who were likely to be penalized by the AFM's policies were African American underscores how the residua of Jim Crow ideology and social structures affected jazz musicians during the period of bebop's birth.

8. I use terms like "Parker and company" in this chapter, when referring to bebop's early pioneers, in the interest of narrating the development of the music through the metonymic example of its greatest innovators, while acknowledging the fact that its progress depended so heavily on the group interaction of Harlem's jam sessions.

9. Baraka changed his name from LeRoi Jones in 1968. His early essays on African American music were published under the former name, and are listed as such in the bibliography.

10. Perhaps the most common example of misguided reduction in histories of bebop is the tendency to ignore the social factors that influenced the music's development. As Scott DeVeaux argues, the emergence of bebop is often constructed as a result of "jazz [being] an organic entity that periodically revitalizes itself through the upheaval of stylistic change" ("Constructing" 540). That is, jazz historiographers depict changes in the music as a natural result of some essential call from within the music's aesthetics, neglecting the fact that it is people who engender these changes for reasons that may include the social, the political, the economic. DeVeaux cites examples of this line of thinking as found in Ross Russell's articles on bebop in the magazine *The Record Changer*, and Barry Ulanov's 1952 survey *A History of Jazz in America*.

11. Ironically, Gillespie himself was at various times accused of the same kind of "tomming" for which both he and Davis criticized Armstrong. For example, Davis writes in his autobiography: "I love Dizzy, but I hated that clowning shit he used to do for all them white folks" (163). Addressing the matter in his memoirs, Gillespie, however, reverses his earlier criticism of Armstrong:

> Hell, I had my own way of "Tomming." Every generation of blacks since slavery has had to develop its own way of Tomming, of accommodating itself to a basically unjust situation. [. . .] Later on, I began to recognize what I had considered Pops's grinning in the face of racism as his absolute refusal to let anything, even anger about racism, steal the joy from his life and erase his fantastic smile. Coming from a younger generation, I misjudged him. (296)

Gillespie's comments here are fundamentally similar to Baker's description of "mastery of form" as a mode of African American cultural performance. Scott DeVeaux reads Gillespie's onstage antics as strategic play with white expectations: "Onstage, he was constantly in motion, animated by a barbed humor that drew most of its edge by signifying on the traditional role of the black entertainer—keeping the squares amused at their own expense" (*Birth* 172).

12. The list of bop and post-bop jazz compositions that use the changes to "I Got Rhythm" as their harmonic foundation is incredibly lengthy, and includes well-worn standards like Thelonious Monk's "Rhythm-a-ning" and Sonny Rollins's "Oleo." The term "rhythm changes" is itself short-hand in the jazz improviser's vocabulary for the sequence, used in jam sessions and pick-up gigs for easy reference to the pattern the group will follow in a particular solo round. Parker was perhaps the most frequent reviser of standard chord progressions for his own compositions, using "Indiana" to compose "Donna Lee," "Lover Come Back to Me" for "Bird Gets the Worm," "Cherokee" for "Warming Up a Riff" and "Ko Ko," and "Honeysuckle Rose" for "Marmaduke" and "Scrapple from the Apple."

13. Ingrid Monson echoes Gates's thinking when she writes that "[t]he modernism of the beboppers explicitly sought to carve out a new space for a specifically African American creativity" ("Problem" 411).

14. By the late 1920s, appropriation of the styles of earlier jazz virtuosi was further aided by the commercial sheet music industry. In this I am referring to the Melrose Music Company's 1927 publication of two collections of transcribed Louis Armstrong solos and cadenzas, *125 Jazz Breaks for Cornet* and *50 Hot Choruses for Cornet.* The books were intended to let the consumer capture Armstrong's improvisational genius by reading a fixed musical text. As the publishers urged in one collection, "If you want to get hot and stay hot, memorize these breaks. They will prove invaluable to jazz cornetists as they may be used in playing any and all dance melodies" (qtd in Bergreen 293).

15. An example of bebop's origins as being explained as racial narrative occurs in 1961's *The Jazz Scene,* by noted British jazz critic, Francis Newton. Addressing the bop "revolution," Newton writes that "from the late thirties the coloured musician became increasingly ambitious [. . .] to establish his superiority over the white musician" (205).

16. Some white jazz critics seem especially hard-pressed to consider the relationship of race to the music at all. For example, former *Down Beat* editor Gene Lees writes in the title essay to his collection, *Waiting for Dizzy,* that he "never was able to accept the story that [Gillespie and company] 'invented' bebop at Minton's as a thing the 'white boys' couldn't steal" (227). Similarly, responding to critic Frank Kofsky's suggestion that the title of Charlie Parker's famous blues, "Now's the Time" (1946), was a call for an immediate end to Jim Crow, jazz critic Ira Gitler claims, "I deny the 'obvious social implication.' The title refers to the music and the 'now' was the time for the people to dig it" (qtd in Kofsky 56).

17. *Blues People,* Baraka's famous study of African American music is founded on the notion that black social history and black music are completely inseparable—that African American musical aesthetics have always been informed by the material history of black people in the United States. As Baraka asserts: "if the music of the Negro in America, in all its permutations, is subjected to a socio-anthropological as well as musical scrutiny, something about the essential nature of the Negro's existence in this country

ought to be revealed, as well as something about the essential nature of this country, *i.e.,* society as a whole" (*Blues* ix-x).

18. In his memoirs, Dizzy Gillespie perhaps best expresses his own connection to what Lott calls "the militancy of the moment" in the following anecdote about his interview with the United States draft board during WWII:

> [T]hey started asking me my views about fighting. "Well, look, at this time, in this stage of my life here to the United States whose foot has been in my ass? The white man's foot has been in my ass hole buried up to his knee in my ass hole!" I said. "Now, you're speaking of the enemy. You're telling me the German is the enemy. At this point, I can never even remember having met a German. So if you put me out there with a gun in my hand and tell me to shoot at the enemy, I'm liable to create a case of 'mistaken identity,' of who I might shoot." They looked around at one another. [. . . T]hey finally classified me 4F because I was crazy enough not to want to fight, in anybody's army. And especially not at that time. (120)

19. Ingrid Monson shows in detail how the beboppers' assertion of black difference through style was often misinterpreted by white onlookers, and in many ways rehearsed the unsettling essentialism of Harlem's earlier Negro vogue. As Monson writes: "To the extent that well-meaning white Americans have confused the most 'transgressive' aspects of African American culture with its true character, they fall into the trap of viewing blackness as absence. Whether conceived as an absence of morality or of bourgeois pretensions, this view of blackness, paradoxically, buys into the historical legacy of primitivism and its concomitant exoticism of the 'Other'" ("Problem" 398). This legacy was particularly troubling amidst the emergence of bebop:

> The modernism in the self-conception of bebop musicians partook deeply of the image of the avant-garde artist as outside and social critic, and of the accompanying expectation of "mad" or "bad" behavior. On the one hand, this image mediated racial difference through a common vocabulary of an artistic modernism; on the other hand, the historically close associations between madness, pathology, and racial difference made the image of the jazz avant-garde artist especially prone to appropriation by primitivist racial ideologies. (412)

20. The following anecdote from white trumpet player Johnny Carisi highlights how black musicians' fear of economic exploitation by the white mainstream could at times manifest itself in calls for racial exclusion:

> "The only [racial] 'thing' I ran into [at Minton's] was really
> a backhanded kind of compliment, in a way. There was a
> lotta getting loaded there. I remember one time we took a
> walk outside, and Joe Guy was pretty stoned. I guess the
> previous set I'd managed to keep up with them, whatever
> they were doing, and Joe Guy, half-hostile, and half-famil-
> iar, family kinda style, grabbed me and says, 'You ofays
> come up here, and you pick up on our stuff.' And the other
> cats were saying, 'What're you doing, Joe?' They cooled
> him out. He was loaded and everything. But it was kind of
> a compliment, because he was really saying, 'Man, you're
> doing what we're doing.'" (qtd in Gillespie 143)

Carisi's punchline in this anecdote—taking the accusation of creative threat
as a compliment—seems indicative of the white musician's lack of awareness about economic imbalances along racial lines in the music business.

21. Among the innumerable bebop tunes based around the blues's I-IV-V chord
     orientation are "Parker's Mood" and "Now's the Time" by Charlie Parker,
     and "Straight, No Chaser" and "Blue Monk" by Thelonious Monk. The
     beboppers' relationship to the blues, though, was certainly a Signifyin(g)
     one. Consider for example, Dizzy Gillespie's comments on the blues:

> I'd tell [other musicians], "Man, [the blues are] my music,
> that's my heritage." The bebop musicians wanted to show
> their virtuosity. They'd play the twelve-bar outline of the
> blues, but they wouldn't *blues it up* like the older guys
> they considered unsophisticated. They busied themselves
> making changes, a thousand changes in one bar. Why
> make one change in a bar if you could put a thousand
> there? (*To Be* 371, my emphasis)

In addition, as Floyd notes, "the use of the flatted fifth [blue note] was not
new. . . . The beboppers were simply reviving and emphasizing it" (138, n.3)

22. The emphasis on toasts and cutting contests in bebop further underscores its
     place within the Signifyin(g) expressive matrix that Gates outlines as including
     verbal contests like rhymed toasts and the dozens (*Signifying* 68–71).

23. The biggest innovator in changing the role of the drum in jazz was likely
     Kenny Clarke, whose "technique of keeping a shimmering pulse on the ride
     cymbal, occasionally punctuated by vigorous accents on the bass and snare
     drums, earned him the onomatopoeic nickname Klook-mop, or Klook"
     (DeVeaux, *Birth* 218). DeVeaux highlights the specific modifications
     Clarke introduced in jazz:

> By the late 1930s Clarke was already an experienced big-
> band drummer, content with his specialized professional
> role. "I always concentrated on accompaniment," he told an

interviewer. "I thought that was the most important thing, my basic function as a drummer, and so I always stuck with that. And I think that's why a lot of the musicians liked me so much, because I never show off and always think about them first." He began studying arrangements carefully, playing rhythms along with the brass: "I knew exactly what they were playing because I saw it on the music, and I put what I thought was a good support for them, a special passage." Where there were "holes" in the arrangement, he filled them with drum interpolations. This practice provoked criticism from musicians used to a steady rhythmic foundation. "They said, 'Oh, that little guy is crazy, he's always breaking up the tempo.' [. . .]" (218)

24. Hughes seems to have condensed a number of Gillespie recordings in the musical quotation he provides in the story, combining the lyrics from many of the trumpeter's vocal tunes into one record. Some of the obvious examples from which Hughes was working are "Oop Bop Sh' Bam" (composed by Gillespie and Gil Fuller, recorded for Savoy Records in 1946), "Oop-Pop-A-Da" (composed by Babs Brown, recorded for RCA Victor in 1947), and "Ool-Ya-Koo" (composed by Gillespie, also recorded for RCA Victor in 1947). Interestingly, Hughes collapses the distinction he makes between Calloway's scat and Gillespie's vocalizations in his children's history, *The First Book of Jazz*, published in 1955, just six years after the Simple piece. There Hughes excises any suggestion of political importance to the "non-semantic" vocals of bebop artists and instead writes:

> Sometimes for fun, singers sing "oo-ya-koo" syllables to boppish backgrounds today, as Cab Calloway in the 1930's sang "hi-de-hi-de-ho-de-hey," meaning nothing, or as Lionel Hampton sang "hey-baba-re-bop" in 1940, or as Louis Armstrong used to sing "scat" syllables to his music in Chicago in the 1920's, or as Jelly Roll Morton shouted meaningless words to ragtime music in the early 1900's, or as the Mother Goose rhyme said, "Hey-diddle-diddle, the cat and the fiddle," even before that—for fun. Nonsense syllables are not new in poetry or music, but they are fun. (59)

This undoing of his earlier explanation of bebop's "nonsense" lyrics is possibly a capitulation to market concerns: the difference perhaps between publishing in a progressive African American newspaper and in a children's book aimed at a "mainstream" audience.

25. Early in the music's development, in the mid-1940s, the terms "bebop" and "rebop" were used almost interchangeably as names for the new music. Both are semantic "vocables [. . .] used [. . .] to accompany [a] distinctive

two-note rhythm" that recurs throughout the music (Owens 137). "Bebop" and "bop" are the names that endured.

26. Harlem's 1943 riot, "the worst disturbance that had ever occurred in the community," occurred on the evening of August 1, after word spread among African American residents that a white police officer had shot and killed a black soldier (Anderson 295). The shooting occurred at the Hotel Braddock, on 126th Street, after the soldier, Robert Bandy, intervened in an altercation between white police constable James Collins and an African American female guest. Bandy managed to secure Collins's nightstick in the melee and clubbed the police officer over the head with it, before trying to run from the hotel. Collins halted Bandy's escape by shooting him in the left shoulder, and then took the soldier into custody at Sydenham Hospital. When no word about Bandy's condition followed, some bystanders erroneously assumed that he had died from his wounds. In the wake of this assumption thousands of Harlemites erupted in an angry protest, destroying property and assaulting police and firefighters (Anderson 295–98).

27. Throughout this section I refer to the individual pieces that comprise *Montage of a Dream Deferred* as "lyrics" or "segments," but not as "poems" in themselves. I do this in keeping with Hughes's conception of the book as one long, if not fragmentary, poem.

28. This lyric provides the title of Lorraine Hansberry's famous drama, *A Raisin in the Sun* (1958), itself an exploration of failed promise for urban African Americans at mid-century.

29. I call bebop "disjunctive" after DeVeaux, who uses it to register bebop musicians' characteristic propensity for intermusical juxtaposition in improvisation. Bebop, DeVeaux suggests, is disjunctive in its ironic incorporation of other styles, either across genres (in its allusions to classical or popular music) or time (as in its incongruous use of clichés from earlier jazz styles). While this ironic intertextuality may suggest a "postmodern" aesthetic in its deconstructive impulses, I read both bebop and Hughes's writing (as well as Ellison's, in Chapter Three) as being more "conventionally" modern for the assertive faith they place in the individual artist's ability to give shape to these fragmented elements.

30. As Robinson notes, Glenn Miller's "In the Mood" (1939) may be the best known "riff tune" of the Swing Era, composed as it is around a "stock jazz riff at least as old as Wingy Manone's 'Tar Baby Stomp,'" from 1930 (1047).

31. As an example of Gillespie's "witty" and "punning" riffs, DeVeaux cites a figure from the trumpeter's 1943 recording of "Sweet Georgia Brown," which features "a change in emphasis [that] momentarily transforms a previously underemphasized chromatic neighbor note into [. . .] a blue note" (*Birth* 269). In other words, Gillespie's riff is continuous with his bop-style chromaticism, but also accents one of the signature notes in the blues scale—so much a part of blues and early jazz. This Signifyin(g) gesture seems all the more clever for its placement in an improvisation on an early jazz standard.

32. My emphasis on the bebop riff as a Signifyin(g) figure here is not intended to underestimate its musical functionality. Rather, I acknowledge that, as

Paul Berliner notes in *Thinking in Jazz,* improvisers frequently turn to riffs as "discrete patterns in their repertory storehouses"—which they refer to alternately as "vocabulary, ideas, licks, tricks, pet patterns, crips, cliches, and, in the most functional language, things you can do" (102). As musician Tommy Turrentine adds, "The old guys used to call those things crips. That's from crippled [. . .] . In other words, when you're playing a solo and your mind is crippled and you can't think of anything different to play, you go back into one of your old bags and play one of your crips" (qtd in Berliner 102).

33. It is worth noting here that Hughes's inclusion of this segment in a sequence that both pays deference to the importance of bebop and celebrates black community effectively, if implicitly, constitutes a pre-emptive critique against any suggestion that gays should be excluded from the subcultural fraternity of modern jazz or from a broad vision of African American community. In this way, Hughes problematizes the slippages between jazz and masculinity, and between African American racial pride and strong male identity, slippages that I call attention to in the introduction.

NOTES TO CHAPTER THREE

1. In less public contexts—namely, his correspondence with Albert Murray—Ellison was even more querulous in his estimation of bebop's aesthetic legacy. For example, in a September 28, 1958 letter, Ellison remarks that Charlie Parker sounded "miserable, beat and lost [. . .] most of the time" (qtd in Murray and Callahan 193).

2. While the idea that *Invisible Man* is influenced by jazz is almost universally accepted among critics, different commentators compare the book's design to different jazz styles. Horace A. Porter, for instance, suggests that "Ellison's manipulation of sound recalls [Duke] Ellington's," while A. Timothy Spaulding examines the novel "through the cultural and aesthetic framework of bebop," as I do here (Porter 84; Spaulding 481).

3. As Ellison biographer Lawrence Jackson reports, the book that Wright suggested for review was the novel *These Low Grounds* by the black American novelist Waters Turpin. Initially, Jackson writes, Ellison shied away from the request, but later conceded when "Wright pressed him with the responsibility of examining contemporary black writers from the literary perspective of the radical" (187).

4. Lawrence Jackson reports that Ellison originally intended to study sculpture with Augusta Savage, to whom his art professor at Tuskegee, Eva Hamlin, had written a letter of introduction. Upon landing in New York, however, and meeting Langston Hughes, Ellison decided to study with Barthé, introduced to him by Hughes. On Ellison's early days in New York, including his association with Hughes and Wright, see Jackson, Chapters Seven and Eight.

5. An example of Ellison's later denials of Marxist ideology in his fiction occurs in the interview, "A Very Stern Discipline," published in the March 1967 issue of *Harper's Magazine,* and later reprinted in Ellison's essay collection,

Going to the Territory (1985) and in his posthumously published *Collected Essays* (1995). There Ellison contends:

> I never wrote the official [Party] type of fiction. I wrote what might be called propaganda having to do with the Negro struggle, but my fiction was always trying to be something else, something different even from Wright's fiction. I never accepted the ideology which the *New Masses* attempted to impose on writers. They hated Dostoevsky, but I was studying Dostoevsky. They felt that Henry James was a decadent snob who had nothing to teach a writer from the lower classes, and I was studying James. I was also reading Marx, Gorki, Sholokhov and Isaac Babel. I was reading everything, including the Bible. Most of all, I was reading Malraux. I thought so much of that little Modern Library edition of *Man's Fate* that I had it bound in leather. This is where I was really living at the time, so perhaps it is the writers whose work has most impact upon us that are important, not those with whom we congregate publicly. Anyway, I think style is more important than political ideologies. (742–43)

This disavowal of the viability of integrating Marxist ideas with modernist fiction seems to be a mindset that Ellison arrived at by the 1940s, and perhaps contributed to his creative break from Richard Wright. For a more complicated discussion of Ellison's relationship to Communism, see Jackson, Chapter Eight.

6. In this instance, I intend "parodically" in the popular sense, to mean reflective of comic imitation. Ellison was, of course, a master of a more formal parody—the repetition and revision Henry Louis Gates identifies as central to Signifyin(g)—but in the case of "Hymie's Bull," the writer seems to bring no hints of irony or political comment to his imitative practice. As well, I want to note here that my comparison of this story to Hemingway's fiction is hardly novel; Robert O'Meally, for example, in *The Craft of Ralph Ellison,* argues that the piece is "overly influenced" by Hemingway's work (30).

7. The manuscripts for these stories, which were collected in the posthumous volume *Flying Home and Other Stories,* do not bear dates of composition. However, Ellison's literary executor, John F. Callahan, surmises that they were composed around 1937 or 1938 (basing his argument on the return addresses they feature and the print of the typewriter they bear).

8. Zora Neale Hurston offers a version of this rhyme in Chapter Seven of *Mules and Men,* her collection of African American folklore. There, a speaker begins a folktale with "Once upon a time was a good ole time— monkey chew tobacco and spit white lime" (121). Roger D. Abrahams also includes a version in *Jump–Rope Rhymes: A Dictionary,* 145.

9. The lyric here is of course an homage to Jack Johnson, the first African American to be crowned heavyweight champion in boxing. After Johnson ascended to the championship in 1908, many white fans of the sport called for Jim Jeffries, a white boxer who had retired with a perfect record, to return to the ring and dethrone the black champ. A contest between the two was finally arranged in 1910, and was perceived by many to wield much more than athletic significance. Jeffries was hailed as "the hope of the white race" by the white press; the *Chicago Defender*, on the other hand, argued that "[t]he future welfare of [Johnson's] people form[ed] a part of the stake." When the two finally met in the ring on July 4, 1910, Johnson easily outperformed Jeffries in an epic fifteen–round battle that ended not by a referee's decision, but by Johnson's own mercy after he nearly knocked a dazed Jeffries out of the ring. Johnson's victory was widely celebrated among African Americans and inspired a number of secular songs like the one sung by Buster and Riley here (Levine 430–32).

10. Lawrence Jackson adds: "The de facto segregation of the WPA, where black writers worked exclusively on the black community, continued to provide Ellison with a rich, even academic perspective on black history" (210). Jackson also notes that one of the tales he collected in Harlem was "Sweet the Monkey," a tale about a "black man in antebellum South Carolina who could turn himself invisible" (223). In this, we see the young Ellison compiling material that would go on to influence directly the development of *Invisible Man*. For more on Ellison's tenure with the WPA, see Jackson, Chapter Eight. Eric Sundquist includes Ellison's transcription of Leo Gurley's "Sweet-the-Monkey" in *Cultural Contexts for Ralph Ellison's* Invisible Man, and notes that a number of Ellison's recorded narratives are reprinted in Ann Banks's 1980 edited collection, *First Person America*. See Sundquist, *Cultural*, 132–35.

11. "Indivisible Man" is actually a collaborative effort between Ellison and James McPherson, with whom Ellison conducted a number of interviews and exchanged correspondence.

12. The comparison of Ellison's 1930s social realism to Steinbeck's work here is not merely my own evaluation. Rather, as Robert O'Meally notes, Ellison expressed a fondness for Steinbeck's work in his book reviews for leftist periodicals (*Craft* 39).

13. I make this comparison between Buster and Riley and Huck and Tom with complete awareness of the dizzying complications that Shelley Fisher Fishkin's thesis in *Was Huck Black?: Mark Twain and African American Voices* adds to my suggestion. Fishkin argues that Twain's real–life model for Huckleberry Finn's characterization was likely an African American boy, "Sociable Jimmy," about whom the writer composed an article for the *New York Times* in 1874. She maintains that the similarities between Jimmy's characterization and speech in the newspaper piece and Huck's in the 1884 novel are so striking as to contradict Twain's own assertion in his autobiography that Huck was based on Tom Blankenship, a poor, white boy the writer had encountered in Hannibal, Missouri. In my opinion, the possibility

that Buster and Riley are variations on a "white" character who, in fact, may have been based on a black person—and through whom Twain first experimented with writing African American dialect—is more conclusive proof of the organic hybridity in American culture which I am proposing.

14. Ellison frequently noted Eliot's influence, especially *The Waste Land,* on his literary sensibility. As Horace A. Porter argues, even Ellison's unfinished epic second novel, published posthumously and abridged as 1999's *Juneteenth,* signifies on Eliot's famous poem. See Porter, *Jazz Country,* 114–17.

15. A version of this oral narrative, entitled "A Flying Fool," is collected in Roger D. Abrahams's *African American Folktales,* 280. The tale is also referenced in Richard Wright's novel, *Lawd Today,* and Sterling Brown's poem, "Slim in Hell."

16. The lyric to "Black and Blue," composed by Andy Razaf, is dominated by ironic turns-of-phrase in which the singer expresses the pain of being African American:

> No joys for me, no company,
> Even the mouse ran from my house,
> All my life through, I've been so black and blue.
> I'm white inside, it don't help my case,
> 'Cause I can't hide what is on my face.

Moreover, the song's genealogy compounds its ironic content. Razaf originally composed it for the 1929 New York production, *Hot Chocolates,* to satisfy the demand of the show's financial backer, the white mobster Dutch Schultz, who wanted a comic lament about African American hardship. As Eric Sundquist writes, the song instead "came to be regarded as one of the first overt instances of racial protest in American popular music" (*Cultural* 115).

17. The Invisible Man's physicality in the violent anecdote recalls Baker's "deformation of mastery" for me as it evidences a determination to assert a distinguishable presence. Indeed, Baker conceptualizes the term as a performance that "distinguishes rather than conceals" (*Modernism* 51). This seems in line with the Invisible Man's motivations when he confesses that sometimes, against the threat of invisibility, "you strike out with your fists, you curse and you swear to make them recognize you" (*Invisible* 4). I wish to emphasize the speaker's own admission of a need to be *recognized* that at times manifests itself through violence, while I maintain sight of Baker's assertion that deformation of mastery "advertises [. . .] unabashed *badness,*" but "is not always conjoined with violence" (50, original emphasis).

18. These are only some of the references in the novel that I feel confident suggesting refer to specific moments or people in the history of African American music. Ellison himself makes the connection between "They Picked Poor Robin Clean" and Kansas City jazz in his essay, "On Bird, Bird–Watching and Jazz" (264–65), and admits that Rinehart comes from

the Jimmy Rushing lyric to "Harvard Blues" in "The Art of Fiction: An Interview" (223).

19. As DeVeaux argues, the ambivalence of urbane Northern musicians of the 1940s "is often overlooked in the history of jazz because it does not fit the prevailing paradigm. In contemporary criticism, the blues is more often than not celebrated as the center of an essentialist conception of black identity" (*Birth* 345).

20. Two examples of bebop tunes that "make changes" on the blues are Charlie Parker's "Blues for Alice," which modifies blues harmony by briefly modulating from the key of F to D in the second measure, and then gradually reassumes the original key through a series of ii-V(7) cadences, and Bud Powell's "Dance of the Infidels," which also supplements the blues base I-IV-V harmonic structure with a series of ii-V(7) substitutions.

21. Two excellent essays that further discuss Ellison's relationship to "canonical" texts are Sandra Adell's "The Big E(llison)'s Texts and Intertexts: Eliot, Burke, and the Underground Man," and William Lyne's "The Signifying Modernist: Ralph Ellison and the Limits of the Double Consciousness."

22. Gabbard's discussion uses as a representative example a solo by James Moody in which the saxophonist cites a recognizable phrase from Percy Grainger's "Country Gardens."

23. Monson is especially germane to my discussion of Ellison's jazz–inspired intertextuality here since her conceptualization of intermusicality is heavily indebted to Bakhtinian notions of dialogism and heteroglossia.

24. In keeping with Callahan's reading of Ellison's attempt to create a "continuous present" in *Invisible Man,* it seems fitting that on a syntactical level Ellison's narrator moves from the past tense to the present in his discussion of the black subject's place in history here.

25. In the early days of bebop's development, its young creators and their innovations were quite literally outside the "groove" of history—that is, unrepresented on record because of a ban on recordings lodged by the American Federation of Musicians in the early 1940s. It is likely that bebop's lack of representation on record in its early stages helped feed the myth of its creation that followed: that it appeared as if by magic among its young performers.

26. Mark Anthony Neal and Robin D.G. Kelley also explore the subversive quality of hipster style among African American men in the 1940s. Neal sees the sartorial extravagance of the zoot suit as necessarily related to bebop's revolutionary energy, and part of a larger culture of "social improvisation" among African American men. As he summarizes: "Zoot suits, the lindy–hop, and jive all provided opportunities for African-American youth to be active participants in the subculture that bebop music provided" (201). Kelley suggests, in *Race Rebels,* that the "language and culture of zoot suiters represented a subversive refusal to be subservient. Young black males created a fast–paced, improvisational language which sharply contrasted with the stereotype of the stuttering, tongue–tied Sambo" (166). See Kelley, Chapter Seven.

NOTES TO CHAPTER FOUR

1. I am conceptualizing the mature period of the Civil Rights Era as spanning from 1954's Brown vs. Board of Education decision through to the end of the 1960s.

2. I use "deformative" here to recall my discussion of bebop as "deformation of mastery" from Chapter Two.

3. The "settling" of bebop as the sound of mainstream jazz occurred, of course, with more controversy then I suggest in this statement. Bebop's initial appearance on record, for instance, incensed critics and fans of traditional jazz styles. Bernard Gendron's essay, "A Short Stay in the Sun," offers a productive discussion of bebop's troublesome critical reception. As Gendron writes, bebop "was born in the midst of one of the most divisive disputes in the history of jazz, between the partisans of swing music, on the one hand, and on the other, the 'dixieland' revivalists who were proposing a return to the classic New Orleans jazz of the 1920s. [. . .] The revivalist–swing war so subtly transposed itself into the bebop war that many of the criticisms, once directed against swing by the 'anti–modern' revivalists, were now being leveled against bebop, though in different circumstances and with different inflections" (137–38).

   As well, I wish to note here that there were, of course, other notable stylistic developments launched by jazz musicians after bebop, and beyond the free jazz storm of the 1960s. Other less revolutionary sub–styles of jazz in the 1950s and sixties, for example, are hard bop and soul jazz, both of which tempered the erudition of bebop with a more accessible rhythm and blues groove. The most novel jazz form after the 1960s is likely "fusion," an amalgamation of jazz and rock music pioneered by Miles Davis with his late 1960s records, *In a Silent Way* and *Bitches Brew*. However, many critics regard fusion as such an aesthetic departure from an "accepted" jazz tradition as to preclude its place within that tradition. Reasons for this exclusion would include fusion's focus on the electric guitar and electronic keyboards (rather than on horns and the piano-bass-drum combo of the acoustic rhythm section) and its rhythmic departure from the lilting swing of earlier jazz in favor of beats borrowed from rock and popular rhythm and blues. As Mark Gilbert summarizes, "Purists tended to see it as diluted jazz; others resented what they perceived as blatant commercialism" (420). I discuss fusion in more detail in Chapter Five.

4. I summarize only Coleman's most influential innovations. For detailed discussions of Coleman's musical development, see John Litweiler's *The Freedom Principle* and Ekkehard Jost's *Free Jazz*.

5. By "dynamics" here I mean the musical term: namely, the use of variations in intensity and volume for expressive effect.

6. The examples Gioia cites constitute only a sample of the moments and movements that marked this ethos of freedom. Other examples include the early 1960s motto of the NAACP, "Free by '63," and "Freedom to the Free," the

title of the United States Commission on Civil Rights's 1963 report to the president on the history of civil rights (Franklin and Moss 501–02).

7. For a brief discussion of Graettinger and Tristano's relationship to African American free jazz, see Litweiler, 17–18 and 29–30.

8. For an excellent discussion of the longstanding forced separation of African American jazz from "white" avant–garde music, see George E. Lewis's "Improvised Music after 1950: Afrological and Eurological Perspectives." As Lewis argues, "Eurological modernist music criticism, while erasing the practitioners of Afrological improvised music from postwar histories of 'contemporary' music, has nonetheless felt obliged to present a series of ongoing critiques of its construction of 'jazz.' Such critiques may represent an attempt to create [. . .] an 'epistemological other'" (143).

9. Other notable examples illustrate the economic disenfranchisement of free jazz musicians as the music was coming into its own. Tenor saxophonist Archie Shepp, for instance, was forced to work as a merchandiser for Abraham and Strauss, even after attaining critical interest and recording contracts. In 1966, after giving up his New York "day job" to take a number of playing engagements in California, Shepp fell into such financial hardship that he was forced to pawn his horn and was thus temporarily left without an instrument to play (Kofsky 142–43).

10. While I cite this quote from Baraka to mark the Black Arts movement's attraction to free jazz's apparent separatism, I cannot help but argue that his narration of jazz history is rhetorically opportunistic. As I have tried to maintain all along, at no point in its history has jazz been isolated from "Western popular forms."

11. The Art Ensemble of Chicago came out of a signal development in free jazz in the later 1960s, the emergence of artist collectives aimed at supporting the new music in the face of mainstream indifference. Perhaps the first notable collective was Bill Dixon's Jazz Composers Guild, founded in California in 1964. Others surfaced in various cities throughout the last half of the decade: Los Angeles's Underground Musicians' Association, St. Louis's the Black Artists Group, Detroit's Creative Musicians Association. As Ted Gioia writes, though, "the Chicago–based Association for the Advancement of Creative Musicians (AACM) would prove to be the most influential of these groups" (354). Established in 1965, "with the aim of helping progressive musicians find performing opportunities, rehearsal space, and other career support," the AACM included, at various times, free jazz luminaries like the pianist Muhal Richard Abrams, saxophonist Anthony Braxton, and AEC founding members Roscoe Mitchell, Joseph Jarman, and Lester Bowie (354). As members Abrams and John Shenoy Jackson expressed in 1973: "The Association for the Advancement of Creative Musicians' (AACM) primary concerns are about survival, accountability and achievement. The Black creative artist must survive and persevere in spite of the oppressive forces which prevent Black people from reaching the goals attained by other Americans" (72). Eric Porter offers a detailed discussion of the relationship between jazz

artist collectives and the Black Arts movement in *What Is This Thing Called Jazz?* See Chapter Five.

12. I single out Davis and Coltrane here as mainstream jazz musicians who adopted free jazz stylistics because of their noteworthy place in jazz throughout the 1950s and sixties. However, many other established musicians who were not necessarily aligned with the young jazz avant–garde looked to the new music for inspiration in the 1960s as well. Bebop musicians like Sonny Rollins and Jackie McLean flirted with jazz freedom as the new music gained cachet. Consider, for instance, Rollins's *On the Outside* (Bluebird, 1963), recorded with Coleman's longtime sideman Don Cherry, and McLean's *Let Freedom Ring!* (Blue Note, 1962).

13. In 1958, *Life* magazine named Davis among the black professionals and celebrities they regarded as most influential in advancing civil rights; the trumpeter's 1962 interview with Alex Haley for *Playboy* inaugurated the magazine's now–famous monthly celebrity interview feature. Also, it is worth noting here that Davis's wealth was not merely fortuitous but an effect of the musician's shrewd business sense and negotiation. Davis was an active investor on the stock market, for example, and a relentless voice in confronting managers and venue–owners about unfair practices. As Jack Chambers summarizes, "Davis demanded all his rights and a few privileges too, and he considered them his due; he was not interested in bargaining for what was his due or in presenting his case tactfully, which was a waste of breath" (I: 230).

14. Intriguingly, Davis cast many of his early dismissals of free jazz in racialized tones, appealing to a sense of "authentic blackness" that the trumpeter suggested Coleman and his bandmates exploited. For instance, commenting in the early 1960s on Coleman's trumpet player, Don Cherry, Davis sneered: "Anyone can tell that guy's not a trumpet player—it's just notes that come out, and every note he plays, he looks serious about, and people will go for it—especially white people. They go for anything. They want to be hipper than any other race, and they go for anything like that" (qtd in Chambers II: 20). Similarly, "[w]hen a supporter of Ornette Coleman declared that [bebop drummer] Art Blakey was 'old–fashioned,' Davis snapped, 'If Art Blakey is old–fashioned, then I'm white'" (Chambers II: 24).

15. Davis's young sidemen in his 1960s quintet—Wayne Shorter on tenor saxophone, Herbie Hancock on piano, Ron Carter on bass, and Tony Williams on drums—all seemed to have internalized stylistic developments from free jazz. Hancock, for example, worked Cecil Taylor's stormy percussiveness into an otherwise blues– and bop–steeped keyboard approach. The rhythm foundation of Carter and Williams fed off of an open antagonism in their combined feel, with the bassist intentionally lagging behind the young drummer's perpetual tendency to rush the beat.

16. Amidst the Civil Rights Era, Davis's politics tended to be less "visible," expressed less through explicit social protest than through "practical" gestures like benefit concerts and donations. Despite these moves though, Davis came under criticism from some of his more militant contemporaries

in the 1960s. For example, drummer Max Roach—a bandmate of Davis's in Charlie Parker's 1940s quintet—crashed the trumpeter's high–profile 1961 concert at Carnegie Hall with placard–bearing protesters to demonstrate against Davis's reserved involvement in black politics. (Roach himself had integrated music and politics to striking effect with his 1960 record, *We Insist! The Freedom Now Suite* for Nat Hentoff's Candid Records label.) And though Davis did not attach himself to causes, nor to movements, one could argue that his individualist conduct enacted a version of radical politics. Consider the trumpeter's aggressive efforts to redress exploitative practices in the music business, even acting on behalf of other black artists like the singer Robert Flack, for whom Davis negotiated significantly higher profits in the 1970s. As well, Davis appeared the quintessential "race man"—fearless in the face of white threat—when confronted by racist police officers outside New York's Birdland club in a famous 1959 incident.

17. Kimberly Benston writes: "The 'Coltrane Poem' has, in fact, become an unmistakable genre of contemporary black poetry to which a host of accomplished black poets have contributed—Ebon, David Henderson, Haki Madhubuti, Sharon Bourke, Sonia Sanchez, Jerry Ward, Jayne Cortez, Carolyn Rodgers, A.B. Spellman, and Michael Harper, to list but a few—and it is in this genre that the notion of music as the quintessential idiom, and of the word as its annunciator, is carried to its technical and philosophical apex" (*Performing* 120).

18. Explaining the connections that he sees between Coltrane and Malcolm X in the formation of black nationalism, Kofsky writes:

> Both men perceived the ultimate reality about this country—the reality that you could know only if you were black and you were exposed at close quarters to the jazz club-narcotics-alcohol-mobster-ghetto milieu. Both men escaped being trapped in that milieu; both sought to use lessons they had learned from it to show us not just the necessity for creating a society without ghettos of any sort, but also how to go about it; both, that is exhorted us to make maximum use of our *human* potentialities, our reason and emotions. (223, original emphasis)

19. Coltrane's connection to the new black politics was more material at times, too, as with his 1965 San Francisco benefit concert for Amiri Baraka's Black Arts Repertory Theatre/School. It is worth noting here that in the staging of benefit concerts for political causes, Coltrane and his seemingly less–engaged colleague Miles Davis were perhaps not so different after all. The fact that Coltrane was more often taken up as a figure of political engagement by the Black Power movement might be explained by the saxophonist's more overt acknowledgment of African cultural elements in his music.

20. Joe Goldberg notes in the original liner notes to that recording how much of the then contemporary emphasis on Coltrane as a key figure in the emerging "free jazz" scene missed the fact that his work was "quite firmly based in jazz tradition." Even "as the *avant–garde* controversy rages around him," Goldberg writes, "some tend to forget that Coltrane's great initial reputation was made as a blues player" (liner notes, original emphasis). In addition, Coltrane's use of soprano on this blues date may be a telling marker of the musician's self–styled mastery of tradition and innovation. Many commentators regard his adoption of that horn around 1960 as symbolic of a move away from traditional jazz and a step toward the avant–garde. For example, in Philip Larkin's review of *My Favorite Things,* the British poet and jazz critic equates Coltrane's use of soprano with a rejection of traditional jazz aesthetics, describing the musician's tone on the horn as a "thin, keening noise, sometimes sour as an oboe, at times expiring in an upper–register squeak, possessed continually by an almost Scandinavian unloveliness" (141). However, Coltrane's turn to soprano as a second horn might well have come from commemorative intentions. Richard Cook and Brian Morton, for example, speculate in *The Penguin Guide to Jazz on CD* that his use of the soprano was influenced by his attention to Bechet, whose recordings Coltrane had been absorbing in earnest throughout the last half of the 1950s (320).

21. In *The Signifying Monkey,* Henry Louis Gates draws attention to the well–known Coltrane–Ellington session, citing it as an example of Signifyin(g) as an "unmotivated mode of revision" (xxvii). The fact that the set list for the date comprised signature tunes from both musicians (Coltrane's "Big Nick," Ellington's "In a Sentimental Mood") marks the venture as an instance in which Signifyin(g) revises material not to "critique [. . .] but to engage in refiguration as an act of homage" (xxvii). Coltrane's "traditional" sessions with Johnny Hartman and Duke Ellington have not been looked at so favorably by some, though. Bill Cole reads the two records as a "compromise" by the saxophonist amidst an otherwise important transitional period in his style that led him into progressively more experimental territory. Cole hypothesizes that the traditional sessions were an attempt by Coltrane to placate critics who had attacked his moves toward the avant–garde. Reading the sessions as a backwards step in the development of Coltrane's style, Cole disparages them as "deficient" and "lacking in the strength and vitality" the saxophonist had otherwise shown in the early 1960s (149).

22. Werner reads the Redding performance as a signal moment in the development of "gospel politics." Midway through his set at the Monterey International Pop Festival, Redding announced his intention to do a "soulful number." Over Booker T. Jones's church–like organ accompaniment, the singer prefaced "I've Been Loving You Too Long" with the preacherly exhortation, "This song is a song, you know, we all ought to sing some time. This is the love crowd, right? We all love each other." Then raising the intensity of his voice, Redding called out, "Am I right? Let me hear you

say yeah." The crowd of forty thousand, most of them white Californians, roared back in affirmation, executing a moment of antiphony that Werner argues constituted a very high–profile intersection of popular culture and civil rights activism in the Summer of Love.

23. As I did when quoting Langston Hughes's poetry, I provide line numbers in any incomplete citations of Harper's poems.

24. See Chapter One for my discussion of Fanon's argument in light of the sexualization of jazz throughout the 1920s, particularly Maxim Gorky's vision of the Negro jazz orchestra as the sound of a phantasmagoric assault from a phallic Other.

25. This is, of course, a far from exhaustive list. Self–naming in titles was certainly an essential rite of passage among the beboppers. Examples from other musicians include Duke Jordan's "Jordu," Tadd Dameron's "Dameronia" and "Tadd's Delight," Miles Davis's "Miles Ahead" and "Milestones," and various Charles Mingus album titles, such as *Mingus Ah Um, Mingus Presents Mingus,* and the especially overstated, *Mingus Mingus Mingus Mingus Mingus.*

NOTES TO CHAPTER FIVE

1. In his role as artistic director for New York's Jazz at Lincoln Center (JALC) program, Murray (along with his associates Wynton Marsalis and Stanley Crouch) has been accused of conservatism by several American critics, for preferring works by older figures in the jazz pantheon, such as Louis Armstrong and Duke Ellington. In 1993, the *Village Voice* ran two high–profile critiques of the JALC program, one by Kevin Whitehead and another by Gary Giddins. When Wynton Marsalis responded with a 2500–word response, the *Voice* did not publish his letter (Piazza 166–67). As Tom Piazza summarizes, the program's critics "argue that Jazz at Lincoln Center should make room for a music with a more diffuse set of esthetic concerns, encompassing the work of such musicians as the reed virtuoso Anthony Braxton (who insists that his music is not jazz) and others who base their approaches in funk and world music" (168). As well, other critics have accused Murray of racism for ignoring much of the contributions of white musicians to the jazz tradition. Murray defends his choices by asserting his commitment to foregrounding the achievements of those who defined the jazz tradition: "we're talking here about fundamentals, the mythical style. In opera, you aspire to the sound of the Italian tenor [. . .] In jazz, you need to sound like a Negro" (qtd in Gennari, "Slumming" 62).

2. The closeness of Murray's biography to the narrative details of *Train Whistle Guitar* is striking. Henry Louis Gates's snapshot biography of the writer in a 1996 *New Yorker* magazine profile reads almost like a summary of the novel, especially in the details concerning Murray's academic precociousness and the unusual circumstances of his parentage:

Murray was born in 1916 and grew up in Magazine Point, a hamlet not far from Mobile, Alabama. His mother was a housewife, and his father, Murray says, was a "common laborer," who sometimes helped lay railroad tracks as a cross–tie cutter and at other times harvested timber in the Turpentine woods. "As far as the Murrays were concerned, it was a fantastic thing that I finished the ninth grade," he recalls, "or that I could read the newspaper." But he had already decided that he was bound for college. Everyone in the village knew that there was something special about him. And he knew it, too.

He had known it ever since an all–night wake—he was around eleven at the time—when he had fallen asleep in the living room, his head cradled in his mother's lap. At one point, he surfaced to hear himself being discussed, but, with a child's cunning, he pretended he was still asleep.

"Tell me something," a relative was saying. "Is it true that Miss Graham is really his mama?"

"She's the one brought him into the world," Mrs. Murray replied. "But I'm his mama." ("Cats" 74–75)

The reminiscence is recreated almost identically in the novel. Scooter, asleep in his mother's lap after a wake, overhears this exchange:

Some of them saying he really belongs to [Edie Bell Boykin], Miss Minnie Ridley Stovall said.

He belong to *me,* Mama said.

See there, Mister Horace Upshaw said.

But before anybody else could say anything else Mama's stomach was vibrating again and I felt the sound start and heard it go and then it came out through her mouth as words:

She brought him into the world but he just as much mine as my own flesh and blood. I promised her and I promised God. (180–81, original emphasis)

Despite these similarities, Murray has always been quick to express distance from his autobiographical character, Scooter, maintaining that he is merely making good on the modernist–aesthetic imperative to stylize one's own experience. Responding, for example, to the question, "How much of Scooter is Albert Murray?" in a 1992 interview, he states:

Well, a lot of him is Albert Murray. The way he feels and his outlook on life represent either my own outlooks or my aspirations, but you handle these things in a literary fashion. The whole idea of literature is *to stylize the raw*

experience of your everyday life into aesthetic statement.
In order to do that you're really trying to make a story. It
has to have a certain design. Just as a painting has to
have a design, so does narrative have to have a design.
You have the freedom, then, of doing all kinds of things.
You can give some of your characteristics to other characters, other people in the book; you can appropriate
some of their ideals and characteristics and their skills
and so forth to yourself. But overall you want to make a
statement. So in a sense Scooter represents a lot of Albert
Murray, but a lot of other people in those books represent a lot of Albert Murray. (qtd in Seigenthaler 57–58,
my emphasis).

Murray's comments here are very similar to his own aesthetic notion of
the "vernacular imperative," which I discuss in this chapter.
3. And the idea of the jam session—of disparate voices coming together in a
ritual of communal aesthetic practice—certainly influences Murray's fiction–writing, by his own acknowledgment. In a 1951 letter to Ralph Ellison, describing the manuscript that would eventually become *Train
Whistle Guitar,* Murray writes:

As you know, from the point of view of composition it is
(in texture) a jam session on the theme of old Jack the Bear,
and I'm supposed to be in there blowing a little of everything that I can think of, blowing it as I feel it and think I
know it, not as I was taught and not as anybody else
thinks I should. Boy, I really think I got me some soloists in
there nearbout as good as [Duke Ellington sidemen] old
Cootie and Rex and Johnny and Ben Webster and Harry
Carney; but you also got to have a pianist–arranger like
old Duke to make them cats really blow, and naturally
THAT'S got me worried. (*Trading* 22–23)

4. Indeed, the trend toward giving jazz ensembles "band" names in fusion
seems to underscore the form's turn toward rock and roll. In the past, jazz
groups had usually appeared under the aegis of their leader: the Duke
Ellington Orchestra, for example, or the Miles Davis Quintet. As jazz
became less distinguishable from rock, its high–profile groups began to
adopt names that downplayed the repertory tendency of the past and
accentuated the status of these combos as pop–style bands. Other examples of fusion's band names from the 1970s, beyond the three I cite above,
are Lifetime, the Crusaders, and Mahavishnu Orchestra.
5. Amidst the popularity of fusion, many of the free jazz musicians who had
come of age in the 1960s continued to perform and explore their own iconoclastic genre. However, the efforts of artists like Coleman, Cecil Taylor,

and the Art Ensemble of Chicago unsurprisingly did not approach the market dominance of the new plugged–in sound during that time.

6. Writing about Marsalis's role in the jazz "renaissance" of the 1980s and nineties, Tom Piazza summarizes:

> The main catalyst in this renaissance has been the trumpeter Wynton Marsalis. Early in the 1980s, Marsalis appeared, age twenty, insisting on playing acoustic jazz and lecturing his elders about selling out. His integrity, sharp appearance, and musical wizardry caught the eyes and ears of young musicians and fans alike. Suddenly, someone their age, or just a little older, was playing a kind of music that was more interesting, and more demanding, than rock, and being cool doing it.
>
> Marsalis has been an important role model for young musicians. Everywhere he goes in a very active touring schedule, he makes time for appearances in local schools. He spends hours talking backstage after his concerts. If students have brought their instruments, Marsalis asks them to play something for him; he stays in touch with the best, and he offers encouragement and advice to all. (107)

7. Crouch is quite open in marking his intellectual debt to Albert Murray, especially in his own move from black nationalist politics to a pluralistic view of American culture. For example, in the introduction to his essay collection, *The All-American Skin Game*, Crouch writes:

> My intellectual apprenticeship of hard knocks and illumination didn't come out of nowhere. Albert Murray and the late Ralph Ellison are the two figures who, as far as I'm concerned, brought it all back home. They pulled in all of the highest intellectual aspirations and achievements from the world over, then combined them with the democratic complexities so inherent to our nation, realizing in their separate work quite bold expressions of reflective insight and aesthetic creation. [. . . For me, they were] the twin towers of a Southern and Southwestern one–two punch that flattened all of my former involvements with black nationalism and liberated me from the influence of LeRoi Jones, whose work I once copied as assiduously as Sonny Stitt did Charlie Parker's. (x)

Commenting on his ongoing "independent study" with Murray, Crouch calls Murray his "mentor and far more [his] father than the fellow whose blood runs in [his] veins" (x).

8. Rourke was a self–fashioned historian of American culture, famous in the 1930s for her bestselling biographies of Davy Crockett and John James Audubon. As well, she organized the 1934 National Folk Festival in St. Louis and for a period in 1937 served as editor of the Federal Art Project's Index of American Design.

9. Among the specific social science studies Murray targets for critique in *The Omni-Americans* is the Moynihan Report (*The Negro Family: A Case for National Action*), which he condemns as "a notorious example of the use of the social science survey as a propaganda vehicle to promote a negative image of Negro life in the United States" (27). The report, prepared by Daniel Patrick Moynihan in 1965 for the Department of Labor's Office of Policy Planning and Research, proposed that African American urban life was a "tangle of pathology," predominantly because of a supposed breakdown in so–called traditional family structures that had left the black family as a matri-archal organization (qtd in Berger 412). Critics of the report took offense at Moynihan's representation of black men as emasculated, supplanted by their female partners. In his constant assertion of maleness in African American achievements, which I discuss throughout this chapter, Murray responds to the attack on black masculinity that this school of social science represents, but also problematically reaffirms the slippages between masculinity and prideful African American identity, which I discuss in the introduction.

10. As discussed in Chapter Four, the Black Arts intellectuals championed African American artists whom they perceived as the embodiment of black national-ism's separatist ethos. Those swing musicians Murray celebrates, such as Duke Ellington or Count Basie, who are so consistently at the center of American popular music on a national level, never approached the Black Arts move-ment's "radical reordering of the western cultural aesthetic" or its "separate symbolism, mythology, critique, and iconology" (Neal, "Black Arts" 184).

11. Cholly himself asserts Scooter's and Buddy's place in the expressive tradi-tions and extended community he maps with his folk blues. As Scooter recalls at one point,

> Sometimes we would come upon him sitting somewhere by himself tuning and strumming his guitar and he would let us stay and listen as long as we wanted to, and some-times he would sneak our names into some very well known ballad just to signify at us about something, and sometimes he would make up new ballads right on the spot just to tell us stories. (10)

NOTES TO THE CODA

1. For example, in a January 16, 2001 interview with Eleanor Wachtel for CBC Radio's *Arts Tonight,* Burns says:

> I realized that this was not just this epic story and its sequel, but a trilogy that had to approach the only art

form that Americans have invented—one that's suffused
with the American story and the American experience. So
the film I would make would not be just about the music
and the extraordinary musicians who made it, but, having
larger fish to fry, about two World Wars and the devastat-
ing Depression, and the music that got people through the
toughest of times.

In that same interview, Burns, by his own admission a less-than-knowl-
edgeable jazz fan, reports that his decision to make *Jazz* the trilogy's third
part was influenced by African American cultural critic Gerald Early who,
while being interviewed for the *Baseball* documentary, told Burns that
"when they study our American civilization two thousand years from
now, Americans will only be known for three things—the Constitution,
baseball and jazz music. He said they're the three most beautiful things
that Americans have ever designed."

2. I discuss Burns's film in mainly positive terms here because ultimately its
    celebratory attention seems preferable to me than the various types of den-
    igration to which jazz was subjected historically. But I also wish to make
    note of the controversy the documentary stirred. Many viewers—includ-
    ing myself—were put off by the film's lopsided chronology, with three of
    ten episodes focused on the Swing Era, but only one—the final episode—
    covering jazz from 1960 to the present. The fact that this rushed ending to
    Burns's long narration of the music's history summarily dismissed the
    importance of free jazz—by racing through its period of emergence—
    enraged many of the same critics of the JALC's representation of the tradi-
    tion. Also, given Burns's relative inattention to jazz's most politically
    radical period, with the black nationalism of the sixties and seventies, it
    seems the filmmaker appears least interested in the music when it is most
    "threatening" to the American mainstream.

3. These various cross–promotions were certainly lucrative. For instance, as
    Steven F. Pond notes, halfway through the initial airing of *Jazz* on PBS in
    January 2001, "sales of related merchandise had already topped fifteen
    million dollars," at a time when "domestic jazz sales [. . .] were roughly
    twenty million dollars" annually (12).

4. I do not mean to seem overly anecdotal in arguing that the occasional pres-
    entation of jazz on a half–hour sitcom constitutes a widescale re-emergence
    of the music in the popular imagination. But indeed, I am perennially sur-
    prised when teaching undergraduates how few students know who Dizzy
    Gillespie is until I remark that he portrayed Vanessa's balloon–cheeked
    music teacher on Cosby's show. Invariably, at that point, the number of
    students in the class familiar with the famed trumpeter doubles or triples.

5. *Saturday Night Live* had featured a number of jazz musicians in the past,
    before the Marsalis appearance, but these were generally very avant–garde
    features in the early days of the show or spots by artists working with elec-
    tric or electronic groups, that offered some pop crossover appeal. (Of the

former type I am thinking, in particular, of Sun Ra's May 20, 1978 appearance and Ornette Coleman's spot on April 14, 1979; and of the latter, the plugged–in appearances by Miles Davis and Herbie Hancock that appeared on October 17, 1981 and December 8, 1984, respectively.) In the 1970s, the show had featured a few performances by acoustic jazz musicians like vocalist Betty Carter (March 13, 1976), the Preservation Hall Jazz Band (July 24, 1976), and Keith Jarrett (April 15, 1978), but by the 1980s, its music segments were almost purely devoted to pop acts like Simple Minds, Bryan Adams, and Frankie Goes to Hollywood. The Marsalis appearance seems so significantly anomalous, then, because by the time of its airing on March 28, 1987, viewers of *Saturday Night Live* had not seen any kind of "traditional" jazz act since pianist Eubie Blake's appearance with dancer Gregory Hines on March 10, 1979.

6. I single out Lee's film here because its presentation of jazz musicians is remarkably different from the representations that dominate jazz films by white directors in the 1980s, namely, Bertrand Tavernier's *Round Midnight* (1986) and Clint Eastwood's *Bird* (1988). While the latter films thrive on the mythology of the self–destructive jazz genius (emphasizing the alcoholism of the Lester Young–like protagonist in Tavernier's film, or the heroin addiction of Charlie Parker in Eastwood's project), Lee's movie portrays jazz musicians as an industrious, straight–shooting faction, without a whiskey bottle or syringe in sight.

Works Cited

Abrahrams, Roger D., ed. *Jump–Rope Rhymes: A Dictionary.* Austin: U of Texas P, 1969.

———. *African American Folktales: Stories from Black Traditions in the New World.* New York: Pantheon, 1999.

Abrams, Muhal Richard and John Shenoy Jackson. "The Association for the Advancement of Creative Musicians." *Black World* 23.1 (1973): 72–74.

Adell, Sandra. "The Big E(llison)'s Texts and Intertexts: Eliot, Burke, and the Underground Man." *CLA Journal* 37.4 (1994): 377–401.

Anderson, Jervis. *This Was Harlem: A Cultural Portrait, 1900–1950.* New York: Farrar, 1981.

Armstrong, Louis, trumpet, vocal. "King of the Zulus." *The Complete Hot Five and Hot Seven Recordings.* Disc 1. Rec. June 23, 1926. Columbia, C4K 63527, 2000.

———, trumpet, vocal. "West End Blues." *The Complete Hot Five and Hot Seven Recordings.* Disc 4. Rec. June 28, 1928. Columbia, C4K 63527, 2000.

———, trumpet, vocal. "St. Louis Blues." *Louis Armstrong Collection, Vol. 6: St. Louis Blues.* Rec. December 13, 1929. Columbia, CK 46996, 1991.

———. *Swing that Music.* 1936. New York: Da Capo, 1993.

Baker, Houston A., Jr. *Blues, Ideology and Afro-American Literature: A Vernacular Theory.* Chicago: U of Chicago P, 1984.

———. *Modernism and the Harlem Renaissance.* Chicago: U of Chicago P, 1987.

Bakhtin, M.M. "Discourse in the Novel." 1934–35. *The Dialogic Imagination: Four Essays by M.M. Bakhtin.* Ed. Michael Holquist. Trans. Caryl Emerson and Michael Holquist. Austin: U of Texas P, 1981. 259–422.

Barksdale, Richard K. "Hughes: His Times and His Humanistic Techniques." 1981. *Langston Hughes: Critical Perspectives Past and Present.* Ed. Henry Louis Gates, Jr. and K.A. Appiah. Amistad Literary Series. New York: Amistad, 1993. 94–106.

Barrett, Lindon. "African-American Slave Narratives: Literacy, the Body, Authority." *American Literary History* 7.3 (1995): 415–42.

Bell, Bernard. *The Afro-American Novel and Its Tradition*. Amherst: U of Massachusetts P, 1987.

Bell, Clive. "'Plus de Jazz.'" *The New Republic* 28 (1921): 92–96.

Benston, Kimberly W. "I yam what I am: the topos of (un)naming in Afro-American literature." *Black Literature and Literary Theory*. Ed. Henry Louis Gates, Jr. New York and London: Routledge, 1984. 151–72.

——, ed. *Speaking for You: The Vision of Ralph Ellison*. Washington, D.C.: Howard UP, 1990.

——. *Performing Blackness: Enactments of African-American Modernism*. New York: Routledge, 2000.

Berger, James. "Ghosts of Liberalism: Morrison's *Beloved* and the Moynihan Report." *PMLA* 111.3 (1996): 408–20.

Bergreen, Laurence. *Louis Armstrong: An Extravagant Life*. New York: Broadway, 1997.

Berliner, Paul. *Thinking in Jazz: The Infinite Art of Improvisation*. Chicago: U of Chicago P, 1994.

Bhabha, Homi. "Signs Taken for Wonders: Questions of Ambivalence and Authority under a Tree Outside Delhi, May 1817." *Critical Inquiry* 12.1 (1985): 144–165.

Bowen, Barbara E. "Untroubled voice: call and response in *Cane*." *Black Literature and Literary Theory*. Ed. Henry Louis Gates, Jr. New York: Routledge, 1984. 187–203.

Boynton, Robert S. "The Professor of Connection." *New Yorker* November 6, 1995: 95–116.

Bradbury, Malcom and James Mcfarlane. "The Name and Nature of Modernism." 1976. *Modernism: A Guide to European Literature 1890–1930*. London: Penguin, 1991. 19–56.

Breton, Marcela, ed. *Hot and Cool: Jazz Short Stories*. New York: Plume, 1990.

Burns, Ken. Interview with Eleanor Wachtel. *The Arts Tonight*. CBC Radio 1. January 16, 2001.

Butler-Evans, Elliott. "The Politics of Carnival and Heteroglossia in Toni Morrison's *Song of Solomon* and Ralph Ellison's *Invisible Man*." *The Ethnic Canon: Histories, Institutions and Interventions*. Ed. David Palumbo-Liu. Minneapolis: U of Minnesota P, 1995. 117–39.

Callahan, John F. "Chaos, Complexity and Possibility: The Historical Frequencies of Ralph Ellison." 1979. In Benston, ed., *Speaking for You*. 125–43.

——. "The Testifying Voice in Michael Harper's *Images of Kin*." *Black American Literature Forum* 13 (1979): 89–92.

——. "Frequencies of Eloquence: The Performance and Composition of *Invisible Man*." *New Essays on* Invisible Man. Ed. Robert O'Meally. Cambridge, Mass.: Cambridge UP, 1988. 55–94.

——. "Introduction." *Flying Home and Other Stories*. By Ralph Ellison. Ed. John F. Callahan. New York: Random, 1996. ix–xxviii.

——. "Introduction." *Trading Twelves: The Selected Letters of Ralph Ellison and Albert Murray*. New York: Modern Library, 2000. vii–xiii.

Carby, Hazel. *Race Men*. Cambridge, Mass.: Harvard UP, 1998.

Carmichael, Stokely (Kwame Ture) and Charles Hamilton. *Black Power: The Politics of Liberation in America*. 1967. New York: Vintage, 1992.

Carson, Warren. "Albert Murray: Literary Reconstruction of the Vernacular Community." *African American Review* 27.2 (1993): 287–95.

Chambers, Jack. *Milestones: The Music and Times of Miles Davis*. 1983, 1985. 2 vols. New York: Da Capo, 1998.

Chinitz, David. "Literacy and Authenticity: The Blues Poems of Langston Hughes." *Callaloo* 19.1 (1996): 177–92.

Clar, Mimi. "The Style of Duke Ellington." 1959. *The Duke Ellington Reader*. Ed. Mark Tucker. New York: Oxford UP, 1993. 303–11.

Cole, Bill. *John Coltrane*. 1976. New York: Da Capo, 1993.

Coltrane, John. Liner notes, *A Love Supreme*. 1964. John Coltrane, tenor saxophone. Impulse Records, MCAMD-5660.

Cook, Richard and Brian Morton. *The Penguin Guide to Jazz on CD*. 4th ed. London: Penguin, 1998.

Cullen, Countee. "Rev. of *The Weary Blues*." 1926. *Langston Hughes: Critical Perspectives Past and Present*. Ed. Henry Louis Gates, Jr. and K.A. Appiah. Amistad Literary Series. New York: Amistad, 1993. 3–5.

Davis, Francis. *Bebop and Nothingness: Jazz and Pop at the End of the Century*. New York: Schirmer, 1996.

Davis, Miles, with Quincy Troupe. *Miles: The Autobiography*. New York: Simon, 1989.

DeKoven, Marianne. "Modernism and gender." *The Cambridge Companion to Modernism*. Ed. Michael Levenson. Cambridge: Cambridge UP, 1999. 174–93.

DeVeaux, Scott. "Constructing the Jazz Tradition: Jazz Historiography." *Black American Literature Forum* 25.3 (1991): 525–60.

———. *The Birth of Bebop: A Social and Musical History*. Berkeley: U of California P, 1997.

Douglas, Ann. *Terrible Honesty: Mongrel Manhattan in the 1920s*. New York: Farrar, 1995.

Douglass, Frederick. *Narrative of the Life of Frederick Douglass, an American Slave, Written by Himself*. 1845. Ed. David W. Blight. Boston: Bedford, 1993.

Du Bois, W.E.B. *The Souls of Black Folk*. 1903. Ed. Henry Louis Gates, Jr. and Terri Hume Oliver. New York: Norton, 1999.

———. "Criteria of Negro Art." 1926. In Du Bois, *Reader*. 509–15.

———. "On Carl Van Vechten's *Nigger Heaven*." 1926. In Du Bois, *Reader*. 516–20.

———. "Two Novels." *The Crisis* 35 (1928): 202.

———. *W.E.B. Du Bois: A Reader*. Ed. David Levering Lewis. New York: Holt, 1995.

Eliot, T.S. "Tradition and the Individual Talent." 1919. *The Sacred Wood: Essays on Poetry and Criticism*. 1920. London: Methuen, 1964. 47–59.

———. *The Waste Land*. 1922. *Collected Poems 1909–1962*. London: Faber, 1963. 61–86.

Ellington, Duke. "Certainly it's music!" *Listen* October 1944: 5–6.

Ellison, Ralph. "Hymie's Bull." 1937. In Ellison, *Flying Home*. 82–88.

———. "The Black Ball." 1937–38. In Ellison, *Flying Home*. 110–22.

———. "I Did Not Learn Their Names." 1940. In Ellison, *Flying Home*. 89–96.

———. "Afternoon." 1940. In Ellison, *Flying Home*. 33–44.

———. "Mister Toussan." 1941. In Ellison, *Flying Home*. 22–32.

———. "That I Had the Wings." 1943. In Ellison, *Flying Home*. 45–62.

———. "Flying Home." 1944. In Ellison, *Flying Home*. 147–73.

———. *Invisible Man*. 1952. New York: Vintage, 1982.

———. "Brave Words for a Startling Occasion." 1953. In Ellison, *Collected Essays*. 151–54.

———. "Twentieth–Century Fiction and the Black Mask of Humanity." 1953. In Ellison, *Collected Essays*. 81–99.

———. "The Art of Fiction: An Interview." 1955. In Ellison, *Collected Essays*. 210–24.

———. "Living with Music." 1955. In Ellison, *Collected Essays*. 227–36.

———. "The Charlie Christian Story." 1958. In Ellison, *Collected Essays*. 266–72.

———. "The Golden Age, Time Past." 1959. In Ellison, *Collected Essays*. 237–49.

———. "On Bird, Bird–Watching, and Jazz." 1962. In Ellison, *Collected Essays*. 256–65.

———. "What These Children Are Like." 1963. In Ellison, *Collected Essays*. 542–51.

———. "The World and the Jug." 1963–64. In Ellison, *Collected Essays*. 155–88.

———. "Introduction: *Shadow and Act*." 1964. In Ellison, *Collected Essays*. 49–60.

———. "Hidden Name and Complex Fate." 1964. In Ellison, *Collected Essays*. 189–209.

———. "'A Very Stern Discipline.'" 1967. In Ellison, *Collected Essays*. 726–54.

———. "Indivisible Man." 1970. In Ellison, *Collected Essays*. 353–95.

———. "Remembering Richard Wright." 1971. In Ellison, *Collected Essays*. 659–75.

———. "A Completion of Personality." 1974, 1987. In Ellison, *Collected Essays*. 783–817.

———. "Introduction." In Ellison, *Invisible Man*. vii–xxiii.

———. *Flying Home and Other Stories*. Ed. John F. Callahan. New York: Random, 1996.

———. *The Collected Essays of Ralph Ellison*. Ed. John F. Callahan. New York: Modern Library, 1995.

Fanon, Frantz. *Black Skin, White Masks*. 1952. New York: Grove, 1967.

Faulkner, Anne Shaw. "Does Jazz Put the Sin in Syncopation?" *Ladies Home Journal* 38 (1921): 16, 34.

Fauset, Jesse. "Our Book Shelf." *Crisis* 31 (March 1926): 239.

Feinstein, Sascha. *Jazz Poetry: From the 1920s to the Present*. Westport, Conn.: Greenwood, 1997.

Fischlin, Daniel and Ajay Heble. *The Other Side of Nowhere: Jazz, Improvisation, and Communities in Dialogue*. Middletown, Conn.: Wesleyan UP, 2004.

Fisher, Rudolph. "The Caucasian Storms Harlem." 1927. *Voices from the Harlem Renaissance*. Ed. Nathan Irvin Huggins. New York: Oxford UP, 1976. 74–82.

Fishkin, Shelley Fisher. *Was Huck Black?: Mark Twain and African-American Voices*. New York: Oxford UP, 1993.

Floyd, Samuel A., Jr. *The Power of Black Music: Interpreting Its History from Africa to the United States*. New York: Oxford UP, 1995.

Frank, Waldo. *In the American Jungle (1925–1936)*. New York: Farrar, 1937.

Franklin, John Hope and Alfred A. Moss, Jr. *From Slavery to Freedom: A History of African Americans*. 7th ed. New York: Knopf, 1994.

Freundlich, Roger. "Psyching Out Improv Demons." *Down Beat* June 1998: 62–63.

Gabbard, Krin. "The Quoter and His Culture." *Jazz in Mind: Essays on the History and Meanings of Jazz*. Ed. Reginald T. Buckner and Steven Weiland. Detroit: Wayne State UP, 1991. 92–111.

———. "Introduction: The Jazz Canon and Its Consequences." *Jazz Among the Discourses*. Ed. Krin Gabbard. Durham, N.C.: Duke UP, 1995

———. *Jammin' at the Margins: Jazz and the American Cinema*. Chicago: U of Chicago P, 1996.

Garrison, William Lloyd. "Preface." In Douglass, *Narrative*. 1845. 29–35.

Gates, Henry Louis, Jr. "Editor's Introduction: Writing 'Race' and the Difference It Makes." *"Race," Writing and Difference*. Ed. Henry Louis Gates, Jr. Chicago: U of Chicago P, 1985. 1–20.

———. *The Signifying Monkey: A Theory of African-American Literary Criticism*. New York: Oxford UP, 1988.

———. "King of Cats." *New Yorker* April 8, 1996: 70–81.

———. "The Trope of a New Negro and the Reconstruction of the Image of the Black." *Representations* 24 (1998): 129–55.

Gelfand, Marvin. "Taking a Leaf: A Talk with Albert Murray." In Maguire, *Conversations*. 8–11.

Gennari, John. "Jazz Criticism: Its Development and Ideologies." *Black American Literature Forum* 25.3 (1991): 449–523.

———. "Slumming in High Places: Albert Murray's Intercontinental Ballistics." *Brilliant Corners* 1.1 (1996): 59–67.

Gilbert, Mark. "Fusion." *The Blackwell Guide to Recorded Jazz*. Ed. Barry Kernfeld. Oxford: Blackwell, 1991. 419–42.

Gillespie, Dizzy, with Al Fraser. *To Be, or not . . . to Bop*. Garden City, NY: Doubleday, 1979.

Gilroy, Paul. *The Black Atlantic: Modernity and Double Consciousness*. Cambridge, Mass.: Harvard UP, 1993.

Gioia, Ted. *The History of Jazz*. New York: Oxford UP, 1997.

Goldberg, Joe. Liner notes, *Coltrane Plays the Blues*. 1960. John Coltrane, tenor saxophone. Atlantic CD, 1382-2.

Gorky, Maxim. "from *The Music of the Degenerate*." 1929. *The Picador Book of Blues and Jazz*. Ed. James Campbell. London: Picador, 1995. 119–21.

Green, Abel. "Cotton Club Review." 1927. *The Duke Ellington Reader*. Ed. Mark Tucker. New York: Oxford UP, 1993. 31–32.

Griffin, Farah Jasmine. *If You Can't Be Free, Be a Mystery: In Search of Billie Holiday.* New York: The Free Press, 2001.

Harper, Michael S. "Brother John." 1970. In Harper, *Songlines.* 3–4.

———. "Dear John, Dear Coltrane." 1970. In Harper, *Songlines.* 25–26.

———. "Elvin's Blues." 1970. In Harper, *Songlines.* 7–8.

———. "*'Bird Lives'*: Charles Parker in St. Louis." 1971. In Harper, *Songlines.* 50–51.

———. *History Is Your Own Heartbeat.* Chicago: U of Illinois P, 1971.

———. "Blue Ruth: America." In Harper, *History.* 3.

———. "Here Where Coltrane Is." In Harper, *History.* 32.

———. "Last Affair: Bessie's Blues Song." 1972. In Harper, *Songlines.* 63–64.

———. "My Poetic Technique and the Humanization of the American Audience." *Black Literature and Humanism.* Ed. R. Baxter Miller. Lexington: UP of Kentucky, 1981. 27–32.

———. "Bandstand." 1985. In Harper, *Songlines.* 168.

———. "A Narrative of the Life and Times of John Coltrane: Played by Himself." 1985. In Harper, *Songlines.* 187–88.

———. "Polls." 1985. In Harper, *Songlines.* 170.

———. "Solo." 1985. In Harper, *Songlines.* 171.

———. "Pulp Notes." 1985. In Harper, *Songlines,* 178–79.

———. *Songlines in Michaeltree: New and Collected Poems.* Chicago: U of Illinois P, 2000.

Harper, Philip Brian. *Framing the Margins: The Social Logic of Postmodern Culture.* New York: Oxford UP, 1994.

———. *Are We Not Men?: Masculine Anxiety and the Problem of African-American Identity.* New York: Oxford UP, 1996.

Hartman, Saidiya V. *Scenes of Subjection: Terror, Slavery, and Self-Making in Nineteenth–Century America.* New York: Oxford UP, 1997.

Heble, Ajay. *Landing on the Wrong Note: Jazz, Dissonance and Critical Practice.* New York: Routledge, 2000.

Hentoff, Nat. "Crazy Like a Fox." 1952. *Down Beat* July 1999: 14.

———. *Listen to the Stories: Nat Hentoff on Jazz and Country Music.* New York: Harper, 1995.

Hersch, Charles. "'Let Freedom Ring!': Free Jazz and African-American Politics." *Cultural Critique* 32 (1996): 97–123.

Hine, Darlene Clark. "'In the Kingdom of Culture': Black Women and the Intersection of Race, Gender, and Class." *Lure and Loathing: Essays on Race, Identity, and the Ambivalence of Assimilation.* Ed. Gerald Early. New York: Penguin, 1993. 337–51.

Huggins, Nathan Irvin. *Harlem Renaissance.* New York: Oxford UP, 1971.

Hughes, Langston. "I, Too." 1925. In Hughes, *Collected.* 46.

———. "Jazz Band in a Parisian Cabaret." 1925. In Hughes, *Collected.* 60.

———. "Negro Dancers." 1925. In Hughes, *Collected.* 44.

———. "The Weary Blues." 1925. In Hughes, *Collected.* 50.

———. "The Cat and the Saxophone (2 A.M.)" 1926. In Hughes, *Collected.* 89.

———. "Harlem Night Club." 1926. In Hughes, *Collected.* 90.

———. "The Negro Artist and the Racial Mountain." 1926. *Within the Circle: An Anthology of African American Literary Criticism from the Harlem Renaissance to the Present.* Ed. Angelyn Mitchell. Durham, N.C.: Duke UP, 1994. 55–59.

———. "Saturday Night." 1926. In Hughes, *Collected.* 88.

———. "Gypsy Man." 1927. In Hughes, *Collected.* 66.

———. "My Man." 1927. In Hughes, *Collected.* 67.

———. "Suicide." 1927. In Hughes, *Collected.* 82.

———. "Young Gal's Blues." 1927. In Hughes, *Collected.* 123.

———. "Advertisement for the Waldorf-Astoria." 1931. In Hughes, *Collected.* 143–46.

———. "Goodbye Christ." 1932. In Hughes, *Collected.* 166–67.

———. *The Big Sea.* 1940. Introduction by Arnold Rampersad. New York: Hill, 1993.

———. "Bop." 1949. *Simple Takes a Wife.* New York: Simon, 1953.

———. *Montage of a Dream Deferred.* In Hughes, *Collected.* 387–429.

———. *The First Book of Jazz.* 1956. Hopewell, NJ: Ecco Press, 1995.

———. "Jazz as Communication." *The Langston Hughes Reader.* New York: George Braziller, 1958. 492–94.

———. *The Collected Poems of Langston Hughes.* Ed. Arnold Rampersad and David Roessel. New York: Vintage, 1994.

Hutchinson, George. *The Harlem Renaissance in Black and White.* Cambridge, Mass.: Belknap P of Harvard UP, 1995.

Isaacs, James. Liner notes, *Stan Getz & Bill Evans.* 1964. Stan Getz, tenor saxophone, and Bill Evans, piano. Verve 833 802–2.

Jackson, Lawrence. *Ralph Ellison: The Emergence of Genius.* New York: Wiley, 2002.

Jazz. "Episode Three: 'Our Language.'" Dir. Ken Burns. PBS. WTVS, Detroit. January 10, 2001.

Johnson, Bruce. "Hear me talkin' to ya: problems of jazz discourse." *Popular Music* 12.1 (1993): 1–12.

Johnson, Charles. "Jazz Poetry and Blues." *Carolina Magazine* 58.7 (1928): 16–20.

Johnson, James Weldon. *The Autobiography of an Ex-Colored Man.* 1913. *Three Negro Classics.* New York: Avon, 1965. 393–511.

———. "Preface to the First Edition." 1922. *The Book of American Negro Poetry.* Rev. Ed. New York: Harcourt, 1931. 9–48.

———. *Black Manhattan.* 1930. Introduction by Sondra Kathryn Wilson. New York: Da Capo, 1991.

Jones, Gayl. *Liberating Voices: Oral Tradition in African American Literature.* Cambridge, Mass.: Harvard UP, 1991.

Jones, LeRoi (Amiri Baraka). *Blues People: The Negro Experience in White America and the Music That Developed From It.* New York: Quill, 1963.

———. *Black Music.* New York: Quill, 1967.

Jost, Ekkehard. *Free Jazz.* Graz: Universal Edition, 1974.

———. "Free Jazz." *The Blackwell Guide to Recorded Jazz.* Ed. Barry Kernfeld. Oxford: Blackwell, 1991. 385–418.

Karrer, Wolfgang. "Nostalgia, Amnesia, and Grandmothers: The Uses of Memory in Albert Murray, Sabine Ulibarri, Paula Gunn Allen, and Alice Walker." *Memory, Narrative, and Identity: New Essays in Ethnic American Literatures.* Ed. Amritjit Singh, Joseph T. Skerrett, Jr., and Robert E. Hogan. Boston: Northeastern UP, 1994. 128–44.

Kelley, Robin D.G. *Race Rebels: Culture, Politics, and the Black Working Class.* New York: The Free Press, 1994.

Kent, George E. "Ralph Ellison and Afro-American Folk and Cultural Tradition." 1972. In Benston, *Speaking for You.* 95–104.

Kernfeld, Barry, ed. *The New Grove Dictionary of Jazz.* New York: St. Martin's, 1991.

Kofsky, Frank. *Black Nationalism and the Revolution in Music.* New York: Pathfinder, 1970.

Lange, Art and Nathaniel Mackey. "Editor's Note." *Moment's Notice: Jazz in Poetry and Prose.* Ed. Art Lange & Nathaniel Mackey. Minneapolis: Coffee House, 1993. i–ii.

Larkin, Philip. *All What Jazz: A Record Diary 1961–1971.* New York: Farrar, 1985.

Lees, Gene. *Waiting for Dizzy.* New York: Oxford UP, 1991.

Levine, Lawrence. *Black Culture and Black Consciousness: Afro-American Folk Thought from Slavery to Freedom.* New York: Oxford UP, 1977.

Lewis, David Levering. *When Harlem Was in Vogue.* New York: Oxford UP, 1981.

Lewis, George E. "Improvised Music after 1950: Afrological and Eurological Perspectives." In Fischlin and Heble, eds., *Other Side of Nowhere.* 131–62.

Litweiler, John. *The Freedom Principle: Jazz After 1958.* New York: Morrow, 1984.

Locke, Alain. "The New Negro." *The New Negro: An Interpretation.* Ed. Alain Locke. New York: Albert and Charles Boni, 1925. 3–16.

Long, Richard A. "Interactions between Writers and Music during the Harlem Renaissance." *Black Music in the Harlem Renaissance.* Ed. Samuel A. Floyd, Jr. Contributions in Afro-American and African Studies, Number 128. New York: Greenwood Press, 1990. 129–37.

Lott, Eric. "Double V, Double–Time: Bebop's Politics of Style." 1988. *The Jazz Cadence of American Culture.* Ed. Robert G. O'Meally. New York: Columbia UP, 1998. 456–68.

Loy, Mina. "Modern Poetry." 1925. *The Lost Lunar Baedeker.* Ed. Roger L. Connover. New York: Farrar, 1996. 157–61.

Lyne, William. "The Signifying Modernist: Ralph Ellison and the Limits of the Double Consciousness." *PMLA* 107.2 (1992): 319–30.

Lyons, Len. *The Great Jazz Pianists: Speaking of Their Lives and Music.* New York: Da Capo, 1989.

Madhubuti, Haki. (Don L. Lee). "Don't Cry, Scream." 1969. *Directionscore: Selected and New Poems.* Detroit: Broadside, 1971. 94–98.

Maguire, Roberta S., ed. *Conversations with Albert Murray.* Jackson: UP of Mississippi, 1997.

Mailer, Norman. *The White Negro.* 1957. San Francisco: City Lights, 1969.

Malamud, Randy. *The Language of Modernism.* Ann Arbor: UMI Research P, 1989.

Martin, Dellita L. "Langston Hughes's Use of the Blues." *CLA Journal* 22 (1978): 151–59.

Marvin, Thomas. "Children of Legba: Musicians at the Crossroads in Ralph Ellison's *Invisible Man*." *American Literature* 68.3 (1996): 587–608.

McFarlane, James. "The Mind of Modernism." 1976. *Modernism: A Guide to European Literature 1890–1930*. Ed. Malcolm Bradbury and James McFarlane. London: Penguin, 1991. 71–94.

McMichael, George, et al, eds. *Anthology of American Literature*. Vol. 2: Realism to the Present. Upper Saddle River, NJ: Prentice Hall, 2000.

Meltzer, David. "Pre-ramble." In Meltzer, *Reading Jazz*. 1–34.

———, ed. *Reading Jazz*. San Francisco: Mercury House, 1993.

Mercer, Kobena. *Welcome to the Jungle: New Positions in Black Cultural Studies*. New York: Routledge, 1994.

Miller, R. Baxter. "Hughes: His Times and His Humanistic Techniques." *Langston Hughes: Critical Perspectives Past and Present*. Ed. Henry Louis Gates, Jr. and K.A. Appiah. New York: Amistad, 1993. 94–106.

Milton, John. "At a Solemn Musick." 1633. *John Milton: Complete Poems and Major Prose*. Ed. Merritt Y. Hughes. New York: Macmillan, 1957. 81–82.

Monson, Ingrid. "The Problem with White Hipness: Race, Gender, and Cultural Conceptions in Jazz Historical Discourse." *Journal of the American Musicological Society* 48.3 (1995): 396–422.

———. *Saying Something: Jazz Improvisation and Interaction*. Chicago: Chicago UP, 1996.

Morrison, Toni. *Playing in the Dark: Whiteness and the Literary Imagination*. New York: Random, 1992.

Murray, Albert. *The Omni-Americans: Black Experience and American Culture*. 1970. New York: Da Capo, 1990.

———. *The Hero and The Blues*. New York: Vintage, 1973.

———. *Train Whistle Guitar*. 1974. Foreword by Robert G. O'Meally. Northeastern Library of Black Literature. Boston: Northeastern UP, 1989.

———. *Stomping the Blues*. New York: Da Capo, 1976.

———. "Improvisation and the Creative Process." *Stirrings of Culture: Essays from the Dallas Institute*. Eds. Robert Sardello and Gail Thomas. Dallas: Dallas Institute Publications, 1986. 191–93.

———. "Regional Particulars and Universal Statement in Southern Writing." *Callaloo* 12.1 (1989): 3–6.

———. *The Seven League Boots*. New York: Pantheon, 1995.

———. *The Blue Devils of Nada: A Contemporary Approach to Aesthetic Statement*. New York: Vintage, 1996.

———. "Preface." In Murray and Callahan, eds., *Trading Twelves*. xix–xxiv.

Murray, Albert and John F. Callahan, eds. *Trading Twelves: The Selected Letters of Ralph Ellison and Albert Murray*. New York: Modern Library, 2000.

Neal, Larry. "The Black Arts Movement." 1968. *Within the Circle: An Anthology of African American Literary Criticism from the Harlem Renaissance to the Present*. Ed. Angelyn Mitchell. Durham, N.C.: Duke UP, 1994. 184–98.

———. "Ellison's Zoot Suit." 1970. In Benston, ed., *Speaking for You*. 105–24.

Neal, Mark Anthony. "' . . . A Way Out of No Way': Jazz, Hip-Hop, and Black Social Improvisation." In Fischlin and Heble, eds., *Other Side of Nowhere*. 195–223.

Newton, Francis. *The Jazz Scene*. London: Penguin, 1961.

Nielson, Aldon L. *Writing Between the Lines: Race and Intertextuality*. Athens, GA: U of Georgia P, 1994.

North, Michael. *The Dialect of Modernism: Race, Language and Twentieth–Century Literature*. New York: Oxford UP, 1994.

O'Brien, John. "Michael Harper." *Interviews with Black Writers*. New York: Liveright, 1973. 95–107.

Oliver, Paul and Barry Kernfeld. "Blues." In Kernfeld, ed., *Grove Dictionary*. 121–29.

Oliveros, Pauline. "Harmonic Anatomy: Women in Improvisation." In Fischlin and Heble, eds., *Other Side of Nowhere*. 50–70.

O'Meally, Robert G. *The Craft of Ralph Ellison*. Cambridge, Mass.: Harvard UP, 1980.

———. "Introduction." *New Essays on* Invisible Man. Cambridge, Mass.: Cambridge UP, 1988. 1–24.

———. "On Burke and the Vernacular: Ralph Ellison's Boomerang of History." *History and Memory in African-American Culture*. Ed. Geneviève Fabre and Robert O'Meally. New York: Oxford UP, 1994. 244–60.

———. "Preface." *The Jazz Cadence of American Culture*. Ed. Robert G. O'Meally. New York: Columbia UP, 1998. ix–xvi.

———. "Introduction, Part 2: One Nation Under a Groove, or the United States of Jazzocracy." *The Jazz Cadence of American Culture*. Ed. Robert G. O'Meally. New York: Columbia UP, 1998. 117–19.

Owens, Thomas. "Bop." In Kernfeld, ed., *Grove Dictionary*. 137–39.

Peretti, Burton W. *The Creation of Jazz*. Chicago: U of Illinois P, 1992.

———. *Jazz in American Culture*. American Ways Series. Chicago: Ivan R. Dee, 1997.

Phillips, Wendell. "Letter." In Douglass, *Narrative*. 1845. 36–38.

Piazza, Tom. *Blues Up and Down: Jazz In Our Time*. New York: St. Martin's, 1997.

Pond, Steven F. "Jamming the Reception: Ken Burns, *Jazz*, and the Problem of 'America's Music.'" *Notes* 60.1 (2003): 11–45.

Porter, Eric. *What Is This Thing Called Jazz?: African American Musicians as Artists, Critics, and Activists*. Berkeley: U of California P, 2002.

Porter, Horace A. *Jazz Country: Ralph Ellison in America*. Iowa City: U of Iowa P, 2001.

Pound, Ezra. "Preface to *Some Imagist Poets 1915*." 1915. *Imagist Poetry*. Ed. Peter Jones. London: Penguin, 1972. 134–36.

Rampersad, Arnold. *The Life of Langston Hughes. Volume 1: I, Too, Sing America*. New York: Oxford UP, 1986.

Randall, James. "An Interview with Michael S. Harper." *Ploughshares* 7.1 (1981): 11–27.

Reini-Grandell, Lynette. "Langston Hughes's Invocation of the Blues and Jazz Tradition under the Double-Edged Sword of Primitivism." *West Virginia University Philological Papers* 38 (1992): 113–23.

Robinson, J. Bradford. "Riff." In Kernfeld, ed., *Grove Dictionary*. 1047.

Rogers, J.A. "Jazz at Home." *The New Negro: An Interpretation.* Ed. Alain Locke. New York: Albert and Charles Boni, 1925. 216–24.

Rowell, Charles H. "'Down Don't Worry Me': An Interview with Michael S. Harper." *Callaloo* 13.4 (1990): 780–800.

Sabatella, Marc. "Improvisation." *A Jazz Improvisation Almanac.* May 9, 2005. <http://www.outsideshore.com/school/music/almanac/html/Improvisation/>.

Scherman, Tony. "What is Jazz?: An Interview with Wynton Marsalis." *American Heritage* October 1995: 66–85.

Schuller, Gunther. "Ornette Coleman." In Kernfeld, ed., *Grove Dictionary.* 229–31.

Seigenthaler, John. "An Interview with Albert Murray, Author of *The Spyglass Tree.*" In Maguire, *Conversations.* 57–65.

Shapiro, Irvin. "Langston Hughes a Young Poet of Great Promise: Wardman Park Bellhop Author of Volume of Verse Sponsored by Carl Van Vechten." *Washington Herald* 31 January 1926: 6D.

Sheppard, Richard. "The Crisis of Language." 1976. *Modernism: A Guide to European Literature 1890–1930.* Ed. Malcolm Bradbury and James McFarlane. London: Penguin, 1991. 323–36.

Smith, Bessie, composer and vocalist. "Backwater Blues." Rec. February 17, 1927. *The Essential Bessie Smith.* 2 discs. Columbia C2K 64922, 1997.

Smith, Julie Dawn. "Playing Like a Girl: The Queer Laughter of the Feminist Improvising Group." In Fischlin and Heble, eds., *Other Side of Nowhere.* 224–43.

Southern, Eileen. *The Music of Black Americans: A History.* 3rd ed. New York: Norton, 1997.

Spaulding, A. Timothy. "Embracing Chaos in Narrative Form: The Bebop Aesthetic in Ralph Ellison's *Invisible Man.*" *Callaloo* 27.2 (2004): 481–501.

Spencer, Jon Michael. *The New Negroes and Their Music: The Success of the Harlem Renaissance.* Knoxville: U of Tennessee P, 1997.

Spillers, Hortense J. "Mama's Baby, Papa's Maybe: An American Grammar Book." 1987. *Within the Circle: An Anthology of African American Literary Criticism from the Harlem Renaissance to the Present.* Ed. Angelyn Mitchell. Durham, N.C.: Duke UP, 1994. 454–81.

Stallybrass, Peter and Allon White. *The Politics and Poetics of Transgression.* Ithaca, NY: Cornell UP, 1986.

Stepto, Robert. "Narration, Authentication, and Authorial Control in Frederick Douglass' *Narrative* of 1845." 1979. *African American Autobiography.* Ed. William L. Andrews. Englewood Cliffs, NJ: Prentice Hall, 1993. 26–35.

Summers, Martin. *Manliness and Its Discontents: The Black Middle Class and the Transformation of Masculinity, 1900–1930.* Chapel Hill: U of North Carolina P, 2004.

Sundquist, Eric J. "Red, White, Black and Blue: The Color of American Modernism." *Transition* 6.2 (1996): 94–115.

———. *Cultural Contexts for Ralph Ellison's* Invisible Man. Boston: Bedford, 1995.

Taylor, Clyde. "'Salt Peanuts': Sound and Sense in African/American Oral/Musical Creativity." *Callaloo* 5:3 (1982): 1–11.

Tracy, Steven C. *Langston Hughes and the Blues.* Chicago: U of Illinois P, 1988.

———. "To the Tune of Those Weary Blues." *Langston Hughes: Critical Perspectives Past and Present.* Ed. Henry Louis Gates, Jr. and K.A. Appiah. New York: Amistad, 1993. 69–93.

Tucker, Sherrie. "Bordering on Community: Improvising Women Improvising Women-in-Jazz." In Fischlin and Heble, eds., *Other Side of Nowhere.* 244–67.

Turner, Victor. "Liminality and the Performative Genres." *Rite, Drama, Festival, Spectacle: Rehearsals Toward a Theory of Cultural Performance.* Ed. John J. MacAloon. Philadelphia: Institute for the Study of Human Issues, 1984. 19–41.

Van Vechten, Carl. *Nigger Heaven.* New York: Knopf, 1926.

Wagner, Linda Welshimer. *Interviews with William Carlos Williams: "Speaking Straight Ahead.* New York: New Directions, 1976.

Waldron, Edward E. "The Blues Poetry of Langston Hughes." *Negro American Literature Forum* 5 (1971): 140–49.

Wall, Cheryl. "Whose Sweet Angel Child? Blues Women, Langston Hughes, and Writing During the Harlem Renaissance." *Langston Hughes: The Man, His Art, and His Continuing Influence.* Critical Studies in Black Life and Culture, Vol. 29. New York: Garland, 1995. 37–50.

Watson, Steven. *The Harlem Renaissance: Hub of African-American Culture, 1920–1930.* New York: Pantheon, 1995.

Werner, Craig. *A Change Is Gonna Come: Music, Race & the Soul of America.* New York: Plume, 1998.

Wiegman, Robyn. *American Anatomies: Theorizing Race and Gender.* Durham, N.C.: Duke UP, 1995.

Williams, Martin. Liner notes, *The Shape of Jazz to Come.* 1959. Ornette Coleman, alto saxophone. Atlantic CD, 1317-2.

Williams, William Carlos. *Spring and All.* 1923. *Imaginations.* New York: New Directions, 1971. 85–154.

———. *Paterson.* 1963. Ed. Christopher MacGowan. New York: New Directions, 1992.

Wilmer, Valerie. *Jazz People.* 1970. New York: Da Capo, 1977.

———. *As serious as your life: John Coltrane and beyond.* 1977. London: Serpent's Tail, 1992.

Wilson, Olly. "The heterogeneous sound ideal in African-American music." *New Perspectives on Music: Essays in Honor of Eileen Southern.* Ed. Josephine Wright, with Samuel A. Floyd, Jr. Warren, Mich.: Harmonie Park Press, 1992. 327–38.

Wintz, Cary D. *Black Culture and the Harlem Renaissance.* Houston: Rice UP, 1988.

Wood, Joe. "The Soloist: Albert Murray's Blues People." *VLS* February 1996: 17–22.

Woolf, Virginia. *Mr. Bennett and Mrs. Brown.* London: L. and V. Woolf, 1924.

Worth, Robert. "*Nigger Heaven* and the Harlem Renaissance." *African American Review* 29.3 (1995): 461–73.

Wright, Beryl J. "Back Talk: Recoding the Body." *Callaloo* 19.2 (1996): 397–413.

Yeomans, W.E. "T.S. Eliot, Ragtime and the Blues." *The University Review* 34.4 (1968): 267–75.

Young, Al, Larry Kart and Michael S. Harper. "Jazz and Letters: A Colloquy." *Tri-Quarterly* 68 (1987): 118–158.

Young, Robert J.C. *Colonial Desire: Hybridity in Theory, Culture and Race.* London: Routledge, 1995.

Index